Central Pacific Sesquicentennial Edition

Alfred A. Hart's Stereoscopic Views
of the Central Pacific Railroad
1863 – 1869

3D Anaglyphs by Howard Goldbaum   Text by Wendell W. Huffman

Nevada State Railroad Museum

Carson City, Nevada

2012

Waiting for the Cars
Alfred A. Hart's Stereoscopic Views
of the Central Pacific Railroad

Nevada State Railroad Museum
2180 S. Carson St.
Carson City, Nevada 89701

2012

Copyright ©2012 Nevada State Railroad Museum
ISBN 978-0-97287733-6 52995
The Waiting for the Cars website, waitingforthecars.com, features stereo cards and anaglyphs not included in this book, as well as other interactive features. There are links to order additional paper 3D glasses, or professional models.

The lenticular 3D image on the front cover is an illustration derived from Alfred Hart's stereo card "First Construction Train passing the Palisades." This image may be seen in its authentic stereo effect on page 407.
    The front cover background photo was adapted from Hart's stereo card of CP Locomotive no. 1, 'Gov. Sanford.' See pp. 24-25.
    The illustration on the end sheets is a composite made from two of Hart's stereo cards, "The Monarch from the East," and "The Monarch from the West." See pages 434-435.

Printed in China

123456789 15 14 13 12
First printing 2012

CONTENTS

Introduction	5
Alfred A. Hart, Artist	7
Map	10
The Photographs	
Sacramento	12
Newcastle	50
Colfax	84
Blue Canyon	156
Cisco	200
Donner	234
Truckee	280
Reno	316
Wadsworth	342
Palisade Canyon	378
Elko	412
Promontory	426
Notes	448
Sources	468
Index	475

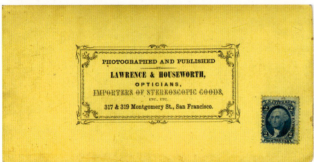

Alfred A. Hart's stereo cards, published by the artist and others, featured different colors and designs on their reverse sides.

INTRODUCTION

In April 1867, according to a piece in the *Sacramento Bee*, "a little fellow was looking through a stereoscope at a lot of California views, when by and by he came to that which represents the Bloomer Cut on the Pacific Railroad. He held it to his eyes a long, long time, when those around wondered why he dwelt so extensively on that one, asked him, and he answered, 'I am waiting for the cars to come along'".

The present work is an album of these same stereoscopic views that commanded that youngster's attention, including that of Bloomer Cut, along with many more that date from the following two years. While most of the views will be familiar to aficionados of the Central Pacific, few people have had the opportunity to see them reveal their full three-dimensional detail as photographer Alfred A. Hart intended. Our hopes in presenting these images in a stereographic format are that they will be more pleasing and meaningful that the ordinary "flat" presentation, and that Hart's art will find renewed appreciation. We hope that this "sense of place" media will make history come alive for our readers. A selection of the Alfred A. Hart CPRR stereo views not included in this book may be seen on our website: http://waitingforthecars.com.

We also call attention with the publication of this book to the 150th anniversary of the start of construction of the Central Pacific Railroad in 1863.

This project began in 2005 when we worked with a very small selection of the Hart images in the preparation of a web-based 3D gallery of historical images. The impact of peering back into the past through the red and cyan lenses led us to explore other Hart images. This soon became a quest bordering on an obsession: to acquire high-resolution scans of all the Hart railroad images and make them all available to a modern audience with the same vivid dimensional space that the photographer envisioned. When the photography professor and the railroad historian combined their research in 2007, this book began to take shape.

The conversion of the 150-year-old stereo cards into digital anaglyphs of high quality presented a number of challenges. Some of the photographs, due to improper storage or other factors, suffered from age spots (foxing), mildew, or bleed-through of the glue. Others evidenced water spots or other staining, emulsion tears, and even pen or pencil markings. When these imperfections were found in areas of continuous tone, such as the sky, they were repaired using pixel cloning so that the imperfections would not adversely impact the 3D effect. When serious defects were found within important image details, pixels from the corresponding area on the other side of the stereo card were utilized.

Hart's published stereo cards were intended to be viewed in the wooden frame of the stereoscope popular in the 1860s and still to be found on occasion in antique shops. This device positioned the stereo card just inches from the user's eyes, permitting an immersive effect that completely filled the field of view. In an effort to replicate as much as possible the visual impact of this nineteenth-century technology, we have cropped some of the anaglyphic images to secure the most immersive 3D effect. In all cases the original images, full-frame and with any imperfections intact, may be seen in the stereo card reproductions on the text pages.

Several views, deemed important to the narrative, were found to be assembled as stereo cards with identical images on each side of the card, and thus had no 3D quality. These may have resulted from an error in the 19-century manufacture of the card, or may have been a mistake on the part of the photographer. However to preserve the continuity of the 3D images we introduced a depth effect into these images, noted as such in the text.

In preparing the captions for these images, our intent has been to either explain whatever activity Hart may have recorded, place what is seen in the context of the construction or early operation of the CP, or recount some subsequent event related to a particular location. Just as the railroad wound through a variety of landscapes, the subjects of the captions sometimes range far and wide, though they are all relate in some way to the scenes that Hart recorded. A considerable effort has been made to establish the precise location of each view, often confirmed through on-site visits. In this work, the photographs are arranged geographically, west to east, so the scenes will unfold as if one were making a train trip from Sacramento to Ogden. While the dating of many of the photographs can be determined, a geographic continuum was felt to have more value to the reader than one that was strictly chronological.

Anyone who appreciates this work will owe gratitude to a number of people. Undoubtedly foremost among these are Mead Kibbey and Barry Swackhamer. Both generously provided access to their extensive collections of original Hart stereo cards, allowing them to be scanned for this project. We also would like to acknowledge the financial support provided this publication by the Kibbey family and by other donors to the Nevada State Railroad Museum. Other Alfred A. Hart images are used courtesy of Tom Gray, Brian Welton, the Library of Congress, the Special Collections Department at the University of Nevada, Reno Library, the Nevada Historical Society, the Crocker Art Museum, and the Stanford University Archives.

Also, Lynn Farrar and the family of Ron Hancock deserve special note as well for their role in preserving and freely sharing a plethora of railroad records. Farrar was the last Southern Pacific valuation engineer, while Hancock was the last civil engineer of the Southern Pacific's Salt Lake Division. Most of Farrar's material is now at Stanford University and the California State Railroad Museum, while Hancock's collection is at the Nevada State Railroad Museum.

Among the several specialists who provided assistance are: Sue Fawn Chung of the University of Nevada, Las Vegas, Doug Ferrier and Russell Towle of Dutch Flat, Nelson Van Gundy of Truckee, trails and wagon road historians William Bagley and Edward Hodges, Promontory authority Robert L. Spude of the National Park Service, Alfred Hart scholar Glenn G. Willumson of the University of Florida, and railroad historians Kyle Wyatt of the California State Railroad Museum, and Randy Hees of the Society for the Preservation of Carter Railroad Resources. Stephanie Hees provided an invaluable service in obtaining the Heuer material at the National Archives. James Barkley, G.J. Chris Graves, Alan Hardy, and Paul Pace also added information or provided leads. Thanks also goes to Larry K. Hersh for doing a lot of the groundwork in establishing the locations of many of the Hart photographs in Nevada, and for his guidance in leading the way to several of those sites.

We are grateful as well for the research assistance provided by Donnelyn Curtis, Jacquelyn Sundstrand, and Kathryn Totton of the Special Collections Department at the University of Nevada, Reno Library; Joyce Lee, Mona Reno, and Hope Williams of the Nevada State Library and Archives; Diana Daniels at the Crocker Art Museum; Maggie Kimball at the Stanford University Archives; and Eric Moody, Michael Maher, Lee Brumbaugh, and Arline Laferry of the Nevada Historical Society.

Glee Willis, Larry Mullaley and Steve VanDenburgh read early drafts of the manuscript, and we greatly appreciate their well-considered comments. As the project came to completion the editing and design contributions of Nancy Peppin proved invaluable. This book could not have been completed without the enthusiastic support of Peter Barton, Administrator of the Division of Museums and History of the Nevada Department of Tourism and Cultural Affairs.

And finally, but certainly not least, we acknowledge the support and encouragement of our wives, Lisa Huffman and Robin Goldbaum, as we pursued this project.

Wendell W. Huffman
Howard Goldbaum

Wendell W. Huffman is curator of history at the Nevada State Railroad Museum in Carson City. Previously he was a librarian at the Carson City Library and at the History of Science Collections of the University of Oklahoma. He has graduate degrees in the history of science and in library and information studies from the University of Oklahoma and training from the Rare Book School at Columbia University. He has published a number of articles on historic western railroads and the history of astronomy, and has served as a consultant for PBS and History Channel programs. His particular interests are early trails, roads, and railroads across the Sierra and the Great Basin.

Howard Goldbaum is an Associate Professor at the Reynolds School of Journalism at the University of Nevada, Reno. He has also worked as a photojournalist, photography professor, and multimedia producer and taught at Bradley University in Illinois for 26 years before moving to Nevada in 2003. He has also served as a consultant in multimedia and digital imaging in education and has won numerous awards for his web sites and virtual-reality environments, such as his Nevada documentation project (www.allaroundnevada.com). His 30 years of research on the ancient monuments of Ireland and their folklore culminated in his 2010 sabbatical project (www.voicesfromthedawn.com).

ALFRED A. HART
Artist
by Mead B. Kibbey

Trained as a painter in New England, Alfred A. Hart became an influential figure in the development of Western landscape photography. But the artist has been an elusive and shadowy figure until rather recent times. In 1918, ten years after Hart's death, Charles B. Terrill mentioned him in connection with his study of photographer Carleton E. Watkins. In 1969, George Kraus devoted half a page of the forward to his book, *High Road to Promontory*, to the historical importance of Hart's photographs and lamented the lack of recognition he had received. Finally a trained art historian, Glenn Willumson, became focused on Hart when he conducted the research for his 1982 Master's thesis.

Alfred A. Hart was born March 28, 1816, in Norwich, Connecticut, and received his first training as a fine arts painter, later making his living as a portrait painter in nearby Hartford. In 1852, he painted a long panorama portraying Biblical scenes of the Holy Land on a roll of canvas. In New York, the panorama was unrolled from one vertical spool to another at the opposite side of a stage, pausing while "Professor" Hart lectured about the scene depicted.

In the early 1860s he moved his family to Cleveland, Ohio, where he operated an art store. Although the reasons for his next move are not clear, by 1863 he had left his family in Cleveland and was taking photographs in California. Hart was already 46 years old and an experienced photographer and artist at the time the Central Pacific Railroad commenced construction in Sacramento on January 8, 1863. There is no evidence of Hart's presence at the ceremony, although we know from a surviving newspaper advertisement that he was already in California at that time. It may have been there that Hart saw an advertisement from the optical firm of Lawrence & Houseworth offering stereoscopic equipment for sale, realized the potential opportunity, and decided to contact them.

In stereo photography, in order that the eye and brain can work the miracle of depth perception, two images must be taken, usually with about the same separation as human eyes (i.e. around 2-5/8 in). Usually the two images were taken on a single negative at the same instant, using a special camera equipped with two lenses.

An experienced stereo photographer tended to seek camera locations that would exploit the camera's ability to record depth. Interiors of snowsheds, tunnels, and bridges were obvious targets. Hart understood that stereo scenes could be vastly improved by including something distinctive, or dramatic in the immediate foreground, usually within 15 feet of the lens. For Hart the unbeatable "something" was the top of a locomotive boiler, or the railroad rails traversing a cliff near his camera with a valley far below.

Hart's energetic approach and almost total disregard for his personal safety while taking photographs is not immediately apparent in every CP stereo, but it is clearly demonstrated in a number of his views. In fact, getting his heavy camera and tripod to high places to record scenes from the tops of locomotives, boxcars, and various cliffs was a hallmark of his work. An especially large number

Portrait of Alfred A. Hart, c. 1845, by an unknown artist. (History Colorado, Jerome Family Collection, Denver, Colorado)

of Hart's CP views in Nevada and Utah are taken from the tops of boxcars, which required climbing a narrow vertical ladder. Likewise the difficulties in getting from the tracks to the camera location at the very top of the Palisades (see pages 402-3 and card pictured below) must have been a story in itself.

Wet-plate stereo camera of the 1860s. The lens caps in the foreground were used to time the exposure, and the slits to accommodate the removable diaphragm stops are just above the focus-knobs.

In the 1860s, when Hart was first taking his railroad views, the pioneering daguerreotype method of photography had already declined in popularity and the wet collodion process was in vogue.

This involved carrying glass plates, which were, just before use, coated with iodized collodion (a viscous mixture of gun-cotton dissolved in alcohol and ether) and sensitized by dipping in a silver nitrate solution. The sensitizing had to be done in a dark tent by the dim light from a small translucent panel of yellow or orange silk.

Coating, sensitizing, exposing, and developing had to be completed before the plate dried, (a total period of five to ten minutes) or the emulsion would crystalize and lose its sensitivity. The 5-inch x 8-inch glass plates were heavy (three and one half ounces each) and fragile, but photographers utilized this messy process because the resulting negatives displayed a beautiful tonal range, required a shorter exposure than the earlier methods, and could be used to make any number of positive paper prints.

Lawrence & Houseworth became the first to publish Hart's CP stereo photographs and regularly purchased other CP negatives from him as construction progressed. In the summer of 1865, the CP directors bought over 500 of these stereoscopic prints from Lawrence & Houseworth. But in January of 1866, the CP purchased 32 stereoscopic negatives from Hart, and from then on he acted as the railroad's de-facto photographer.

Throughout his working association with the Central Pacific, Hart's sponsor was Judge E. B. Crocker, legal counsel to the CP. The Judge approved payment for Hart's first invoice and he also selected and favorably commented on later Hart views. Because of this influential connection, Hart had the ability to halt trains at photo opportunities and even to stop and pose the rushing construction workers on the job. He was also allowed to have his small photo-darkroom-wagon hauled to the end-of-track on a railroad flat car where he hitched it to a horse and pushed ahead to capture scenes of the early stages of excavation for the roadbed. Because he was on site well before the completion of the famous snowsheds in 1869, and before the tracks were in such heavy use, Hart was able to take advantage of photographic opportunities not available to other photographers of that era. His photographs taken along this route during the actual process of building trestles, constructing enormous embankments, and digging tunnels can never be duplicated.

Unfortunately, Judge Crocker suffered a stroke and retired from the Central Pacific board of directors in the latter part of 1869, and Hart's special connection with the railroad terminated within a few months. A long-time friend of CP Director Collis P. Huntington, Carleton E. Watkins, soon replaced Hart. By 1870 Watkins was publishing most of the Hart CP negatives, with Hart's original numbers and nearly identical titles, but without any credit to Alfred Hart. This was not an unusual practice for the time, and would seem to indicate that the negatives were actually owned by the CP. Watkins mounted the prints from the Hart negatives on cards identified variously as "Watkins' Pacific Railroad", "Central Pacific Railroad," "Watkins' Pacific Coast," and others. While also making his own images of the CP, Watkins continued to sell Hart's stereocards under his own name until the negatives were all lost in the San Francisco earthquake of 1906.

Alfred A. Hart, 1886
(Photo from a private collection)

Alfred Hart pursued a number of careers after completing his work with the CP, as an author, an inventor, a painter, and a dealer in photographic materials. He moved to St. Louis, to Denver, and back and forth between New York and San Francisco. In the year of the great earthquake, at the age of 89, Alfred Hart was on the opposite coast, listed in a New York business directory as a publisher of artistic blueprints. In his ninetieth year he returned to California where he later died in the Alameda County Infirmary on March 5, 1908, a few days before his ninety-second birthday.

After spending many years looking at Alfred A. Hart's fascinating photographs and visiting more than 50 of the sites where he placed his camera along the Central Pacific, I can say that it is quite disappointing that Hart is not better known today. When seen in 3D as the photographer intended, and as *Waiting for the Cars* facilitates, Hart's stereographs transform one's visual space into an exciting reproduction of the scene itself. An almost uncanny feeling of time-travel occurs when one views a Hart stereograph of a bustling railroad settlement as it appeared in the 1860s and compares it to the now deserted location.

Based on the titles for his photographs that he wrote, it is clear that Hart never belittled the people depicted, as other photographers of the period occasionally did, never complained about the conditions under which he worked, and consistently displayed respect and admiration for the accomplishments of the builders of the railroad. For generations to come the photographs of Alfred A. Hart will delight and inform us. As the architect Sir Christopher Wren had inscribed near his tomb in London's St. Paul's Cathedral: *Lector, si monumentum requiris, circumspice* ("Reader, if you seek a memorial, look around.")

Mead B. Kibbey

Mead B. Kibbey is the author of the first published Alfred A. Hart monograph, *The Railroad Photographs of Alfred A. Hart, Artist* (1996).

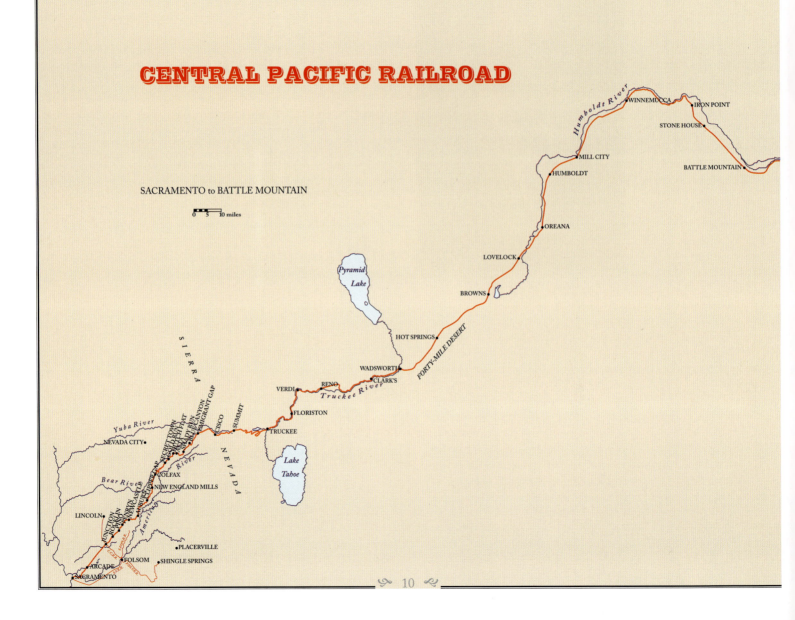

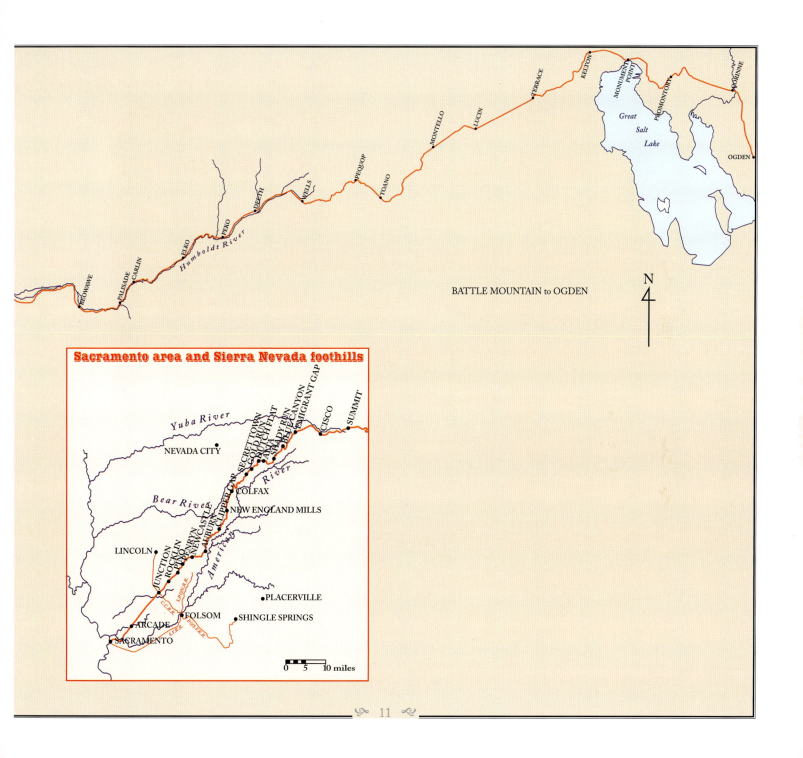

FRONT STREET, SACRAMENTO

The groundbreaking ceremony of the Central Pacific Railroad (CP) was held at Front and K streets in Sacramento on January 8, 1863, a now-forgotten holiday commemorating the Battle of New Orleans. This view of that intersection dates from two years later. The train, however, does not belong to the CP but to a company that was, until 1865, a rival for the trans-Sierra commerce: the Sacramento Valley Railroad (SVRR).

The SVRR was the West's first railroad enterprise. It commenced construction in 1855, building toward Marysville in the expectation that it would someday become a link in a chain of railroads extending around the north end of the Sierra Nevada and on toward the Missouri River. In 1860, the SVRR's former chief engineer, Theodore D. Judah, was inspired by the Comstock excitement to promote a new route for a Pacific railroad directly over—rather than around—the Sierra Nevada. This soon became the CP. Meanwhile, the SVRR never laid track beyond Folsom, but by the date of this photograph it was allied with other companies developing a trans-Sierra railroad via Placerville. The competition for the Comstock trade made the SVRR and the CP rivals, and that drove the CP to build more quickly than it might have otherwise done.

Adjacent to the train, in this scene, is the freight shed of the California Steam Navigation Company, which operated riverboats between Sacramento and San Francisco. The CP's freight house and passenger depot are north of K Street.

CENTRAL PACIFIC DEPOT, SACRAMENTO
Elevation 35 feet

The CP inaugurated passenger service in April 1864 and opened this depot the following month. At that time, the railroad extended only from Sacramento to Junction, where it crossed the California Central Railroad. The town of Roseville sprang up around Junction, and the station name was changed to "Roseville" in 1890.

The railroad brought several changes to Sacramento's Front Street. Not only were passenger and freight depots built, but the street itself was raised. When the CP first built its track, the city front sloped down to the river, little changed from the natural river bank. The embankment for the CP's track became the basis for the city's 1864 levee, and the street was soon raised to the level of the track. Shortly before this winter 1865 view was made, the CP commenced construction of an extensive wharf adjacent to the depot, and the tower of the pile driver used on that project can be seen beyond the baggage car.

Beyond the depot are the masts of a schooner—one of the many that delivered railroad material from San Francisco. A stern-wheel riverboat is moored across the Sacramento River, just downstream from the wagon road bridge to Yolo County. In this era, stern-wheel boats generally operated in the shallow waters upstream from Sacramento, while larger side-wheel boats operated between Sacramento and San Francisco.

SACRAMENTO WATERFRONT from RIVERBOAT

Hart made this photograph of the CP's wharf from the top of the starboard paddle box of the river steamer *Capital*.

The crates at the near end of the wharf contain locomotive components. Among those that can be recognized are a smoke stack, an upside-down pilot, and a boiler encased in protective packing. The large semicircular crates hold "saddle tanks"—water tanks that straddled the boilers of switch engines in lieu of separate tenders. The CP had only four locomotives with this distinctive style of tank, and of them, only nos. 32 and 33, *Ajax* and *Achilles*, also had pointed wood pilots like those seen on the wharf. Thus, the newspaper report of the arrival of these particular locomotives from the New Jersey Locomotive & Machine Company of Paterson, New Jersey, dates this image to early 1868. All of the locomotives imported from eastern factories were shipped broken down into units small enough to fit into the holds of sailing vessels.

Farther up the wharf can be seen the derricks used to unload river vessels. Kegs of spikes are piled at the base of the closest crane, while a man stands next to it on a stack of timbers. The schooner moored upstream appears to be loaded with long timbers, likely being delivered from a coastal sawmill.

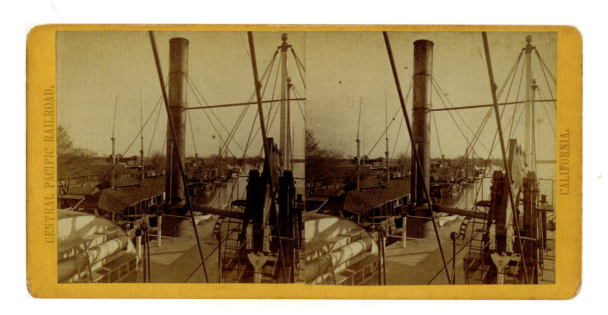

SACRAMENTO WATERFRONT from RIVERBOAT

Hart understood that foreground objects enhance the visual effect of stereo photographs, and he often went out of his way to include them in his views. He made many pictures from inside snowsheds and tunnels, with foreground elements completely framing the scene. In this view, he achieved the same effect by shooting through the *Capital*'s rigging.

The round-topped enclosure in the left foreground is the cover of the *Capital*'s starboard paddlewheel, from which the preceding view was made. The walking-beam, which transmitted motion from the boat's single cylinder's piston to the paddles, is prominent on the right.

Visible through the trees on the left in the background is the CP's Sacramento freight depot. The passenger train shed and depot are out of the view immediately to the left of the riverboat. Just beyond the *Capital*'s stern quarter lies a schooner that has been roofed over and permanently moored for use as a landing stage. Because it rode with the rise and fall of the river and was connected to the levee by a hinged ramp, this floating platform enabled hand trucks to be rolled directly onto a riverboat's deck.

The need to deliver supplies and equipment to Sacramento for the construction of the CP was a boon to river traffic. But once the railroad was extended to San Francisco Bay in 1869, the river business began to decline, and the waterfront became less important to the city.

RAILROAD WHARVES at SACRAMENTO CITY

This view of the Sacramento wharf features flatcars being loaded with rail for transport to the end-of-track. Beyond, locomotive tires and kegs, possibly containing spikes, are ready to be loaded onto cars.

In conformity with the Pacific Railroad Act, all the iron rail used on the mainline of the CP was manufactured in the United States. As there were then no rolling mills in the West, all of this rail had to be delivered from the eastern seaboard. Most was carried the long way around South America in sailing ships, though in 1868 enough rail to lay 58 miles of track was shipped in steamers via Panama. The material transported via Panama had to be unloaded and hauled across the Isthmus via the Panama Railroad, and then reloaded into other vessels on the Pacific side. From San Francisco, schooners carried the rail across the bay and up the Sacramento River to Sacramento.

The task of ordering rail fell to Collis P. Huntington, the CP's vice president, who settled in New York to oversee the company's financial affairs. Huntington wrote that, with competition for rail from other railroads, strikes, and the breaking, burning, and flooding of rolling mills, the problem of getting the rail "has given me more trouble than all the other troubles of my life, and I would not go through the same thing again for the whole road."

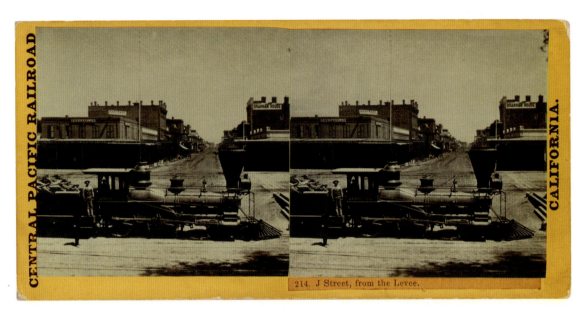

J STREET, SACRAMENTO, FROM THE LEVEE

Locomotive no. 7, *A.A. Sargent*, pauses for Hart's camera at the foot of J Street. The passenger depot is out of frame to the left, the freight house is to the right. This engine was named for Congressman Aaron A. Sargent of Nevada City. Sargent played a key role in the passage of the initial Pacific Railroad Act in 1862, though later he was less supportive of the railroad.

This locomotive had been ordered by the SVRR but was appropriated by the CP when it acquired a controlling interest in the rival road in August 1865. The engine was delivered to Sacramento from the Union Iron Works of San Francisco the following December in full running order. Whereas California factories wanted to build locomotives for the CP, they expected payment in gold. East Coast builders, on the other hand, willingly accepted currency, notes, or bonds as payment. Thus, even with the high cost of shipping locomotives to California, eastern locomotives were less expensive to the company, and the *Sargent* was the only California-built locomotive on the CP until the company began building its own in the 1870s. Nevertheless, California's remoteness spurred local industry, and the CP built many locomotive smoke stacks and two complete tenders during the period of the railroad's construction, in addition to hundreds of cars.

LOCOMOTIVE NO. 1, GOV. STANFORD

The company's first locomotive was the *Gov. Stanford*, named for Leland Stanford, CP president and then governor of California. The engine arrived in San Francisco in September 1863, after a 127-day voyage from Boston on the clipper *Herald of the Morning*. The schooner *Artful Dodger* carried its various components up the river to Sacramento for assembly, and the locomotive operated for the first time on November 10. The *Stanford* was involved in the company's first fatality, backing a train over Flavius Clement in the curve at Sixth and H streets in Sacramento, in January 1864. Clement had worked with Judah on the early surveys.

The *Gov. Stanford* was manufactured by Richard Norris & Son, locomotive builders of Philadelphia. The CP was very happy with this engine: Mark Hopkins, the company treasurer, reported in 1867 that it was "the most serviceable on our road—has been longest in use—less days in the shop for repairs—has cost nearly or quite one half . . . to keep her up in good working condition—is the easiest on the curves, & has never yet been off the track, while [derailments are] an almost daily occurrence with the others, in the winter season where the new road is in uneven bad condition." Hopkins asked Huntington to buy more locomotives just like it, but by then Norris had retired, though a few other Norris locomotives were found.

By 1870, Hart's railroad photographs were being published by Carlton E. Watkins, whose imprint appears on this card.

NORTH of CENTRAL PACIFIC DEPOT, SACRAMENTO

After being relegated from construction-train service, the *Gov. Stanford* became the regular Sacramento switch engine, and it is seen here at the north end of the Sacramento depot. Extra coupler links and a rope for pulling cars on an adjacent track hang at the ready from hooks on the back of its tender. The Wason-built passenger car on the left is one of those delivered overland after the railroad was completed, thus dating this photograph to 1869 and identifying this as one of Hart's last views of the CP.

The draw span of the first Sacramento-Yolo bridge can be seen in the distance on the left. This 1857 bridge was replaced in late 1869 with a new structure, built by the California Pacific Railroad to bring its track from Vallejo into Sacramento. In the far distance, beyond the men, is the silhouette of the Pioneer flour mill, and to the right is the city's waterworks building. It provided water to the city and to the railroad's thirsty locomotives. The rail stacked at the right is destined for the California & Oregon Railroad.

"Sacramento City" appears in the caption of several of Hart's cards. Technically this was correct as the "City" was not dropped by the post office until March 1883. Still, even the earliest CP time schedule referenced "Sacramento" alone, no doubt reflecting what was already by then popular usage.

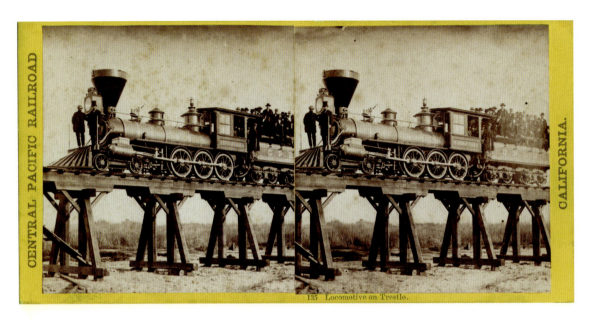

LOCOMOTIVE NO. 6, CONNESS, on AMERICAN RIVER TRESTLE

Locomotive no. 6, *Conness*, built by Mason Machine Works of Taunton, Massachusetts, was the CP's first large engine. It first operated on March 16, 1865, after being assembled in Sacramento. The *Sacramento Bee* reported that the *Conness* was photographed on the American River bridge that very day. The paper also indicated that the photograph was made by CP director Edwin B. Crocker, though it is unclear just what role he played. The camera and darkroom equipment belonged to Hart, and he likely composed the image, prepared the emulsion and developed the negative as well. On the other hand, Crocker sponsored Hart, assuring him of the company's patronage and providing access to the railroad during construction. Crocker developed an interest in art and later assembled a notable art collection that his widow bequeathed to the city of Sacramento.

This engine was named to flatter Senator John Conness of California in the hope that he would assist the company in Washington. All CP locomotives acquired during the construction period were named, but only a handful bore the names of living persons. In 1866 the company considered eliminating the use of names entirely, but names were easily distinguished from part numbers, and using both designations on the various components helped in sorting them as they arrived, especially when parts of different locomotives arrived at the same time. For this reason, CP locomotives continued to be named as long as they were shipped unassembled.

AMERICAN RIVER BRIDGE
3.8 miles from Sacramento

This two-span Howe truss bridge carried the CP's track across the American River just northeast of Sacramento. While the railroad's other bridges were built by the company itself, this structure was erected by contractors Isaac M. Hubbard and Jesse G. Baker. The truss spans had an overall length of 407 feet, plus some three thousand feet of trestle approaches. Work driving the piles for the structure began even before the railroad's official groundbreaking ceremony. The bridge alone required some 44 tons of nuts and bolts. Its timbers were shipped all the way from Puget Sound. The railroad track reached the bridge from Sacramento on November 20, 1863, and the bridge was completed and carrying trains by December 1. It was soon sheathed and painted.

This image is a companion to the preceding view. The *Conness* can be seen in the distance on the far side of the river, its tender still loaded with excursionists. The nearby locomotive is no. 3, *C.P. Huntington*, which the *Bee* reported was photographed on the same occasion as the *Conness*.

Running the CP directly across the American River's floodplain north of town gave the railroad a direct approach to the Sierra, but high water soon caused trouble. In the fall of 1868 the bridge had to be raised and some of the trestlework was replaced with two additional truss spans. This bridge was destroyed by an arsonist in March 1870.

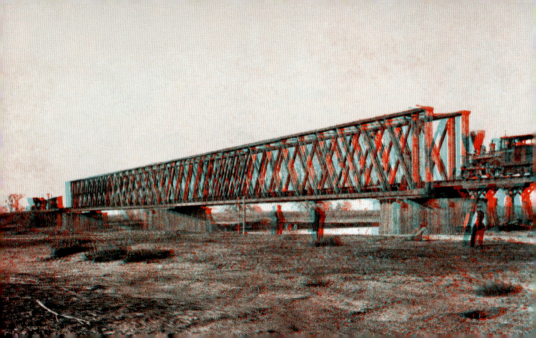

12-MILE TANGENT

Once across the American River, the railroad extended for 12 miles in a straight line across the Rancho del Paso toward the Sierra Nevada. Though often presented as "bound *for* the mountains," the direction of shadows and the placement of the telegraph poles reveal that this view is actually facing back toward Sacramento. The photograph was made from the roof of the cab of one of the early Mason-built 4-4-0s. Though the windblown smoke suggests motion, the locomotive is doubtless standing still so Hart and his camera would not fall off. Hart had an eye for the dramatic story.

Most observers at the time assumed that the CP would commence construction at the eastern end of the Sacramento, Placer & Nevada Railroad, which then extended almost to Auburn from its connection with the SVRR at Folsom. However, the requirement of the Pacific Railroad Act of 1862 that the CP complete 40 miles of railroad on its own to qualify for any federal assistance compelled the company to start construction at Sacramento, giving it as many relatively inexpensive miles as possible before entering the foothills.

Except for the bridge, 16 miles of roadbed were nearly complete by May 1863, though the track itself was not laid until the end of that year, after the first rails finally arrived. The end-of-track was 10 miles from Sacramento on January 8, 1864, the first anniversary of the groundbreaking ceremony.

DRY CREEK BRIDGE
16.7 miles from Sacramento

The 12-mile tangent ended in a gentle reverse curve just west of this four-span Burr-truss crossing of Dry Creek. The whole structure was 218 feet long. The company built a state-of-the-art railroad, laying up stone piers for the bridge and covering the trusses to protect the timbers from the weather. It was a "deck bridge," with the track laid on the top chord. Rails were laid across the bridge in late February 1864.

The locomotive in this view is Mason-built no. 5, which went into service in June 1864. Its name, *Atlantic*, is spelled out on the side of its tank. The round-case headlamp is unusual, though a few other early CP locomotives had them.

The station at Junction, where the CP track crossed the California Central Railroad, was 1.5 miles east of this bridge. The California Central ran from Folsom to Lincoln. After the CP absorbed it in 1868, it became the trunk of the California & Oregon, which was eventually extended north into Oregon. Today, the railroad's vast Roseville classification yard stretches out on both sides of Dry Creek.

Dry Creek drains a considerable foothill watershed, and it is not always dry. The bridge was damaged by storms in December 1866, and it was destroyed by fire in May 1873.

Central Pacific Railroad, Granite Quarry at Rocklin.

ROCKLIN, RAILROAD, and GRANITE QUARRY
22 miles from Sacramento

The railroad track reached Rocklin in March 1864, and the company ran an excursion train to the new terminus on March 19. The special train consisted of every piece of rolling stock then on hand: seven flatcars (equipped with temporary benches for passengers), two passenger cars, and the locomotive *Gov. Stanford*. Hart recorded this scene, of a different train, some time later.

The locomotive in this view, pulling its train into Rocklin from the southwest, is apparently the *Atlantic*; this is probably the same train seen crossing Dry Creek in the preceding image. A derrick belonging to one of the Rocklin stone quarries is seen immediately adjacent to the track.

For a number of years the industry of local granite quarries and the activity at the railroad roundhouse made Rocklin a thriving place. One visitor noted, "Rocklin is celebrated—and by certain bad people, ridiculed—all over this part of the foothills for the superabundance of its juvenile population. If one makes any inquisitive remarks about this fact the Rocklinite addressed will either blush or grin, according to his temperament, and say, 'It's the glorious climate.'"

CUTTING GRANITE at ROCKLIN

It appears that in the early days there was some confusion whether the place was "Rockville," "Rockland," or "Rocklin." Any of those names were appropriate as a mass of underlying granitic rock is exposed at several places in the vicinity. A quarry had been opened at the site before the advent of the railroad, but the CP made the commercial production of the local stone profitable. The railroad company earned its first revenue on March 25, 1864 hauling three carloads of cut stone from Charles A. Bringham's quarry to Sacramento.

Stone from Rocklin was used in many California buildings, including the state capitol, then under construction in Sacramento. To deliver stone blocks to the capitol, a spur track was laid on Sixth Street between H and I streets in Sacramento. The CP also used Rocklin stone in several of its own installations.

In this view, stone cutters are at work squaring large blocks of rock. Behind them is the derrick used to lift and move the blocks.

In time, there were several quarries at Rocklin. They remained active into the 20th century.

ROUNDHOUSE AND TRAIN, ROCKLIN
22.15 miles from Sacramento, elevation 249 feet

At Rocklin the railroad enters the foothills and begins its ascent of the Sierra Nevada. From a maximum gradient of 25 feet to the mile across the valley floor, the rate of climb increases dramatically to over 105 feet in the mile just east of Rocklin, where the railroad begins winding its way up the ridge between Antelope Creek and Secret Ravine. To care for the heavy machines needed to pull trains up this grade, the company established a major locomotive facility at Rocklin. In this late 1868 photograph, the large stone roundhouse and turntable are on the left, while the platform of the passenger depot is on the extreme right. Beyond it, in the distance opposite the roundhouse, is the large shed for locomotive firewood. The view faces east.

Because of the underlying bedrock, deep wells were difficult to bore at Rocklin, and the local water supply was inadequate for the railroad's needs. Locomotive crews made a point of returning from the mountains with tender tanks full of water. Finally, in the late 1880s, a pipe was extended three miles eastward to bring water from Loomis. The dearth of local water was one of the reasons the company relocated its operations to Roseville in 1908.

241 Engine House and Turntable.
Rocklin, 22 miles from Sacramento.

ENGINE HOUSE AND TURNTABLE

Construction of Rocklin's 28-stall roundhouse began late in 1866, using the abundant local stone. Locomotives were first assigned to Rocklin in May 1867, though the structure was not completed to its full configuration for another year. The locomotive seen here on the 51-foot turntable is no. 45, *Majestic*, manufactured by McKay & Aldus of East Boston, Massachusetts. It entered service in the spring of 1868. In 1876, the railroad company employed 80 men at the Rocklin roundhouse. The old roundhouse was demolished in 1913 to make room for baseball diamond.

In the days of wood-burning locomotives, firewood was stockpiled at 21 woodsheds strategically spaced along the railroad from Sacramento to Wadsworth. They ranged in size from two hundred to nearly five hundred feet in length. One of the hazards associated with the use of wood for engine fuel was the propensity of the wood piles to catch fire from sparks thrown from locomotives. In October 1869, fire destroyed Rocklin's first woodshed along with several month's supply of fuel. The replacement shed was more than six hundred feet long. Locomotives running between Sacramento and Truckee burned wood exclusively until late 1886, when coal was introduced. Wood fuel was phased out entirely over the following five or six years.

The 3D effect of this image has been digitally enhanced.

TANGENT BELOW PINO
23 miles from Sacramento

Long tangents, like this 1.3-mile stretch above Rocklin, become less frequent as the railroad enters the mountains.

Photographer Hart's shadow is cast onto the scene in the right foreground, along with that of his large, tripod-mounted camera and an assistant. In the distance, cordwood can be seen stacked alongside the railroad track, where it was delivered by local contractors. Contracting with local woodchoppers for firewood was just one of the ways in which the CP contributed to local economies.

Pino was 25 miles from Sacramento at an elevation of 402 feet, just two miles beyond the location of this photograph. To avoid confusion with "Reno," Pino was renamed "Loomis" in 1884 after local depot operator James Loomis. The CP rarely built and operated its own depots. Rather, concessionaires were allowed to build and operate depots on company property in exchange for providing services to the railroad's passengers. The early CP depots were more than mere ticket offices and waiting rooms. The one at Loomis was also a tavern and post office. Many depots provided lodging rooms, and several offered dining facilities where entire trainloads of passengers could eat while the locomotives were being fueled and watered. Not until after Pullman began operating cars over the CP in 1883 were trains regularly equipped with buffet or dining cars.

GRIFFITH'S QUARRY at PENRYN
28.1 miles from Sacramento, elevation 628 feet

Yet another granite quarry was located at Penryn, established in late 1864 by Griffith Griffith and named by him for his Welsh hometown.

Griffith previously had a quarry located on the Sacramento, Placer & Nevada Railroad (SP&N), which had been organized in 1859 to build from Folsom to Auburn and was operating trains over most of that distance before the CP began construction in 1863. However, when the CP approached Newcastle in the spring of 1864, the SP&N was outflanked and soon ceased to operate. When the Placerville & Sacramento Valley Railroad, then building toward Placerville from Folsom, bought the SP&N rail, the CP attempted to block the dismantlement of the line. The CP recognized the Placerville railroad as a rival for the Comstock traffic, and it wanted the SP&N's American-made iron for its own track. Acting on behalf of the CP, Griffith filed a lawsuit to block the scrapping of the SP&N, arguing that it would kill his business. However, neither legal action nor an exciting little war, with much shouting, some gunfire, and a little bloodshed could save the SP&N, and Griffith, no doubt with the CP's encouragement, soon opened a quarry on the new railroad.

In this March 1865 photograph, the brand new *Conness* is standing on the quarry spur, with the mainline curving away in the background. The bearded man with hands on hips in the foreground is CP Director E.B. Crocker. The man standing next to him may be Griffith himself.

ANTELOPE RIDGE, NEAR NEWCASTLE
30 miles from Sacramento

This eastward-facing photograph was made a mile or so west of Newcastle, where the railroad climbs along the north flank of Antelope Ridge. Trains were running to this point in May 1864.

E.B. Crocker's brother Charles was the contractor who built the first 18 miles of the CP. At the time the company was formed he was a dry goods merchant in Sacramento, but his prior occupation running an iron works in Indiana, and later leading a party of pioneers to California, gave him valuable experience managing men. As the only one of the company's founders to have traveled overland to California, Charles had at least some idea of the nature of the country they were venturing into.

Since he had been one of the company's organizers and one of the first directors, competing bidders complained that Charles had won the first contract unfairly. Responding to this, work on the next 13 miles of railroad was divided among several contractors, with Crocker awarded only the two-mile section below Newcastle, part of which appears in this image. This new arrangement was unsatisfactory, however, as the various contractors competed against each other for laborers, driving up costs and causing delays. Some even failed to complete their sections. Thereafter, all construction was in Crocker's hands. Until September 1869, Crocker also served as superintendent of the railroad, directing all train operations.

NEWCASTLE
31.24 miles from Sacramento, elevation 960 feet

The track reached Newcastle on June 3, 1864, and the following day the company ran an excursion to the new end of the line. Regular operation began on the sixth, with three trains each way Mondays through Saturdays and one each way on Sundays. Sunday trains were discontinued in July 1866, not to be resumed until the CP connected with the Union Pacific (UP) in 1869.

As of 1864, the Comstock mining district of Virginia City, Nevada was the primary source of trans-Sierra commerce. While Donner Pass, toward which the CP was building, had been used in the 1840s by pioneers crossing the Sierra, most of the Comstock traffic in the early 1860s moved between the end of the SVRR at Folsom and Virginia City on a wagon road that ran through Placerville. For the CP to succeed, it had to quickly capture as much of that business as possible. Toward this end, the directors of the company developed the Dutch Flat & Donner Lake Wagon Road as a connection between the CP railhead and Nevada. That road was opened in June 1864, when the railroad reached Newcastle. Until the railroad actually connected with its roadway, traffic between the railroad and Dutch Flat ran on wagon roads already in existence.

Hart may have been the unidentified photographer the *Sacramento Bee* reported taking pictures at Newcastle in January 1865.

LOCOMOTIVE NO. 5 ATLANTIC

Even while the CP was slowly extending its track into the foothills, the Placerville & Sacramento Valley Railroad (operated by the SVRR) was building its own line eastward from Folsom, and competition between the CP and the SVRR became intense. In August 1864, just two months after the CP reached Newcastle, the Placerville railroad was opened as far as Latrobe. To settle which route provided the fastest service, a contest was staged to see which company could deliver San Francisco newspapers to Virginia City in the shortest time, relying on stagecoaches to complete the connections beyond their respective terminals. For the race, the CP used this, its newest locomotive, no. 5, *Atlantic*, a fleet eight-wheeler built by Mason Machine Works.

The CP won the contest, primarily because there was little traffic on the new road, and the storm that merely sprinkled the Donner route turned the Placerville road into mud. Nevertheless, the teamsters were familiar with the Placerville route, and it retained most of the Nevada commerce. Hopkins attributed the teamster's loyalty to the old route to the "waiting girls and friendly barmaids" of its established inns. Not until the CP acquired control of the SVRR in August 1865 was it finally able to divert the bulk of the Comstock traffic to its own line by way of Donner Pass.

The *Atlantic* had other adventures in its life. In November 1865, near Newcastle, it ran into a camel, presumably a stray from those imported to carry hay and salt to the Comstock.

TRESTLE UNDER CONSTRUCTION, NEWCASTLE
31.4 miles from Sacramento

The railroad ascends to Donner Pass along the ridge dividing the American River from the watersheds of the Bear and Yuba rivers. While this divide extends all the way from the valley floor to the summit, it is broken in places with low "gaps" that the railroad had to cross. The first of these gaps was encountered at Newcastle. The railroad crossed the gap at Newcastle on this 528-foot long trestle, laid out on a 4° curve and rising 63 feet above the ravine bottom.

When Hart made this north-facing view, probably in March 1865, the trestle was still under construction. The tall mast was used to lift components into position. The vertical segments of the trestle are called "bents." Once in place, the bents were connected with horizontal timbers to stabilize the structure, and stringers—to carry the track—were laid across the top. The bents, spaced at one-rod intervals, rested either on bedrock or on masonry piers.

Newcastle remained the end-of-track for nearly a year, not because of delay in the construction of the trestle, but because of the company's nearly bankrupt condition. This was a long, discouraging period. Various measures by state and local municipalities to aid the railroad were challenged in court by the SVRR, and the Civil War made paper currency almost worthless. For one 17-day period, the company did not have a single dollar in its treasury.

LOCOMOTIVE CONNESS AT NEWCASTLE

Hart probably made this photograph in March 1865, on the maiden trip of locomotive no. 6 into the hills. More than nine months after the track first arrived, Newcastle was still the end-of-track and the trestle was still unfinished. But finally, after delays and frustration, the company's circumstances were starting to improve.

Until the CP built enough track to qualify for federal bonds, it had to rely on traffic revenue, donations, and the sale of company stock and bonds for financing. However, as long as the railroad's ultimate success remained in doubt, these securities were unattractive to investors and few were sold. In an effort to remedy this situation, the State of California (which had much to gain by the completion of the Pacific railroad) agreed to guarantee the interest on the company bonds. While this was challenged by the SVRR, the California Supreme Court's validation of the act in January 1865 measurably increased the value of the company bonds. This good news was followed by more in March, when the federal government authorized the company to sell bonds on the railroad as much as one hundred miles in advance of the rails, and it subordinated the government mortgage on the property to the mortgage protecting the company-issued bonds. Furthermore, the following month, just as the Civil War ended, the company finally received the voter-approved donation of San Francisco municipal bonds after a hard-fought legal battle.

RAILROAD above NEWCASTLE
32 miles from Sacramento

With the apparent resolution of its financial troubles, the company faced the new problem of finding enough workmen to build the railroad. Jobs were plentiful in California, and many men worked for wages only long enough to finance their next forays to the mines. Although the CP advertised for five thousand workers in January 1865, fewer than half that number was on the job as late as April, when the Newcastle trestle was finished. The company had hired Chinese as early as February 1864, but only in small numbers (only 50 Chinese were employed as of January 1865). Yet, their work was good, and with difficulty obtaining anyone else, more and more Chinese were hired through early 1865. Hopkins acknowledged in May of that year, "without [the Chinese] it would be impossible to go on with the work." By then, already two-thirds of the two thousand men employed were Chinese. Realizing that the local population of Chinese was insufficient to meet the demand, the CP sent recruiters to southern China promising work to any young men who came to California.

The trenches visible on the uphill side of the excavations in this east-facing view were intended to divert rainwater into culverts, protecting the faces of the excavations from erosion and possible collapse onto the track.

EMBANKMENT in DUTCH RAVINE
32.5 miles from Sacramento

This embankment carries the railroad across a swale in Dutch Ravine. The view faces toward the east.

In places in the foothills workers had to scrape over a large area to obtain sufficient material for embankments. The farther the workers had to go to get material, the more time and effort each fill cost. Inspection reports indicate that the tops of embankments were 12 feet wide, but the one in this view appears little wider than the eight-foot crossties. With experience, the standard width for embankments was increased to 14 feet.

All of the embankments were built by hand, and the only compaction they received during construction was from workers and horses walking on them, and later from the passage of trains. Invariably, the first rains caused the banks to settle or wash away entirely. As a consequence, the company found itself constantly rushing repairs to new track during the first weeks of the rainy season. However, once the railroad was built, fill material from distant sources could be delivered by train with relative ease. It took several years of use and repair to get the embankments into a solid state.

APPROACHING BLOOMER CUT

To pass from Dutch Ravine to Baltimore Ravine, the railroad runs through a narrow passage cut in the intervening ridge of conglomerate rock. This excavation, up to 63 feet deep and 800 feet long, was called "Bloomer Cut," taking its name from the adjacent ranch. Work began at Bloomer in February 1864, even before the railroad itself had reached Rocklin. This image looks eastward along the railroad as it turns into the steep-sided excavation.

Before anyone could turn a shovelful of earth for the railroad, the engineers had to first find a suitable route. Later they marked on the ground exactly where the workers were to dig. During construction, engineers periodically checked to see that all was carried out according to plan, and after the roadbed was complete, they staked a centerline for the track layers.

Judah made the initial reconnaissance and preliminary survey of the CP's route, and for about the first 31 miles the railroad followed his line closely, though the location work between Sacramento and Junction was executed under the supervision of his brother Douglas. After Judah's death in 1863, the engineering work was carried on under the leadership of Samuel S. Montague, his former assistant on both the California Central and the CP. Among the engineers working on the CP under Montague's direction were Lewis M. Clement, Charles Cadwalader, Alonzo Guppy, John Kidder, William Hood, John R. Gilliss, Butler Ives, and Joseph M. Graham. Graham lived long enough to attend the ceremony marking the opening of the Golden Gate Bridge in 1937.

BLOOMER CUT
33.5 miles from Sacramento

Given the quantity of explosives used in the construction of the CP, and the number of men engaged, there were remarkably few construction accidents. Bloomer Cut was the scene of the CP's first known construction-related death, which occurred in April 1864. Following the failure of a charge of powder to detonate, construction superintendent James H. Strobridge and some workers commenced reopening the hole to set a new fuse. Inadvertently, they made a spark in striking stone with an iron bar, igniting the powder still in the hole and blasting shards of rock directly into their faces. One Portuguese worker was killed outright, a Frenchman was cut about the face, and Strobridge was blinded in his right eye.

Today, very little of the railroad looks like it did when the CP was built. Embankments and excavations have been widened, in many places to accommodate double tracking, and also to allow access for maintenance-of-way road vehicles. In contrast, except for the establishment of vegetation on the excavation walls, Bloomer Cut has been little altered since 1865. This is thanks to Southern Pacific (SP) President Donald J. Russell, who halted a project to widen the cut, deliberately preserving it as a monument to the CP's early laborers.

This view faces west.

BLOOMER CUT AND EMBANKMENT

To make this view toward the east, Hart placed his camera on a water flume that crossed the center of Bloomer Cut. The resulting image illustrates how material taken from an excavation was used to build an adjacent embankment. The civil engineer's objective was to move as little material as necessary, move it as short a distance as possible, and use all of the material that had to be moved. In this case, material removed from Bloomer Cut was deposited in adjacent Baltimore Ravine, creating a uniform roadbed for the track. Later, the workers were in such a hurry that much material was wasted by simply blasting it out of the way.

All rails laid before October 1866 were connected at their joints with "rail chairs"—wrought iron plates that wrap around the rail base at the joints to hold the adjacent rails in alignment. To accommodate the thickness of the chair beneath the rail, the surface of each joint tie had to be adzed down so the chair base did not lift the rail above the level of the neighboring ties. Wood chips from adzing the joint ties appear in this photograph as light colored material around every tenth tie. Having to adz the ties slowed construction.

Track laying was also slowed by the need to cut a few inches from the rails on the inside of curves to keep the joints directly opposite each other. Keeping the joints "square" simplified rail laying, but even joints were also believed to save wear and tear on rolling stock, and it was the standard of the day.

See an alternate Hart view of this scene on p. 474.

AUBURN STATION
36.24 miles from Sacramento, elevation 1,360 feet

The first CP passenger train ran to Auburn on May 13, 1865. One of the buildings in this image houses the saloon and restaurant run by Furniss & Mahon. The other building is the freight depot operated by George Willment. After his death, Willment's widow continued to run the depot; she was one of several women station agents on the railroad.

The Pacific Railroad Act of 1862 provided that a specific number of United States bonds would be issued to the various companies building the Pacific railroad for each mile of track completed. The requirement that 40 miles of railroad be completed before the first federal bonds would be issued was reduced to 20 miles in 1864, but the CP did not receive any of the federal bonds due it until May 1865, coincident with the opening of the railroad to Auburn.

Upon completion of the railroad in 1869, the CP had received federal bonds with a total face value of $25,885,120. To turn those bonds into cash to pay for construction, the railroad company had to sell them to investors. Because of low confidence in the project during the early years, the bonds rarely sold at par, and the company received a total of only $18,765,047 from their sale. These bonds represented a loan from the government, not a donation, and the entire $25.9 million plus interest was due in 30 years. With the last installment, made in 1909, the CP repaid a total of $58,812,715 to the federal government.

RAILROAD EAST of AUBURN STATION
37 miles from Sacramento

Much of the CP roadbed between Auburn and Clipper Gap was ready for the crossties and rails by May 1865.

This view looks southwestward, back toward Auburn from the first cut east of town. No warning sign protects the crossing just beyond the cut, though signs lettered "LOOK OUT FOR THE LOCOMOTIVE WHEN THE BELL RINGS" are known to have been used at railroad-street crossings in urban areas by this date. On the CP, only the locomotive bell was rung as a warning by trains approaching crossings until February 1882, when the company began to require its engineers to sound the whistle. Until the 1920s the whistle signal for a crossing was two long blasts followed by two shorts, though that last "toot" was probably drawn out until the train reached the road long before the rule was changed to the modern standard. The railroad crossed 20 wagon roads between Newcastle and Colfax.

All the material moved in the excavation of cuts or the building of embankments was shoveled by hand into wheelbarrows or carts. A Placer County tax inventory of October 1865 records that the railroad owned 350 carts, two thousand wheelbarrows, and three thousand shovels. That was nearly as many shovels as the number of workers then employed.

WEST OF CLIPPER GAP
39.3 miles from Sacramento, elevation 1,625 feet

The low points in the ridge the railroad climbs toward the summit controlled its alignment, because the track cannot be higher above the surface of the ground at the gaps than the practical height of trestles—about one hundred feet. But between the gaps, the railroad could run on either side of the intervening highlands, depending upon the economy of earthwork and the location providing the necessary length of line to yield the most suitable rate of ascent. At the location of this Hart photograph, the railroad was built on the north side of the ridge, above Rock Ravine, which drains toward the Bear River.

This view nicely illustrates how stereographic photography enhances the quality of certain views. In this case, the "flat" image does not readily disclose that the man was standing on a ledge well above the level of the track. The photograph also gives some sense of the eastward incline ascended by the railroad. Most of the railroad's gradient from Rocklin to the summit was limited to 105 feet to the mile (about 2%), though in places it reached 116 feet to the mile (2.2%), the federally mandated maximum for the Pacific railroad. Such a sustained ascent required extra locomotives and extra fuel to pull the trains uphill, as well as careful braking on the descent.

TRESTLE at LOVELL'S RANCH
40.3 miles from Sacramento

The CP built 10 big trestles. Nine of them were located between Newcastle and Gold Run, though their greatest concentration was within a four-mile stretch centered on Clipper Gap. In that distance, five trestles spanned a succession of gaps and gulches. The first two of these were a quarter-mile apart at Samuel W. Lovell's ranch; of them, this was the second. The view looks eastward.

Unlike the truss bridges, which were sheathed and painted for protection against the weather, all the components of the trestles were exposed to the elements and they were a continual fire hazard. For this reason, they were replaced by embankments as soon as possible. Two of the five trestles near Clipper Gap were filled or bypassed in 1873, and the others, including the two at Lovell's ranch, were eliminated in 1876. In that same year the big trestles at Newcastle, Auburn, Long Ravine, and Secret Town were also filled in. The big trestle near Cisco was replaced with a bridge in 1869. Thus, within a decade of the completion of the railroad to Donner Pass, all of these notable structures had vanished.

The location of some of these trestles can only be determined with difficulty, as the topography of this district was altered considerably with the construction of the second track between Roseville and Colfax in 1911-12. Building Interstate 80 changed the country even more; it was completed through Clipper Gap in 1960.

CLIPPER GAP
42.8 miles from Sacramento, elevation 1,759 feet

The CP's track reached Clipper Gap on June 7, 1865, with service to that point commencing on June 10. The California Stage Company began connecting with the trains here in July.

The railroad company first tried its hand at town-building at Clipper Gap, even constructing a toll road from Nevada City to feed traffic to the railroad at this point. However, the town project failed, simply because Clipper Gap was not a terminus for long enough to attract any significant development. Before the end of that summer, the railroad had been extended nearly a dozen miles to Colfax. In 1879, Clipper Gap was eclipsed by Applegate, a new station established just three miles farther up the line.

In the early years, while it was functioning as a station, the limited facilities at Clipper Gap consisted of the depot, a 220-foot long woodshed, a 14,000-gallon, four-cistern water tower, and two handcar houses.

In 1880, the California Iron & Steel Company built a blast furnace at Hotaling, three miles west of Clipper Gap. It produced pig iron utilizing local iron ore, marble (used as a flux), and charcoal. Its product was used in the manufacture of wheels for railroad cars but production ceased after a few years. The Excelsior Lime Works was located about two miles above Clipper Gap in 1885.

29. Trestle in Clipper Ravine, near Clipper Gap.

TRESTLE in CLIPPER RAVINE
43.7 miles from Sacramento

Two trestles were built in the mile immediately east of the station at Clipper Gap. Both were about 450 feet long. The first of these was known as the "Clipper Gap" trestle, the second as "Clipper Ravine," though it merely crossed a gulch that drained steeply down into Clipper Ravine proper. The latter structure was the subject of this Hart photograph. This trestle was about 50 feet tall. In 1873 it was one of the trestles that was filled in.

Until July 10, 1865, when the end-of-track was nearly to this point, the CP was the only company engaged in actual construction of the Pacific railroad. However, on that date the UP commenced construction westward from Omaha, Nebraska.

About this same time, the first of the workers recruited in China began to arrive. The Chinese who worked on the CP, whether those recruited directly from China or Gold Rush immigrants, came primarily from the districts around Canton in southern China. Most were in their early twenties and most came from an agricultural background. As it happened, the labor-intensive rice farming practiced in southern China fostered a culture of industriousness that the Chinese easily applied to the demanding work of building the railroad.

DEEP GULCH TRESTLE-BRIDGE
44.25 miles from Sacramento

About 1.5 miles east of Clipper Gap, the railroad crossed Deep Gulch on a spectacular trestle, rising nearly one hundred feet above the gully. Because of its height, it was built to an unusual design, incorporating eight truss bridges, with 50-foot and 80-foot sections of conventional trestlework at either end. This view shows the 40-foot long Palladio "straining-beam" trusses used in the Deep Gulch structure. The use of these truss sections reduced the number of bents, which here required exceptionally long timbers. The mast in the foreground was probably left over from erecting the bridge. The speed limit for trains on all bridges and trestles was six miles per hour.

Both this and the adjacent Clipper Ravine trestle were eliminated in 1873 by shifting the line into the ridge, away from Clipper Creek, a realignment that required a new, 700-foot long tunnel. This was the CP's 16th tunnel, but to preserve the established west-to-east numbering sequence, the new tunnel was assigned "Number 0." Tunnel no. 0 remained in service for 70 years but it was eventually abandoned because of its substandard clearances. The tunnel was originally built the proper size. However, after being lined, there were soon indications of a general cave-in, so a second rock lining was built inside the first, just barely leaving room for trains to transit the tunnel without touching its sides.

CUT near NEW ENGLAND MILLS
46.5 miles from Sacramento

The railroad climbs steadily from Clipper Gap through Wildcat Summit and Star House Gap to George's and Summit gaps and then is nearly level from New England Mills to Colfax, climbing only 130 feet in the last 5.87 miles. Still, there were some major excavations in that section, totaling nearly a mile in length. The cut at George's Gap was 1,150 feet long, and two of the other cuts were more than 50 feet deep.

George's Gap was named for George Giesendorfer, one of the first settlers near what became New England Mills, a station 49 miles from Sacramento at an elevation of 2,280 feet. The sawmill at New England Mills was operated by Massachusetts-born John Starbuck, and his origin is probably what gave the location its name. When building within the first few miles from Sacramento, the CP obtained most of its wood products from sawmills located along the Pacific shore, with the lumber being delivered to Sacramento by schooners. However, once the railroad finally entered the forests of the Sierra, it was able to load products from local sawmills directly onto the cars.

When a post office was established at New England Mills in 1886, it was named "Weimar" after a well-known local Indian. However, the railroad continued to use the original name until the station was closed in the 1970s.

Depot at Colfax.

DEPOT AT COLFAX
54.18 miles from Sacramento, elevation 2,418 feet

The railroad reached Colfax on September 1, 1865. In the five months since track construction had resumed at Newcastle, the rails had been extended 23 miles. This remained the end of operations until July 1866.

Just the month before its track reached Colfax, the CP finally acquired control of the rival SVRR. By reducing service on the SVRR, the CP was able to divert a significant portion of the trans-Sierra commerce to its own line and wagon road, though the railroad did not dominate the Washoe trade until it reached Cisco more than a year later. To accommodate the commerce it expected to transfer from trains to wagons at Colfax, the CP built the 280-foot long freight depot seen in this photograph.

San Francisco's *Alta California* newspaper recorded: "[Colfax] has the largest freight depot of any of the towns on the railroad . . . , and at this point is deposited the greater portion of the freight for the extensive mining district of Grass Valley and Nevada [City]. In passing on the cars you do not get a view of the town, the large depot shutting it off, and a stranger in passing would hardly think it consisted of more than the depot and passenger house, but on going a few steps and turning the corner, Colfax in all of its primitive grandeur burst upon the view. It consists of about 100 business houses, with all the different trades to make it complete."

LOCOMOTIVE NO. 8, NEVADA, AT COLFAX

When the CP reached Colfax it was operating with six locomotives, nine passenger-train cars, 39 boxcars, and 65 flatcars. In December the *A.A. Sargent* was delivered, and in March 1866 locomotives no. 8, *Nevada*, and no. 9, *Utah*, arrived. They were the first pair of eight nearly identical mogul-type locomotives built for the CP by Danforth Locomotive & Machine of Paterson, New Jersey.

Due in part to the disruptions of the Civil War economy, the *Nevada* and *Utah* turned out to be the most expensive locomotives on the CP. At $36,438.57 apiece, they cost more than twice the *Gov. Stanford*. Unfortunately, the company was disappointed with them almost immediately. Hopkins complained that they were poorly finished, with their paint flaking off. More seriously, their long wheelbase resulted in rapid wear of the front driver tires and countless broken rails. Eventually the company learned that machining the flanges off the middle drivers provided some relief, but these particular locomotives spent lots of time in the repair shop. All but one of these locomotives were converted to conventional 4-4-0s within a few years.

In the early days, Colfax boasted a turntable, an engine house with capacity for two locomotives, and a woodshed that was two hundred feet long. Throughout the days of steam, Colfax was home to helper engines added to trains for the steeper grade above.

LONG RAVINE BRIDGE
55.8 miles from Sacramento

The deepest gap in the ridge the CP ascended is just above Colfax, where the Bear River and the American River make their closest approach to each other. Long Ravine runs north from the gap to the Bear River, and it gives the bridge its name. Rice's Ravine, which is the more commanding of the two as viewed from a train, drains south from the gap into the American River. The depression at Long Ravine is so deep that the eastward grade is downhill from Colfax to the crossing. To avoid losing any more elevation than necessary, the company built its tallest structure—a combination trestle and bridge that carried the track 115 feet above the gap. Altogether, it consisted of a bridge made up of two 150-foot, and one 128-foot Howe-truss spans, with a 450-foot long approach trestle on the west, and a four-bent trestle on the east. The west approach trestle—the focus of this Hart image—was filled in as a solid embankment in 1876.

In August 1865, as railroad building below Colfax was finished, workers were moved ahead to the alignment between Colfax and Dutch Flat. By late summer the workforce had grown to some four thousand, and moving the camps and all of the equipment took considerable time and effort. Nevertheless, by September, most of the 13 miles of grade between Colfax and Dutch Flat was being worked, and it was almost ready for the track by year's end.

LONG RAVINE BRIDGE from BELOW

One of the four Mason-built 4-6-0s (the group including no. 6, *Conness*) heads a westbound train stopped on the Long Ravine Bridge for the photographer. The men standing on the car tops were brakemen whose jobs were to apply the cars' brakes upon a signal from the engineer.

Rails were laid across the completed bridge in early April 1866. By 1873 the bridge trusses and piers were sheathed with corrugated iron to protect them from the weather and fire. From 1875 until 1942, the track of the Nevada County Narrow Gauge Railroad, connecting Colfax with Grass Valley and Nevada City, passed under the structure. The original bridge was replaced in 1889 by an iron viaduct, which was remodeled just eight years later. In 1914 a parallel structure was built just to the north for the railroad's second track. Interstate 80 was opened under the twin viaducts in 1958.

Hart was very sensitive to artistic composition in his works. This is one of the few images he made with the railroad running directly across the scene. His more typical formula was to arrange the view with the track sweeping off dramatically into the distance, a composition that worked well in stereoscopic photographs because it contributes to the sense of movement and depth. In this picture, Hart relies on the wagon road to lead the viewer's eye into the scene.

ROUNDING CAPE HORN
56.8 miles from Sacramento

Once across Long Ravine, the railroad runs on a narrow shelf carved around the face of a bluff called "Cape Horn." Pioneers who had immigrated by sea around Cape Horn, at the far end of South America, long remembered the difficulty of the months-long voyage and the perilous, fierce storms. Subsequently, they freely applied the name "Cape Horn" to various roundabout detours they encountered, such as this promontory high above the North Fork of the American River, with Rice's Ravine falling away on the west side, and Robbers' Ravine on the east.

In running around Rice's Ravine and doubling Cape Horn, trains describe an "S" curve, making two complete changes of direction within two miles. While the overall curvature in both of these bends exceeds 180°, they originally were composed of small distinct curves interspersed with short tangents.

The eastbound locomotive in this Hart view appears to be one of the Mason 4-4-0s. The whistle, in the immediate foreground, sits atop the steam dome, which encases the engine's throttle high above the boiler's water level. Beyond that is the sand dome, which holds sand to be released onto slippery rails to give the engine traction. The large spark arrestor over the smokestack at the front of the boiler is characteristic of wood-burning locomotives. It was intended to limit the spread of burning embers as much as possible.

CANYON OF THE NORTH FORK OF THE AMERICAN RIVER
57.1 miles from Sacramento

For this photograph Hart posed diminutive locomotive no. 3, *C.P. Huntington*, at the tip of Cape Horn with the canyon of the North Fork of the American River as its backdrop. At this point the river is some 1,300 feet lower than the elevation of the track. The locomotive was named for the CP's vice president.

In November 1866, an inebriated passenger was put off a westbound train at Gold Run. Infuriated at the affront to his dignity, the drunk resolved to continue his journey with the aid of gravity and a boxcar he saw near the depot. After aligning the switch for the main track, he climbed on board and released the car's brakes. Set free on the 2% downgrade, the car was soon rolling ever faster down the mountain railroad, over high trestles and around the bends. Careening around Cape Horn and across the Long Ravine Bridge on the roof of a boxcar must have been exhilarating. It must have been sobering, too, because when the car rolled to a stop on the short upgrade west of Long Ravine, the daredevil climbed down and went directly to the nearest saloon in Colfax for another drink.

The freight car, abandoned where it came to rest on the mainline, was smashed by the next train to come along. The boxcar thief was carted off to jail.

See an alternate Hart view of this scene on p.467.

EXCURSION TRAIN AT CAPE HORN
57.2 miles from Sacramento

Rail laying eastward from Colfax got underway in early April 1866 upon completion of the bridge at Long Ravine. By then, 12 miles of roadbed were ready for track, and by the end of the month the railroad had been extended five miles. The view from Cape Horn was so spectacular that it immediately became a destination for special excursions, as well as a place where, for many years, regular trains stopped to allow passengers to enjoy the view. The excursion train in this Hart photograph is led by one of the Danforth 2-6-0 locomotives. The image probably dates from late April 1866; there were three excursions to Cape Horn in that month alone. Rice's Ravine and Colfax are visible beyond the train.

This particular view gives some indication of the original slope of the face of Cape Horn, which at its steepest dropped off at an angle of 75°. However, in cutting the roadbed its full width into the bluff, to provide a solid footing for the track, the finished slope above the railroad seems nearly perpendicular in places.

When the second track was built at Cape Horn in 1914, it was run through a pair of tunnels (nos. 33 and 34). Because it made something of a shortcut to the original track around the point, the new line was dubbed the "Panama Canal" after the isthmian waterway just then being completed to shortcut the long sea route around Cape Horn at the tip of South America.

SAWMILL AND CUT EAST OF CAPE HORN
58.5 miles from Sacramento

The railroad station just above Cape Horn was known for many years as "Cape Horn Mills." This was the location of yet another sawmill that provided timber products to the railroad. In addition to lumber, stacks of firewood for the locomotives can be seen in this view, which faces northeast. Where possible, firewood was delivered to landings higher than the track, so that it could be tossed downward to the locomotive tenders or wood cars.

CP locomotives averaged about 30 miles to the cord of wood, but they easily burned more than 20 cords working uphill over the 83 miles from Rocklin to Summit. To make that trip, trains had to stop five or six times to "wood up" the tenders (two or more locomotives were almost always required on the uphill trains). In the early days in fair weather, restless passengers sometimes assisted in tossing the two-foot splits of firewood into the tender, but the task generally fell to the fireman and brakemen. Crews often allowed transients free passage over the road in exchange for helping with the wood chores.

In 1902 this station name was changed to "Caporn," and it became "Cape Horn" 12 years later.

SECRET RAVINE, IOWA HILL IN DISTANCE
60 miles from Sacramento

East of Cape Horn the railroad skirts along the south side of Hayford Hill above Secret Ravine. (This is a different Secret Ravine than the one just east of Rocklin.) The locomotive in this view is no. 3, *C.P. Huntington*.

The *C.P. Huntington* and its twin no. 4, *T.D. Judah*, were "single-driver" locomotives designed for pulling light trains. They were built by Danforth Locomotive & Machine, invoiced in October and November 1863 respectively, and placed in service in April 1864. A similar locomotive, the *Oakland*, was acquired second-hand from the San Francisco & Oakland Railroad in about 1874 and became the second no. 93 on the CP. These locomotives proved too light to be of much use as rolling stock became heavier. The *Huntington* was eventually sold to the SP, and the *Judah* was rebuilt with a separate tender and assigned to pull commuter trains in the Oakland-Berkeley area. Both the *Judah* and *Oakland* are long gone, but the *C.P. Huntington* is preserved in Sacramento.

The prominent point in the distance is Iowa Hill, some five miles to the southeast. Another seven or eight miles beyond that was the mining town of Michigan City, where Leland Stanford had a store and got his start in politics as its justice of the peace.

The anaglyph opposite is a composite made from the stereocard above, and another with a different cropping.

SECRET TOWN
62.1 miles from Sacramento, elevation 2,950 feet

The railroad reached Secret Town on May 5, 1866. This was briefly the end-of-track while carpenters completed the massive trestle across the gap just beyond. A temporary turntable was installed when the railroad arrived, but no large freight depot was ever built here because freight trains continued to stop at Colfax until the line was opened to Alta in July. The large building adjacent to the curve is a sawmill used to cut timbers for the Secret Ravine trestle, which is faintly visible through the trees in the middle distance.

In crossing the gap at Secret Ravine the railroad also crossed from the American River side of the ridge to the Bear River watershed on the north. According to Judah's original design, the railroad was to remain on the Bear River side of the ridge all the way from Secret Ravine until it entered the Yuba River watershed at Yuba Pass. Thus, Secret Ravine would have been the last gap the railroad crossed. However, the railroad above was eventually built on a course that brought it back over to the south side of the divide.

Most of the rail laid between Colfax and Secret Town was originally imported to California by the Placerville & Sacramento Valley for use on its projected railroad between Shingle Springs and Placerville. However, when the CP acquired control of the SVRR, the Placerville company abandoned those plans and sold the rail.

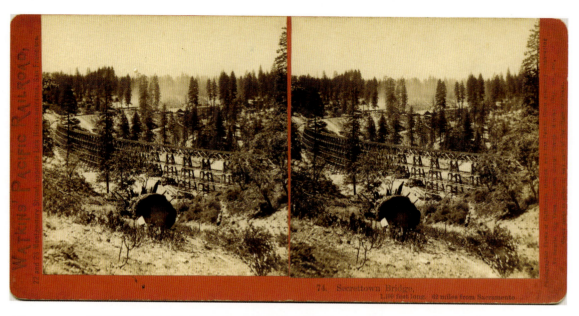

SECRET TOWN TRESTLE, FROM THE EAST
62.4 miles from Sacramento

In this view toward the west, smoke from the sawmill beyond the trees marks the location of Secret Town itself.

At about one thousand feet in length, the trestle at Secret Town was the longest on the railroad other than the approaches to the bridge across the American River at Sacramento. At its highest point, the gracefully curved structure carried the rails some 90 feet above the bottom of the gap. Like the structure at Deep Gulch, the Secret Town trestle was a combination of conventional trestlework and 40-foot straining-beam truss spans. It was nearly as tall as the trestle at Deep Gulch, and the extreme height of both structures accounts for the design used.

The trestle was completed in mid June 1866, concluding Secret Town's brief tenure as the railroad's terminus. Ten years later the trestle was buried in a solid embankment, which was widened in 1914 to make room for the second track. In 1958 Interstate 80 was opened on a parallel embankment built immediately to the south. Perhaps because the modern highway is so close to the level of the track, few recognize the bank with the gentle curve as the vestige of the old CP trestle.

TUNNEL HILL
62.7 miles from Sacramento

Tunnel Hill was located just east of Secret Ravine. In the days when material was moved by shovel and cart, a tunnel was more economical than an open excavation if the cut needed to be more than about 60 feet deep. Accordingly, the company's original plans called for a tunnel at this point. However, when digging began, the ground proved to be too unstable to stand without support, so a large excavation was opened instead. The resulting open cut was 110 feet deep at its extreme.

Keeping this excavation open proved to be as difficult as digging it in the first place. When the soil in this area gets soggy, it loses its strength and begins to flow. Because the winter of 1866 was unusually wet, the excavation sides repeatedly squeezed out onto the roadbed in a spongy mass. As many as five hundred men were put to work shoveling, but for days the sides of the excavation collapsed as fast as the crew could remove the material. The only recourse was to cut back the excavation walls in broad terraces to reduce the overburden. Making the most of the unusually heavy rainfall, workers eventually diverted water from a nearby ditch to flush away unwanted material. By the time Hart took this picture, the cut had been opened much wider than initially envisioned.

BEAR RIVER VALLEY, FROM NEAR GOLD RUN

For the five miles from Secret Town to Alta, the railroad runs along the north side of the ridge dividing the American and Bear rivers. Above Long Ravine, this ridge was known in the 1850s and 60s as the "Dutch Flat Divide," named for what was then the area's principle town. Traveling past Cold Spring Hill passengers were offered some spectacular views overlooking the Bear River Valley and the hydraulic mines at Little York, You Bet, and Red Dog. The scar of one of those mines can be seen in the distance in this Hart photograph.

The most economical method for recovering gold from placer deposits is to wash the material in riffled sluices, leaving the heavy gold trapped in their crevices. In hydraulic mining, streams of water were used, not just for processing, but to flush entire hillsides into the sluices. To accomplish this, extensive water systems were developed. These included upstream reservoirs and networks of flumes and ditches to feed the high-pressure nozzles, known as monitors. While the CP took advantage of the long, continuous ridge between the American and Bear watersheds as a ramp to the summit, credit for first surveying that divide and discovering its features belongs to the mining engineers who developed the water systems that supplied the hydraulic mines around Dutch Flat. Their flumes and ditches were already in place before Daniel Strong of Dutch Flat invited Theodore Judah to determine whether the old wagon above town could be developed as a trans-Sierra thoroughfare.

108

TRAIN in DIXIE CUT
64.25 miles from Sacramento

Just a mile and a half past Tunnel Hill the railroad cuts through Dixie Spur, another excavation that caused considerable problems. As at Tunnel Hill, the ground turned spongy when wet, and the excavation walls repeatedly collapsed onto the grade. Work began here in August 1865, and the track was laid 10 months later, following the completion of the trestle at Secret Town. But, as this westward facing view shows, the work of widening the excavation continued even after the railroad was in place. When this photograph was made, the excavation sides were being cut back into terraces to reduce the pressure on the lower slopes. The company had two full seasons of "infernal slides"—as E.B. Crocker termed them— before this cut and the one at Tunnel Hill were finally stabilized.

A foreman and five workers were killed here by a premature blast of black powder in April 1866. The coincidence of this accident with a devastating explosion of nitroglycerin in downtown San Francisco just the day before led the CP to destroy its own small stock of nitro, with which it had been experimenting. Later, when they were chipping away at the granite of Summit Tunnel, the company reintroduced the use of nitroglycerin. But then, to avoid the hazards of shipping the explosive, it was manufactured on site.

See an alternate Hart view of this scene on p. 448.

55. Flume and Railroad at Gold Run.
64 miles from Sacramento.

GOLD RUN
64.64 miles from Sacramento, elevation 3,227 feet

Gold Run was first established as "Mountain Springs" by Orrin W. Hollenbeck. It received its modern name in 1863 and was a booming mining town before the railroad was built through it in late June 1866.

At Gold Run the railroad ran directly alongside the flume that supplied water to local hydraulic mines. Elisha Bradley was the prominent Dutch Flat ditch owner, and he was one of the few men not associated with the CP who was a stockholder in the Dutch Flat & Donner Lake Wagon Road. Despite the association, Bradley gave no favors to the railroad, charging full price for any water used by men, animals, locomotives, or directly for construction. While the Pacific Railroad Act granted right of way, earth, stone, and timber from public lands for construction, it did not grant water. Hopkins called the ditch companies "water sharks." They were quick to appropriate any water rights they did not already hold.

In the winter of 1866, the mud was so bad that supplies and material for the railroad builders had to be delivered by pack mules rather than wagons. Mules were even used to carry travelers after a stagecoach became stuck in the mud in the middle of Gold Run. The coach remained a fixture in the street for six weeks, and not until March could wheeled vehicles again navigate the wagon roads.

DUTCH FLAT STATION
66.8 miles from Sacramento, elevation 3,390 feet

The little town of Dutch Flat played an important role in the birth of the CP. When the Comstock Lode was discovered in late 1859, Dutch Flat citizens watched with envy as communities on various roads to Nevada prospered from the sudden rush of traffic. Although Dutch Flat was only a few miles from the oldest trans-Sierra wagon trail, the Donner Party had given that route a bad reputation by getting snowbound in 1846, and it had not been used much since. In an effort to develop a road from Dutch Flat to Donner Pass and to bring some of the commerce their way, local druggist Daniel Strong invited Judah to look at their route.

Like nearly everyone else, Judah had initially believed the eventual Pacific railroad would run around one end of the Sierra Nevada or the other. But his brief tour to Donner Pass with Daniel Strong in October 1860 convinced him that the old wagon route through the heart of the central Sierra was suitable for a railroad. Judah quickly recognized that the rich Comstock commerce justified the heavy expense of construction in the mountains and, further, it could finally bring about building the Pacific railroad for which he had agitated for years. Upon his return to Dutch Flat from the summit, Judah drew up the initial charter for the company that would become the CP.

As developed, the railroad did not touch Dutch Flat itself, but the track reached nearby Dutch Flat Station on July 1, 1866.

SANDSTONE CUT NEAR ALTA
68 miles from Sacramento

Above Colfax, solid rock obstructions were increasingly encountered. However, the curtailment of experimentation with nitroglycerin in April 1866 left the CP with only black powder as an explosive agent. The loose powder was poured into holes drilled into the rock and then detonated with a burning fuse. While compressed-air drills existed in the 1860s, none were used by the CP, and all the rock drilling was done by hand.

By the time crews began working above Colfax in late 1865, the company had prepared a special car for transporting blasting powder. It began as an ordinary boxcar, but its sides were sheathed with "Russia iron," with rubber gaskets around the doors to exclude sparks. Its roof was made of thin tin so that, should an explosion occur, the force would go up rather than out. The word "POWDER" was painted on its sides in big letters. The car was no doubt pulled at the very tail end of trains.

The farther the railroad went into the mountains, the harder the rock and the greater the demand for powder. By 1867, the men were using 250-300 kegs of black powder daily, and the demand for it continued to grow until they were well out of the Sierra. The company was in such a hurry to build the railroad that they wasted powder to simply blast earth and rocks off the grade, while the more economical course would have been to break up the rocks with powder and move the pieces by hand. E.B. Crocker explained, "powder is cheaper than muscles."

SUPERINTENDENT STROBRIDGE AND FAMILY

Building the CP was a team effort involving several thousand men, most of whom are entirely unknown to us. Of the top managers, Charles Crocker, the contractor, was the one most often at scenes of activity, visiting at least once a month to distribute the payroll. E.B. Crocker managed to get beyond the end-of-track once or twice a year, while Mark Hopkins only rarely left of Sacramento. Stanford seems to have spent most of his time in San Francisco, and Huntington was in New York.

Construction superintendent James Harvey Strobridge was always at the front, assigning tasks and directing the men. And, Strobridge was the only one associated with the construction of the railroad who was regularly accompanied by his wife. While they had no children of their own, Strobridge and his wife adopted two children while the CP was being built (and eventually, four more). Together, they followed the work continuously until the CP was completed.

While building west of the summit, the work advanced very slowly, allowing the establishment of fixed camps with regular board or log cabins. Strobridge lived in this cabin at Alta with his family during the spring and summer of 1866. Later, when the activity had advanced into Nevada and the track was being extended rapidly, the men lived in tents or in the outfit cars of a camp train. Then, Strobridge and his family lived in a special car fitted out as a house and office.

ALTA
68.65 miles from Sacramento, elevation 3,607 feet

The railroad reached Alta on July 9, 1866. One contemporary report suggests that the station was named to flatter the management of the *Alta California* newspaper. But it seems more likely that the name was recognition of the fact that, when the railroad arrived here, it was the highest point reached by rail in either North America or Europe.

While the railroad opened to Cisco at the end of November 1866, problems with snow, washouts, and the general disruption of new track often made Alta the end of regular operations through March 1867. While the trip to Virginia City from Alta required 12 hours, that was better time than by any other route, and the opening of the railroad to Alta cut deeply into the traffic that remained on the older Placerville road.

In this photograph, facing northwest, the depot-tavern-hotel is in the distance on the left, partially hidden behind the trees. This passenger facility was operated by Edgar M. Banvard, who later became a state senator. That may be the Strobridge cabin behind the trees on the left. The freight depot is on the right.

The spur track leading off the picture to the left went to the turntable. A turntable remained in use at Alta until 1892, when it and the snowplow house were moved to Gold Run.

73. Cut above Alta. Placer County.

CUT ABOVE ALTA
68.8 miles from Sacramento

This view toward the southeast, faces the vantage point from which Hart made the previous photograph. Alta sits atop the Dutch Flat Divide, which the railroad was climbing toward the summit, and this excavation led the railroad back into the American River watershed.

Having experienced the tendency of soil in the vicinity to turn spongy and collapse into excavations, the CP here has resorted to terraced cuts. Still, no more material has been removed than is absolutely necessary to provide clearance for the trains. A special alcove has been carved out to make space for the harp switch-stand on the left.

Fresh-cut railroad crossties are stacked to the right. From 2,200-2,400 ties were used per mile, depending upon the curvature, grade, and length of rails. The headquarters and mill of the Towle Brothers lumbering operation was located just above Alta. It eventually had its own station on the railroad, named "Towle." By the 1880s the local trees had all been cut, and Towle Brothers needed to go farther afield to harvest timber. It eventually built a narrow gauge railroad down into Bear Valley to bring logs up to the sawmill.

BLASTING AT CHALK BLUFFS ABOVE ALTA
69 miles from Sacramento

Several sections of roadbed between Dutch Flat and Emigrant Gap were being worked by April 1866, and track laying eastward from Alta resumed in mid-September.

The caption to this east-facing view suggests that blasting was still being carried out at Chalk Bluffs to prepare the grade. However, as with other earthwork between Secret Town and Canyon Creek, this particular excavation presented trouble for years, and it is possible that the workers seen in the photograph are actually removing debris from a slide. The fact that the terrace is so much wider than seems necessary for the railroad suggests that they were already having trouble with these banks.

A major landslide at this location in 1880 was cleared using a hydraulic mining monitor fed by pipes and a purpose-built flume delivering water from Canyon Creek, which the railroad crosses less than a mile beyond. While free-flowing water was used elsewhere to flush material from excavations, this is the only known instance of a monitor being used by the CP in the Sierra. Modern Interstate 80 crosses the railroad at the point in the near distance where the roadbed curves toward the right.

72. Culvert at Canyon Creek.
185 feet long—12 feet span.

CULVERT AT CANYON CREEK
69.7 miles from Sacramento

The first step in building a railroad embankment was to construct a culvert as long as the finished bank was wide, and of sufficient size to carry the heaviest expected discharge from the upstream watershed. If the culvert was omitted, or the potential freshet underestimated, the embankment would block free drainage and might be washed out. While brick culverts were built west of Rocklin, and some temporary timber trestles were apparently built in Nevada and Utah, the culverts built by the CP in the Sierra were constructed of native stone.

This stone arch culvert, built to carry Canyon Creek under a large embankment a mile above Alta, was the largest such structure on the railroad. Canyon Creek is a tributary of the North Fork of the American River, and at this point it was also carrying the water of Elisha Bradley's Placer Canal. The culvert was 185 feet long with an opening 12 feet wide. The overall height of the culvert structure was 28 feet and it was 54 feet wide. This culvert is still in use, though it has been extended to conform to the width of the modern embankment, which carries two tracks. Another culvert, at Coldstream, 6.5 miles west of Truckee, has the same cross section, but because that embankment is lower, the Coldstream culvert is not as long.

BUILDING EMBANKMENT across CANYON CREEK

This view, looking back toward Alta, shows the embankment being filled in over the finished barrel vault of the Canyon Creek culvert. In the foreground workers are shoveling material into one-horse dump carts for the short haul to the fill. Nearby, some large tree stumps with their masses of roots await removal. Grubbing out stumps and roots was laborious, time consuming, and expensive, but if left in the ground the roots would decay and weaken the roadbed.

During the summer of 1866, when the end-of-track was at Alta, Hart ventured along the path of the unfinished grade as far east as the crest of the Sierra Nevada, photographing scenes of construction activity. Comparing the stages of the work in various views suggests that he made at least two excursions into this section that summer. In some pictures, such as this one, much work remained to be done, while other views show the roadbed ready for the railroad superstructure. On the other hand, adjacent sections of roadbed were not necessarily finished at the same time. Track laying advanced lineally, as the rail and other track hardware were delivered over the railroad itself as it was extended. But the roadbed was prepared in disconnected sections, often far in advance of the railhead, with graders' camps scattered over scores of miles along the engineers' staked line.

153. Hog's Back Cut, 60 feet deep. 2 miles above Alta.

HOG'S BACK CUT
70.26 miles from Sacramento

Immediately past the crossing of Canyon Creek, the railroad turns left through a gap in Hog's Back Ridge, which divides Canyon Creek from the North Fork of the American River. The train in this Hart image is heading east. Today, Hog's Back Ridge is known as "Moody Ridge." Note the splits of firewood neatly stacked on the terrace, and the excursionists watching Hart from the baggage car's gallery. We see this same two-car train in several photographs made in the summer of 1867 between Alta and Cisco.

To gain 6,750 feet in elevation between Rocklin and Summit at a gradient of 105 feet per mile, the CP engineers needed to find the most economical route for at least 65 miles of railroad. In fact, the route needed to be considerably longer than that since the rate of ascent was reduced in every curve to compensate for friction. The original route Judah surveyed for the railroad ran up the Bear River side of the Dutch Flat Divide all the way from Secret Town to the Yuba River. But when the engineers attempted to establish its precise location, the best line that could be developed required 20 miles at a grade of 116 feet to the mile and many 14° curves. While this just barely met the stipulations of the Pacific Railroad Act, the CP sought to hold curvature to 8° or less. Thus challenged, Lewis Clement found a better line on the south side of the divide between Alta and Emigrant Gap, and Judah's line above Dutch Flat was abandoned.

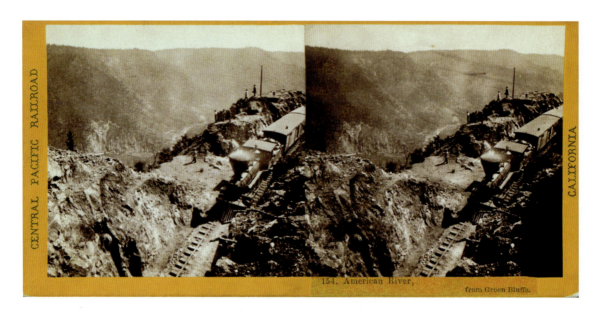

AMERICAN RIVER from GREEN BLUFFS
71.2 miles from Sacramento, elevation 4,016 feet

The railroad emerges on the south side of Hog's Back high above the North Fork of the American River. The track here is nearly half a mile above the river—about twice the elevation differential as at Cape Horn, just a few miles to the southwest. Green Valley is immediately below the overlook while the narrow canyon just downstream is called "Giant Gap."

Green Valley was the scene of considerable mining activity in the 1850s, supporting more than one thousand miners. However, its location deep in the bottom of the American River canyon made it extremely isolated. All supplies had to be delivered on pack animals since the few trails into the canyon were too steep and rough for wagons.

In 1911 the CP established a telegraph station named "Gorge" at this point overlooking the American River canyon. It was vital in controlling train movements over what was then a busy single-track railroad. In 1916 the station was renamed "American." It was provided with a large concrete platform, and until the 1930s, trains stopped to allow passengers to get out and enjoy the view. The second track through here was opened in 1913.

This and the following photograph probably date from the same occasion in the summer of 1867.

FORKS OF THE AMERICAN RIVER

This photograph was taken from nearly the same position as the previous view, with the camera reoriented toward the left, facing up the canyon of the North Fork of the American River. Two branches of the river join immediately below the onlookers. The forks are divided by Sawtooth Ridge, which looms into view from the left.

This view illustrates the importance to the CP of the long ridge that divides the Bear River watershed from the American River watershed. The descending streams of the western slope of the Sierra have carved deep canyons divided by high ridges. Where these streams merge, the intervening ridges end abruptly, as Sawtooth Ridge does here. It was simply beyond the technology and economic resources of the day to bridge such a chasm, and descending to the level of the river for a conventional bridge so close to the summit would have required a gradient too steep for mainline trains. Only those few ridges that divide principle river systems, such as the one the CP followed, provide a generally uniform incline extending all the way from the Sacramento Valley to the crest of the Sierra Nevada—a great enough distance to yield an acceptable rate of ascent.

This is probably the locomotive that we see pulling Hart's two-car excursion train in other photographs between Alta and Cisco. It is no. 22, *Auburn*, a 4-6-0 built by McKay & Aldus. It went into service in March 1867.

VIEW WEST of PROSPECT HILL
75 miles from Sacramento

The embankment that commands the viewer's attention in this photograph carried the track across Little Blue Canyon. The view is from the north, with Sawtooth Ridge and the canyon of the North Fork of the American River in the distance. The condition of the roadbed here and the dating of adjacent photographs suggest that this image was made in September 1866, about the time track building resumed at Alta. This location was fairly accessible from the Dutch Flat & Donner Lake Wagon Road, which was less than half a mile to the north, just behind the ridge where Hart placed his camera to make this and the following photograph.

Shady Run was a construction camp located just around the distant bend of the roadbed at a point 73.49 miles from Sacramento. Rail was laid to Shady Run by September 28. Up to that point, track was built at an average of about one mile per week. But three simple changes doubled the rate of construction: fish bars instead of rail chairs were used for rail joints, eliminating the need to adze joint ties; rail length was increased from 24 to 28 feet; and a portion of the rails were made slightly shorter at the factories, sparing the workers the task of cutting inside rails on curves to keep the joints even.

Shady Run was renamed "Midas" in 1905. Today the nearby community is called "Casa Loma".

PROSPECT HILL
75 miles from Sacramento

Turning his camera just to the left from its orientation for the previous view, Hart here captured some of the activity related to opening an excavation through the ridge separating Little Blue Canyon from Blue Canyon proper.

At the preferred gradient of 105 feet to the mile, the CP faced a half-mile long tunnel through this ridge. In part to avoid this, sections of the ascent above Alta were increased to 116 feet to the mile, raising the elevation of the railroad at this point enough to reduce the length of the expected tunnel to some four hundred feet. At that length and depth, an open excavation was more economical.

Fortuitously, Bradley's Placer Canal, which delivered water to the mines around Dutch Flat, ran just above the railroad's alignment. A great deal of shoveling was avoided by using water from Bradley's ditch to wash material from the cut, much as the miners used the water in their hydraulic mines. To soften the earth, the ground where the cut was to be made was first drilled and blasted, and then water was turned from the ditch to flush away unwanted material.

In this view, the scar of the ditch itself can be seen on the hillside above the railroad grade, beyond the cabin roof.

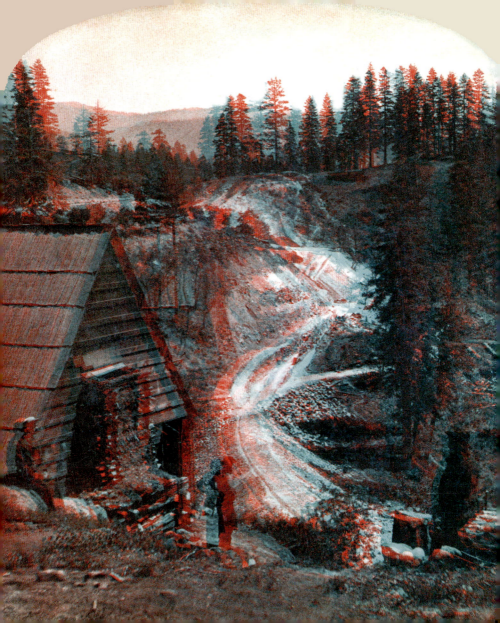

PROSPECT HILL CUT
75.17 miles from Sacramento

Opening the excavation at Prospect Hill was a major undertaking. Its upper slope was 170 feet deep.

The use of water to flush the cuts at Tunnel Hill and Prospect Hill was only possible because of the proximity of ditches conveying water to the nearby mining works. We know of the water system only through written accounts. By the time Hart arrived on the scene at Prospect Hill, the hydraulic excavation system had apparently served its purpose as his photographs show only the workers excavating material with shovels and one-horse dump carts. This view was taken from the top of one of the side banks; the track will run through this scene from side to side.

Blasting, hand loading, and hauling by dump cart were the standard means of earthmoving employed by the CP. There was at least one steam shovel used in California by the 1860s, but it would have taken many of them to move material as fast and over as far-flung an operation as was accomplished by the CP's army of workers, and none was used in building the railroad. During the summer of 1866, when these construction scenes were recorded, more than a thousand men were scattered all along the line of grade from Alta to the Yuba River.

PROSPECT HILL CUT
75.4 miles from Sacramento

This view dates from the summer of 1867, after the track was laid and construction at this location was virtually completed. Hart's camera faced back toward the excavation at Prospect Hill from the east.

The two-car train in the foreground appears in a number of Hart's photographs made in this district. In the views of taken at Green Bluffs on its trip to Cisco, the passengers were out of the cars enjoying the view. In this and other westbound views, they remained inside. Perhaps they were growing impatient with Hart stopping for yet another photograph.

Beyond the excursion train is another train of small, four-wheel dump cars. The CP acquired 20 of these dump cars in the fall of 1865, and had nearly one hundred of them by the time the railroad was completed in 1869. They allowed fill material to be moved easily along the railroad far more economically than by horse-drawn dump carts. The scar of Bradley's water ditch can be discerned in the trees on the hillside above the construction train. It passed through the ridge in a tunnel, the mouth of which is seen just to the right of the railroad's excavation. The ditch probably ran the long way around Prospect Hill before the railroad came along, as the tunnel appears to have been necessary simply to move the ditch out of the railroad's way. On the other hand, the water canal did have at least one other tunnel, and it was not related to the railroad's alignment.

CHINA RANCH
75.65 miles from Sacramento

China Ranch was located just east of Prospect Hill. While the CP is noted for its employment of Chinese, this place name predates the railroad by several years. It apparently recalls Chinese who raised vegetables to supply the Green Valley miners and who also built Bradley's water ditch, which can be traced along the hillside above the railroad grade.

China Ranch station was renamed "Orel" in 1898, and it became "Forebay" in 1914. That latter name was derived from the forebay, or holding basin, for the Frank G. Drum Powerhouse, which was built in the bottom of the Bear River canyon to the north. The forebay itself is located on top of the intervening ridge. To facilitate construction of the powerhouse, Pacific Gas & Electric built a standard gauge railroad from the CP at Forebay to the ridge top, with an incline tramway dropping down to the Bear River. Drum, after whom the powerhouse was named, was a key player in the consolidation of various local water and power companies into PG&E. These small companies were themselves the direct descendants of the water systems developed for hydraulic mining. The Lake Spaulding–Drum Powerhouse unit, developed from the old South Yuba water system, was PG&E's first major hydroelectric project. The development of local hydroelectric capability led the railroad company to consider electrifying its Sierra crossing.

FORT POINT CUT
76.7 miles from Sacramento

Just past China Ranch, the builders had to make another large excavation through a spur of the mountain. This location was called "Fort Point." This cut, too, was originally to have been a tunnel, but raising the line allowed it to be developed as an open excavation 70 feet deep by six hundred feet long. When Hart made this picture in the summer of 1866, the work appears to have been nearly complete, though there is the hint of dust in the air at the far end of the cut. Hart's camera was facing toward the east.

Many of the geographical names recorded in Hart's stereo card labels predate the CP. The name "Fort Point" goes back to a stockade corral built by Elkanar Gay in the 1850s during the preliminary construction of the water ditch. The name was probably a parody of the well-known Fort Point on the south side of the Golden Gate. Gay sold his project to Elisha Bradley and Melvin Gardner long before the railroad was built, but the memory of his "fort" remained fixed in the local nomenclature.

While the railroad cut directly through the mountain spur, the water ditch ran the long way around, following the contour.

VIEW NORTH of FORT POINT CUT
76.9 miles from Sacramento

This view faces back toward the cut at Fort Point from the east. On this side of the ridge the terrain drops off steeply into Blue Canyon.

The Placer Canal was carried around Fort Point itself in the flume seen to the left of the railroad bed. Wooden flumes, such as those on the eastern slope of the Sierra that delivered lumber, were often built with fairly steep gradients. But where water was moved in ditches, the rate of fall had to be limited to restrict the water to a gentle flow to prevent the erosion of the earthen ditch walls. Generally, ditches were limited to a fall of less than 16 feet per mile. Even the flumes associated with ditches were kept at the shallow gradient to keep the motion of the water even. By comparison, the railroad here was dropping at a rate of 116 feet per mile. This difference in gradient is apparent in comparing the relative elevations of the railroad and the ditch in this view at Fort Point and in those at Prospect Hill. Here, the railroad is above the level of the flume, while the ditch was well above the railroad at Prospect Hill, less than a mile away. The railroad crossed the ditch just on the other side of Fort Point cut.

Where topography dictated that the ditch needed a steep fall, its water was emptied into a natural stream, such as Canyon Creek, and then diverted into a new ditch at a lower elevation.

HORSE RAVINE WALL and GRIZZLY HILL TUNNEL
77 miles from Sacramento

This photograph is nearly the opposite view as the preceding image; the two locations are just a few feet apart, though on the opposite sides of the railroad grade. The images were made on the same occasion in the late summer of 1866 when the roadbed was almost ready for the track. Running northeast of Fort Point, the railroad passes Horse Ravine and then transits Grizzly Hill through a tunnel.

Generally, when the roadbed had to cross a ravine or gully, a simple embankment was made by filling in the opening with material from nearby excavations. To assure the stability of these embankments, they were finished with faces that had a 1 vertical to 1.5 horizontal ratio. However, in some places, the ravine floor fell off so steeply that an ordinary embankment was impractical, and stone retaining walls were constructed to support an embankment with a steeper face. Along the course of the CP, workers built several such massive stone walls. In many cases, they still support the railroad track but here the old wall is buried in earthwork built in 1913 to support the second track. Because these walls were built by Chinese, and no doubt, too, because China has a famous wall, they are invariably referred to as "Chinese wall," or "China wall."

WEST PORTAL TUNNEL NO. 1, GRIZZLY HILL
77.02 miles from Sacramento

Work on tunnel no. 1 commenced about the end of 1865, while the end-of-track was still at Colfax. The headings were connected on the following July 4, and the rails were laid through it in October 1866.

Mileage figures used throughout this work are taken from the Corp of Engineers' 1876 resurvey of the Pacific railroad conducted by William H. Heuer and James F. Gregory, who with assistants measured the track with odometer-equipped handcars and steel surveyor's chains. Hewer recorded distances from the south line of K Street at Sacramento, and Gregory from the south end of the Ogden depot. They recorded distances to the nearest foot, and their field books document the locations of many key features not included in timetables or station lists, such as curves, bridges, and tunnels.

Shortly after the railroad was extended to Oakland, the railroad's 0 milepost was moved from Sacramento to San Francisco. Through the years, mileage figures were adjusted as the route itself was changed and the alignment improved. The rebuilding of the railroad and construction of the second track between Rocklin and Colfax in 1913 resulted in a considerable shortening of the line. New mileposts were installed west of tunnel no. 1, but not to the east. As a result, between the tunnel and Blue Canyon, nearly half a mile was skipped in the mileage on the original track and more than a mile was skipped on the eastbound track.

GRIZZLY HILL TUNNEL FROM THE NORTH
77.12 miles from Sacramento

Tunnel no. 1 is still in use, but it was enlarged for the second track in 1913. The original tunnel at Grizzly Hill was 508 feet long. Do to the relative softness of the conglomerate material, both ends of the tunnel were timber lined for a short distance.

West of tunnel no. 12 track laying was performed by a relatively small crew. The men first hauled all the rails, ties, and track hardware needed for a short section of track to the end-of-rails on a squat tracklaying car. They would first unload, distribute and set the ties and then lay, splice, and spike the rails. Except perhaps for the foreman, everyone participated in each task. Remarkably, the names of a few of the tracklayers are known. Three of them were: Ayres, Herrick, and Madden. Of them, we are told, one had been laying track for 25 years, including work on the government railroads during the Civil War. Another was Ned Hussey, who had previously worked on the Freeport Railroad, and perhaps the SVRR. The master track layer was D.D. McWade, who later became the roadmaster of the CP's Western division. Not until early 1868 was the track-laying force increased and divided into specialized teams.

This photograph places Hart on the scene between the August 1866 date of the completion of the tunnel and the laying of ties and rail here in early October. This dates at least one of Hart's visits to the work above Alta to about September of that year.

158. Across Blue Canyon, looking East.

LOOKING EAST across BLUE CANYON

Past Grizzly Hill the railroad skirts Blue Canyon, making a notable horseshoe curve at its head. In this view, Hart's camera faces east across the narrow valley, and one can make out the railroad, and another train on the far side. The head of the canyon, where the railroad crosses Blue Canyon Creek, is to the left.

The passenger car in the foreground is probably the one we see in the two-car excursion train in other photographs. It is one of the original-style CP passenger cars, distinguished by their "flat" roofs. The little square openings in the letter board are ventilators. In August 1867 Huntington described to his partners the new style passenger cars being introduced in the East, with "raised" clerestory roofs.

Thereafter, the modern style was adopted by the CP. The company's passenger cars were painted yellow until the mid-1880s when it adopted the dark "Pullman" color. Its freight cars were painted brown.

The first cars ordered by the CP came as complete kits, including all the woodwork, but in 1866 the company conducted tests and found that Oregon fir was just as good as the wood that came from the East. Thereafter, the CP used local wood and ordered just the iron parts from the East. It sent patterns for the iron components to the various factories in an effort to impose some standardization. Later, as its shops were developed, the CP made even the ironwork locally.

BLUE CANYON EMBANKMENT
77.9 miles from Sacramento

Confronted by the steep gradient and sharp curves of Judah's original line on the north side of the Dutch Flat Divide, Clement sought and found an alternate route on the American River side of the ridge. However, while his first line had a gradient of only 105 feet to the mile, it required a curve at the head of Blue Canyon that was unacceptably sharp. By increasing the gradient to 116 feet to the mile, the line turned the head of the canyon with a curve of only 9°, and it was on this line that the railroad was built. While a few miles of the constructed line were as steep as Judah's line, it had broader curves, and it eliminated all but one of the tunnels on Clement's first line.

The constructed railroad crossed the head of Blue Canyon on a fill, seen in this photograph. The embankment was 600 feet long by 85 feet high, and contained 120,000 cubic yards of material.

The average of all the curves on the railroad was 3°, with only a few 10° curves required in constrained locations. Altogether, about 60% of the entire railroad between Rocklin and the summit was composed of curved track. As built, all the curves on the railroad were circular—not until about 1876 were any transitions or spirals curves introduced. In addition to reducing the gradient on curves, short tangents were placed between opposing curves to further minimize train resistance.

BLUE CANYON
78.2 miles from Sacramento, 4,693 feet elevation

Curve no. 235 at the head of Blue Canyon has the greatest total curvature of any single curve on the CP, turning through 210°. Nearly adjacent curve no. 238, where the railroad swings left out of Blue Canyon through Lost Camp Spur has a total curvature of 195°.

The station at Blue Canyon was right in the middle of the horseshoe curve. Until 1905 the station name was officially spelled "Blue Cañon." Later a "y" replaced the tilde. For many years this was an important station, with a day-and-night telegraph office, turntable, small engine house, an hotel, and a three-hundred foot long woodshed for locomotive fuel. The water here was considered the best on the railroad, and the first water tower had six cisterns, with a total capacity of 21,000 gallons. The tenders of helper engines running light back to Rocklin, where water was scarce, would be filled here. The original buildings burned in 1900.

During the initial construction, rails were laid past the Blue Cañon station point by mid-October 1866. Double-tracking the railroad was completed from Colfax to Blue Canyon in 1913. Until the double track was extended eastward a decade later, Blue Canyon remained a picturesque and lively locality.

LOOKING WEST ACROSS BLUE CANYON

This last scene at Blue Canyon looks back across the gorge toward the railroad on the west side. Tunnel no. 1's portal is visible in the distance just to the left of center. Hart recorded this and the preceding view from virtually the same vantage point. The two-car train, seen in several other photographs, is returning to Sacramento from Cisco, then the end-of-track.

Blue Canyon is believed to take its name from Jim Blue, a local miner, but the locality was the scene of much lumbering activity even before the railroad, and the blue smoke from the sawmills obscured the origin of the name as much as it did the vistas. While the CP was a primary customer for the local lumber output, within a few years of the railroad's arrival, six different sawmills here were cutting products carried by rail to the entire western market. Evidence of fresh logging is visible in the foreground of this image. Lumber cut from these logs was probably destined for use in the first-generation snowsheds that were built in the summer of 1867 when this photograph was made.

Blue Canyon was generally the western end of the railroad's snowshed district. The sidings and the turntable were covered in 1874, and a decade later the sheds had been extended nearly half a mile farther west.

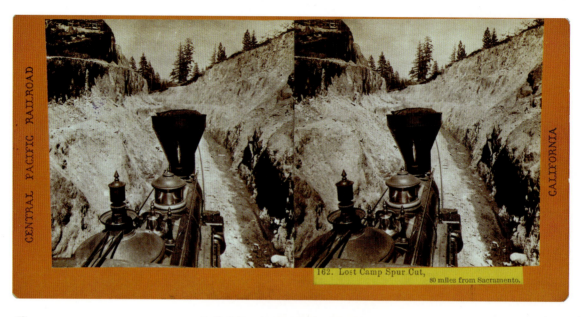

LOST CAMP SPUR
78.8 miles from Sacramento

The railroad leaves Blue Canyon by curving left through Lost Camp Spur into Sailor Ravine. Clement's original line required a three-hundred foot tunnel at this point but increasing the elevation of the railroad to cross Blue Canyon Creek with an acceptable curve also allowed this spur to be breached with an open cut instead of a bore. This was the upper end of the steep grade above Alta. East of Lost Camp Spur the rate of ascent was reduced to less than 90 feet to the mile.

This McKay & Aldus 4-6-0 is probably no. 22, *Auburn*, pulling Hart's two-car excursion train toward Cisco.

Lost Camp itself was located about a quarter mile south of the railroad. The name recalls the "forlorn hope" of Donner Party members who became lost near here in a blizzard in December 1846 while attempting to reach Sutter's Fort. Miners were active at Lost Camp well before the railroad arrived, and Allen, George, and Edwin Towle established their first sawmill near here in 1859. Later, Towle Brothers cut much of the lumber used in the CP's snowsheds. With large timber holdings, Towle Brothers remained a major lumber company in the area until 1902.

BANK and CUT at SAILOR RAVINE
80.6 miles from Sacramento

After running along the north bank of Sailor Ravine for about a mile and a half past Lost Camp, the railroad crosses the ravine on the large fill seen under construction in this view toward the east.

This photograph illustrates the CP's process of building embankments. Carts filled at the face of the excavation in the distance are emptied into the ravine to make the fill. The same process is being carried out on this side of the ravine, though the excavation from which material is being removed is out of sight to the right. The horse-carts made hauling the material relatively easy, but they still had to be filled by hand, one shovelful at a time. Over several weeks the embankment slowly rose and the excavations through the adjoining ridges deepened. When completed, a solid roadbed of the proper width, inclination, and curvature, and at just the correct location, awaited only the laying of track. The track was laid across this embankment in mid October 1866.

Following the unusually severe winter of 1952, a "balloon track" for turning snowplows and flangers was constructed on the broad ridge just east of Sailor Ravine. This and the introduction of diesel-electric locomotives allowed for the retirement of the Emigrant Gap turntable, three miles to the east. Flangers are blade-equipped cars used to clear ice and snow from between the rails.

OWL GAP CUT
80.9 miles from Sacramento

At Owl Gap the railroad was almost back on top of the Dutch Flat Divide. During the days of wood-burning locomotives, this was the location of one of the railroad's several woodsheds, and at various times Owl Gap was called "Camp 27" or "Woodshed." In passing through the cut at Owl Gap, the railroad crosses from Sailor Ravine to Wilson Ravine. Wilson Creek was later renamed "Fulda Creek," and this location was renamed "Fulda" in 1900.

Several of the horse-drawn dump carts used by the CP are seen in this view. The exact number of animals used in building the railroad is unknown. One count tallied nine hundred horses, one hundred oxen, and eight hundred wagons and carts. Nearly all of the company's animals were purchased by Benjamin R. Crocker, who was said to have bought more horses than anyone else in America. Though only remotely related, Ben and Charles Crocker's families had a long association through several generations from Massachusetts to Indiana. Charles and Ben immigrated to California together in 1850, where Ben did very well as a miner. Later he became a liveryman and helped build Sacramento's levee. Ben Crocker is a generally forgotten hero of the CP. During the discouraging days of 1864, when the railroad was broke, he turned his entire personal savings over to the company, enabling it to keep building until it finally qualified for federal bonds.

EMIGRANT GAP RIDGE

In this view of Emigrant Gap from the southwest, the Bear River is out of frame to the left, with the watershed of the upper South Fork of the Yuba River beyond. On the right of the railroad is Wilson's Valley, which drains southward into the North Fork of the American River. Wilson's Valley took its name from Andrew B. Wilson who had a ranch here. Today, Wilson's Valley is known as "Carpenter Flat." While exploring above Dutch Flat in late October 1860, Theodore Judah and Daniel Strong took shelter at Wilson's ranch when they were driven out of Donner Pass by a midnight snowstorm.

Judah began scouting the central Sierra Nevada in September 1860, first investigating a neglected route through Georgetown and then the Henness Pass road above Nevada City. By the time of his third reconnaissance in late October, to the Dutch Flat Divide, Judah began to understand the limitations imposed by the river canyons and seemed to anticipate that the long ridge between the watersheds of the American and Bear rivers would provide a continuous ramp from the Sacramento Valley all the way to Donner Pass. Gathering elevation and distance information from Folsom to the summit, Judah confirmed to his satisfaction that it did indeed offer a long enough run to yield an average gradient suitable for a railroad. At Emigrant Gap, the ramp-like nature of the ridge is most apparent. Judah's original line ran along the north side of the ridge here, somewhat lower than Emigrant Gap itself.

EMIGRANT GAP
83.4 miles from Sacramento, elevation 5,218 feet

The railroad track reached Emigrant Gap in early November 1866. This photograph dates from 1867, before snowsheds were built here.

In the foreground is one of the CP's bucker snowplows. Immediately behind it is the turntable used for turning plows and helper locomotives. In light storms, the snowplows were needed primarily between the Gap and Truckee, while helpers, needed for the steep section above Alta, could be cut off here and returned to Colfax or Rocklin. Though replaced and enlarged over the years, a turntable was maintained at Emigrant Gap until the balloon track was built at Fulda.

Even though the railroad crossed the Dutch Flat-Donner Lake road at Emigrant Gap, no major station was established since track construction did not pause here. The post office was relocated from the Dutch Flat & Donner Lake Wagon Road to the railroad in 1868. When the old trans-Sierra wagon road was revitalized for automobiles in 1911, the portion maintained by the State of California began at Emigrant Gap, connecting with county roads that extended to the Gap from Alta and Nevada City. The state road crossed the railroad directly through a snowshed until an underpass was built in 1930. Interstate 80 was built across the railroad at the Gap in 1962.

EMIGRANT GAP TUNNEL
84.1 miles from Sacramento

Tunnel no. 2 pierced the dividing ridge less than a mile east of Emigrant Gap station. In passing through this tunnel, the railroad departed the American River watershed for the last time. The conglomerate material encountered was fairly soft, and timber lining was needed for the entire three-hundred foot length of the tunnel. It was completed on September 19, 1866. This was just about the time that track construction commenced above Alta, and the resumption of track laying may have been coordinated with the tunnel work to make sure that the workers would not be delayed once they got started.

The tunnel was daylighted when the second track was built eastward through Emigrant Gap in 1923. With the double tracking in the 1920s and highway construction in the 1960s, the topography and railroad alignment at Emigrant Gap have been changed significantly since the railroad was originally built.

While this is not the train with two passenger cars, the locomotive appears to be a McKay & Aldus 10-wheeler. As no McKay 10-wheeler was in service before March 1867, this image, like those taken with the two-car excursion train, must date from the summer of 1867. Hart apparently made several trips to Cisco once the line was opened that far. This image predates the following photograph, which shows nearly the same view with a partially completed snowshed.

EMIGRANT GAP TUNNEL, WALL AND SNOW COVERING
84.1 miles from Sacramento

Wintertime experience in the high Sierra Nevada was limited before the railroad, though the few who crossed (or tried to cross) the range in mid-winter spread word that the snows were deep. Indeed, John C. Frémont's account of his winter crossing in 1844, and the Donner Party's misadventure in 1846-47 forcefully established that the Sierra was a place to avoid in the winter and contributed to the perception that a railroad would have difficulty operating in the heavy snows.

Judah may have been the first to try to quantify the snowfall in his effort to predict the conditions a railroad might expect in operating across Donner Pass. However, the only evidence available was the height above the ground of tree moss and bent branches. While Judah's estimates may have reflected averages, they woefully underestimated the worst conditions. Even by the end of 1865, well before the railroad was into the snowbelt, Judah's successor engineers recognized that some kind of protection from snow would be necessary to keep the line open. Actual experience trying to operate to Cisco in the winter of 1866-67 gave the matter a high priority.

The first snowsheds were built in 1867. The shed in this photograph was so new when Hart visited that it had yet to be sheathed. This view faces eastward.

BEAR VALLEY

Bear Valley, the source of the Bear River, lies just to the north and about six hundred feet below Emigrant Gap. This view looks westward into Bear Valley from what is today called "Smart Ridge," just east of Emigrant Gap. At this point the railroad is one mile above sea level.

This is the same two-car train that appears in several images dating from the summer of 1867, when the railroad was in operation only as far as Cisco. Judging from the fact that the train stopped in several places to allow Hart to take pictures, it was probably a Sunday, when regular trains were not operating. Indeed, this was likely a special train devoted exclusively to Hart's photography. While guests may have occupied seats, they had to wait patiently while Hart took the time to select his views and pack cumbersome camera equipment to various vantage points. The wet collodion process used by Hart required a darkroom and a place to store his glass plates and chemicals. In this case, space in the baggage car was no doubt set aside for Hart's use.

The particular baggage car of this train is an unusual "gallery" car, with an outside passageway—the gallery—along the side of the car. This feature allowed trainmen to pass locked express and mail compartments. It doubtless was a great place to stand and watch the scenery in the days of slow-moving trains. This gallery car probably came to the CP from the SVRR.

LOOKING EAST from EMIGRANT GAP
84.17 miles from Sacramento

Hart made this photograph from a location directly above the eastern portal of tunnel no. 2. He was facing northward.

The distant landscape is part of the watershed of the South Fork of the Yuba River, but the area immediately below the railroad to the left is the eastern end of Bear Valley, drained by the Bear River. In the ancient past, much of the distant watershed also drained into the Bear River. But at some point in time, that drainage was captured by the Yuba, leaving the unusual spectacle of a single mountain valley drained by two streams. Judah called this a "freak of nature." Once past Emigrant Gap, the railroad runs high above Bear Valley to Yuba Pass, where it crosses into the Yuba watershed.

This is probably the same train seen elsewhere emerging from the west portal of the Emigrant Gap tunnel. The buggy on the flatcar of this train is Hart's portable darkroom. It shows up in photographs taken in 1867 on the Dutch Flat & Donner Lake Wagon Road, and the following year near Reno. The photographic process used by Hart required that each glass plate be coated with a cellulose nitrate collodion in a dark environment, and then loaded into the camera and exposed, all before the emulsion dried. This gave the photographer only a few minutes in which to work, and required that he work within a close proximity to his darkroom and chemicals.

170. Cement Ridge—Old Man Mountain in dist.

CEMENT RIDGE
85 miles from Sacramento

For the first four or five miles east of Emigrant Gap construction of the roadbed exposed a hard "lava cement," and for several years the adjacent ridge was called "Cement Ridge." In 1892 the railroad installed a spur track near here to serve the lumbering operation of Birce & Smart, and from 1903 through 1946 the station was called "Smart." In time, people began to call the adjacent ridge "Smart Ridge" instead of "Cement Ridge." Birce & Smart's narrow gauge railroad, which dropped down into Bear Valley, was later used by PG&E in building the dam at Lake Spaulding.

The man sitting on the boxcar ahead is probably Hart's assistant, passing instructions to the engineer, not a brakeman. Still, before all cars were equipped with air brakes, about 1900, riding the tops of cars was the regular duty of brakemen, who had to be ready to apply or release brakes in response to a whistle signal from the engineer. Brakes were set by turning the hand wheels that protrude above the car ends. The brakeman's job was always dangerous. In winter, it was also miserable. The CP began applying air brakes to their freight cars in 1883.

Old Man Mountain is the prominent feature in the distance, seen to the left of the locomotive. The railroad from Blue Canyon to Smart was double-tracked in 1923.

169. Valley North Fork of Yuba—Old Man Mountain.

VALLEY OF THE SOUTH FORK OF THE YUBA RIVER

Beyond Cement Ridge, near the railroad station at Yuba Pass, the railroad traverses from the Bear River watershed to that of the South Fork of the Yuba River.

In October 1904, a misreading of train orders caused a westbound passenger train to collide into the rear of a cattle train stopped on the main line near this point. The crews jumped in time to avoid serious injury, but the locomotive and caboose were demolished and a section of snowshed, which then covered the track, collapsed. Fire broke out almost immediately. Most of the cattle train was pulled clear of the flames, but four damaged cars that could not be moved were soon on fire. Courageous crewmen managed to open the doors, but the cattle inside refused to jump into the flames and so were burned to death. Meanwhile, passengers fled their cars in great confusion, groping their way through the smoke-filled snowsheds looking for an exit, while tongues of fire flickered along the shed roof above their heads. Several of the passenger train's cars, a mile of snowsheds, and the Yuba Pass depot were destroyed in the fire. Sacramento Division Superintendent Robert J. Laws, who had been riding in a business car at the end of the passenger train, suffered a heart attack in the turmoil and died.

Laws had begun working for the CP in 1868. He had surveyed the line of the Carson & Colorado Railroad and is the namesake of Laws, California.

171. Miller's Bluffs, near Crystal Lake. Old Man Mountain in distance

MILLER'S BLUFF
88.4 miles from Sacramento

The name "Miller's Bluff" has disappeared from the modern gazetteer, as has that of nearby Hopkins's Bluff. Those features bore the names of life-long friends and associates Edward H. Miller, Jr. and Mark Hopkins. Hopkins and Miller sailed to California together by way of Cape Horn in 1849 and were partners in a grocery store in Sacramento until Hopkins joined Huntington in the hardware business. Hopkins and Miller remained close, and Miller became the CP's secretary, while Hopkins was treasurer.

The Southern Pacific's (SP) crack streamliner *City of San Francisco* became snowbound adjacent to these bluffs in January 1952, though those old names had long since faded from use. As seen in this view, the original CP line runs around the outside of the bluffs. When the second track was built in 1924-25, tunnels were blasted directly through them. Tunnel no. 36 pierces Miller's Bluff, while tunnel no. 35 runs through Hopkins's Bluff. The railroad quarried rock here even before the tunnels were built.

Rails reached Miller's Bluff on November 21, 1866. In this scene, Old Man Mountain remains in view, but just past Miller's Bluff the track turns to the east, leaving Old Man Mountain behind.

ECHO POINT
89.4 miles from Sacramento

This view looks westward from Echo Point, back toward Sacramento. Miller's Bluff is just around the promontory in the distance. A telegraph pole appears in the lower center of the photograph, with a row of poles extending along the embankment into the distance. While a telegraph already spanned the continent by the time the CP began construction, the company built a new line adjacent to the railroad.

While the crews had worked in fairly soft conglomerate material from Alta to Emigrant Gap, they were now in hard granite. The *Sacramento Bee* reported in the spring of 1866 that the hard rock encountered above Emigrant Gap was leading the company to consider relocating the line to the north via Henness Pass. There was a report in August of that year, when the graders finally got here, that the Chinese were so frustrated by the hard of the rock that many walked off the job.

When the sidings between Roseville and Reno were lengthened in 1907, the Greeks, East Indians, and Italians who then worked in this hard rock had the advantage of air-driven Burleigh drills and electrically-detonated dynamite.

ECHO POINT AND RATTLESNAKE MOUNTAIN

This is virtually the reverse of the preceding view, with Hart's camera facing east toward Echo Point. Red Mountain, which Hart called "Rattlesnake Mountain," rises in the distance on the other side of the South Fork of the Yuba River. The name suggests one could get a strong echo off the bare rock surfaces just across the canyon.

Today the name "Rattlesnake Mountain" is applied to another peak two miles to the east. Red Mountain consists of a cluster of peaks, of which the highest is Signal Peak. In 1877 the CP established an outpost on its flank from which lookouts watched the railroad's line of snowsheds for signs of fire during the dry season. By 1882 a telephone line connected the lookout with Cisco. The lookout was abandoned in the 1930s after most of the wooden snowsheds had been removed.

The railroad's telegraph station at Crystal Lake was a quarter mile east of Echo Point. To accommodate the second track, tunnel no. 37 was bored directly through Echo Point in 1924-25.

Railroading in the mountains required that all rolling stock be in top condition. After the completion of the Pacific railroad, cars interchanged from eastern roads were thoroughly inspected at Ogden before being accepted. Cars with brakes on only one truck—common in the East in the 19th century—were never allowed on the CP.

THE RAILROAD BETWEEN CISCO AND CRYSTAL LAKE

Hart made this photograph looking across lower Butte Canyon from a rocky promontory above the South Fork of the Yuba River. The river itself is out of view to the right, while the fresh scar of the railroad grade is plainly visible on the distant ridge. The Dutch Flat & Donner Lake Wagon Road can be seen winding up the grade in the mid-foreground. By the summer of 1867, when Hart made this image, the CP was operating trains all the way to Cisco, and the wagon road below Cisco had lost all of its traffic. Not a single vehicle is to be seen on the road in this view.

Above Emigrant Gap, the railroad runs along the northwest side of the ridge, high above the Bear and Yuba rivers. But the wagon road remained on the other side of the ridge as far as Crystal Lake, which is located just beyond the low point in the ridgeline at the right margin of the photograph. The railroad's Crystal Lake station was just below that pass, where the road finally crossed the ridge and dropped down across the track. To the left of center one can make out the railroad's trestle across Butte Canyon. The following two views were taken on the railroad just east of that trestle.

Railroad workers began grading this section of roadbed by May 1866. Above Emigrant Gap, much of the roadbed was carved out of solid rock. By the time they had completed the grade to Cisco, they had used up more than one hundred tons of steel just in making rock drills.

FOOT of BLACK BUTTE
90.6 miles from Sacramento

One of the prominent features of the ridge south of the Yuba River is Cisco Butte, or Black Butte as it was known in the days of the CP's construction. This picture was taken where the railroad traverses the foot of Cisco Butte with Hart's camera facing west.

Just beyond the bluff ahead of the train is the trestle across Butte Canyon. The trestle was about four hundred feet long and 75 feet tall. The foundations for this structure were completed on September 24, 1866, and the track was laid across it on November 27 as the builders raced to complete the railroad to Cisco before winter. However, within a month, a torrent of rain and snowmelt pouring down the gulch washed away several of the trestle bents. With most of the railroad closed by weather, there was no way to bring in new timbers, so crews hewed timbers from nearby trees to repair the structure. The replacement trestle was itself replaced by a Howe-truss bridge in 1869.

This image dates from 1867, before the snowsheds (seen in the following view) were erected. This is apparently the same two-car train with the gallery car that we have seen in other views made between Cisco and Alta that summer.

SNOW COVERING BELOW CISCO

Though snowsheds of some kind were anticipated as early as 1865, all of the CP's energy during 1866 was expended just in getting the track to Cisco, and no sheds were built that year. As it turned out, the winter of 1866-67 was very heavy, and soon after the railroad opened to Cisco, storms closed the line. Not until the following April could dependable service be maintained above Alta. The lesson was learned, though, and the following summer an army of carpenters was put to work building snowsheds. Wholly unexpected when the company made its initial plans and estimates, the snowsheds significantly increased the cost of building and maintaining the railroad.

As this view of the snowsheds on either side of Butte Canyon trestle shows, they were not initially continuous structures, but were confined to cuts and sidehills where snow accumulated. While a total of nearly five miles of sheds were built between Lost Camp and Cisco in 1867, the longest single covering was half a mile in length. The snowsheds built that first year were considered experimental, to guide a more extensive effort planned for the following year. The first sheds had open sides. Later they were sheathed, blocking the view and confining the locomotive exhaust. The sheds in this view are so new they had yet to be roofed. This is one of the few locations where snowsheds are still in place on the railroad. This location is known as "Shed 10."

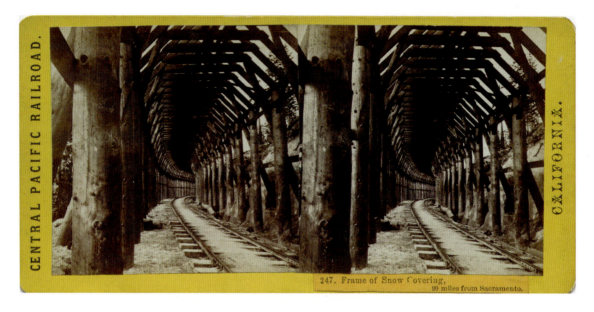

247. Frame of Snow Covering, 90 miles from Sacramento.

FRAME OF SNOW COVERING

This view shows the interior of one of the snowsheds prior to sheathing. The uprights made of un-milled logs identifies this as one of the early sheds, probably built in 1867 before sawmills were available to mill squared timbers. These logs were cut locally and dragged to the railroad by team. The mileage location given in the stereo card caption places this shed between Crystal Lake and Cisco.

The CP officials were determined to complete as many miles of railroad as possible before meeting the UP. To do this, construction would have to be pushed across Nevada during the winter of 1868-69, requiring that the railroad be kept open across the Sierra at all cost. In preparation for this, many more miles of snowsheds were ordered built during the summer of 1868.

Fire was a continual problem with the snowsheds, and the replacement of burned sections was a perennial expense. While passengers generally complained about the sheds shutting out their view, fire presented a more tangible danger. One unfortunate passenger was reportedly asphyxiated by smoke in 1877 as the train he was riding ran through the snowsheds while they were burning. That must have been an exciting trip.

LOWER CISCO

The railroad reached Cisco in late November 1866, just as winter set in. The workers—numbering perhaps as many as 10,000—had built 37 miles of track above Colfax over the previous 12 months. That was the greatest annual advance yet. But Cisco would remain the end-of-track for nearly 19 months while the laborers carved a path through the rugged mountains ahead.

Cisco began life at least two years before the advent of the railroad as a stage and wagon stop on the Dutch Flat & Donner Lake Wagon Road. It was originally known as "Heatonville" or "Heaton's Station" for its proprietor, James Heaton. Heatonville boomed as the jumping off point for Meadow Lake, the scene of a wild but short-lived gold rush in 1865 that attracted many citizens of Virginia City, just then going through a temporary decline. When the railroad arrived, the CP named its own station to honor John J. Cisco, assistant treasurer of the United States during the Civil War. Ironically, J.J. Cisco also served as the treasurer of the UP.

The railroad actually passed a few hundred yards up the hill above Heaton's Station, so a new settlement developed adjacent to the track. As long as there was any life in the old settlement, it was known as "Lower Cisco," while the new railroad town was "Upper Cisco."

UPPER CISCO
91.9 miles from Sacramento, elevation 5,933 feet

This view of Upper Cisco from the west dates from the summer of 1867. On the right, at the higher elevation, a train stands on the main track adjacent to the passenger depot. Leaving the depot toward Sacramento, that track curves in front of the camera, passing just below the stumps in the foreground. The passenger depot was also a hotel, and freshly-washed bedding is hanging out to dry. Before the summer was over, a large woodshed for locomotive fuel was erected adjacent to the main track just beyond the depot.

The freight train at the lower left is on a spur track that curved behind the long freight house, seen just beyond it. The wagons backed up to the freight house are being loaded for Virginia City and other points as far away as Idaho and Montana. The freight house was initially 370 feet long, but was enlarged twice in 1867 until it eventually extended some seven hundred feet. Even that was considered insufficient for the commerce that passed through it that summer.

The locomotive facilities are located between the freight track and the main line. A locomotive is being turned on the turntable in front of the two-stall engine house. One of the company's large snowplows is parked on an adjacent track facing the camera.

The 3D effect of this image has been digitally enhanced.

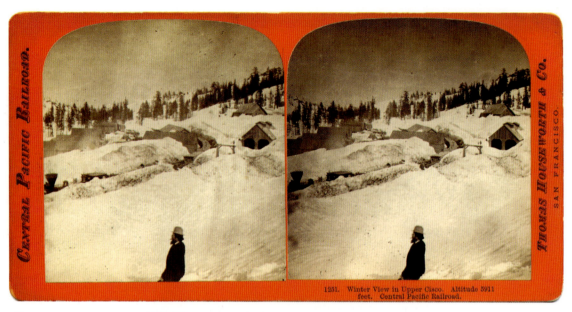

WINTER VIEW in UPPER CISCO

While rain had been the biggest concern in the winter of 1865-66, when construction activity was limited to the lower elevations, snow became the primary problem after the railroad reached Cisco and workers advanced into the high country beyond. As it happened, the winters of 1866-67 and 1867-68 were unusually severe.

Within days of the CP's arrival at Cisco in November 1866, heavy storms with widespread flooding closed the railroad all the way back to Dry Creek, below Rocklin. Not until Christmas were trains from Sacramento again running to Secret Town, and they made it as far as Alta two weeks later. But for days they operated only intermittently above that, ferrying passengers between washed out trestles and embankments. Though service to Cisco was resumed briefly in February 1867, closures were frequent through March. Until well into April, trains ran between walls of snow as high as the car roofs all the way from Emigrant Gap to Cisco.

This photograph was made from approximately the same vantage point as the preceding view. Keeping the unsheltered Cisco turntable clear of snow must have been a full-time job for a large crew. The following summer it was enclosed in a building, but its roof collapsed in March 1868 under the weight of accumulated snow, killing several workers huddled inside.

The 3D effect of this image has been digitally enhanced.

CISCO IN WINTER

The locomotive house is nearly buried by snow in this view from a vantage point near the passenger depot. To the right are some of the commercial buildings facing the freight house. Red Mountain is in the distance. The railroad's line heading west out of Cisco can be traced across the hillside on the left.

These winter scenes date from Hart's first trips to Cisco in April 1867, just after the winter's heaviest snowfall. He is known to have taken photographs at Cisco on at least two occasions that month. The CP did not intend to distribute these views, probably because they might reveal to potential investors that the company would likely face great expenses in operating trains over the Sierra in the winter. Thomas Houseworth, however, unconcerned with such issues, went ahead and published them.

Access by rail changed the perception that the Sierra Nevada were a place to be avoided in the winter into one in which the mountains were now seen as a year-round recreation destination. Then, the railroad had reason to advertise the Sierra's winter recreational opportunities. In later years the railroad operated special trains to carry skiers up to the snow country.

BUCKER SNOWPLOW

Anticipating problems with winter in the high country, the CP began building its first snowplow in September 1866, while the line to Cisco was still under construction. A second plow was built in December, and by the winter of 1868-69, six snowplows were in service.

As many as 12 locomotives were required to push one of these snowplows though heavy drifts. To be effective, the plow had to be driven fast to launch the snow high enough to clear adjacent snowbanks, and it took considerable nerve on the part of the engineers to charge full throttle into a hillside of snow. Eventually the resistance of the snow would slow the snowplow, and the engines would bog to a stop. The train of locomotives and plow would then back up, build up steam pressure, and make a new charge into the snow. Derailments were frequent, and damage to the track and equipment common. But it was all part of the cost of keeping the line clear outside of the snowsheds.

These early snowplows were the railroad's primary weapons against winter, but the company also employed hundreds of men with shovels to dig the snow off switches and telegraph lines. The annual battle was revolutionized in 1888 with the introduction of steam-powered rotary snowplows.

The building behind the locomotives, with its porch extending over the track, is the Cisco passenger depot-hotel.

ENGINES AT CISCO

This view looks down on the same locomotives seen behind the snowplow in the preceding image. Hart and his camera were on top of the snowbank beside the track, not on the plow itself.

Both of the locomotives closest to the camera appear to be Danforth-built 2-6-0s. Note that the wire netting of the spark arrestor of the second locomotive is propped open. The railroad company was very sensitive to the risk of fire to its property and the adjoining forests. Fire was a serious threat in the days of wood burning locomotives, and these smokestack screens were generally kept closed to prevent embers from escaping with the exhaust. However, if clogged with ash, the netting would block the draft like a damper, making it difficult—if not impossible—for a locomotive to generate steam. Fortunately, fires did not pose a particular threat when the ground was covered with snow, and the fireman of this locomotive has opened his stack to ease his job with the fire. However, once the snowsheds were built, these screens had to be kept closed even in the winter.

Due to the corrosive action of smoke, spark arrestor netting eventually burned out, leaving holes through which large, dangerous firebrands could pass. Any locomotive found to be "throwing fire" when out on the road was parked at the first siding until the fault was fixed.

LOCOMOTIVES BEHIND SNOWPLOW

This view of the locomotives behind the bucker snowplow conveys some sense of the great depth of snow in April 1867. Continuous weather records for Donner summit—a thousand feet higher than Cisco—go back only to 1878-79. Since that time, only the winters of 1879-80, 1889-90, 1937-38, and 1951-52 have seen snowfall totals more than 60 feet at that location. With 49 feet of snow at Cisco in 1866-67, it is likely that Donner Pass had more than 60 feet that season as well. The 1867-68 season was equally bad.

In February 1887, two westbound passenger trains were delayed for four days at Cisco because of snow. Five snowplow trains had nearly cleared the line when a section of snowshed at Blue Cañon collapsed in the middle of the night under the weight of wet snow. Unaware of the problem, a train of eight locomotives pushed a snowplow into the wrecked shed in the darkness, derailing and thoroughly blocking the line. The passenger trains waiting at Cisco were protected by sheds, but with 15 feet of snow drifted against them, the only light was from the car lamps. As lamp oil and stove fuel ran out, the passengers and crews were left to huddle in the cold darkness. They lived on beef, biscuits, and coffee available in the Cisco depot.

LOCOMOTIVE NO. 25, YUBA, AT CISCO

The CP commenced service to Cisco with a stable of 13 locomotives, with four more either being assembled or broken in. By December 1867, just more than a year later, the company had 25 engines, the newest of which was no. 25, *Yuba*, a 10-wheeler from McKay & Aldus, which went into service on October 17. This photograph of *Yuba* at Cisco dates from the fall of 1867 when it was brand new.

The hot, pressurized water in a live steam locomotive always possesses the potential to explode. The danger was more acute before the day of modern safety appliances, and the limited pool of experienced engineers on the West Coast from which the CP could hire further increased the risk of accident. On October 8, 1868, the *Yuba* exploded while pulling a freight train uphill near Clipper Gap. Killed were 36-year-old engineer George Albee, 24 year-old fireman J.F. Norman, and a transient working his way over the road passing wood from the tender. The precise cause of the explosion is unknown, but since the fireman had only been over the road once before, the accident was possibly due to his unfamiliarity with the line. If Norman did not allow for the stretch of level track below Clipper Gap, he may not have had enough water in the boiler to cover the firebox when the locomotive topped the grade. When the locomotive leveled off, the crown sheet would have risen above low water, and exposed, it would soon have overheated and failed. With the sudden loss of pressure, the superheated water in the boiler would have instantly exploded into steam, tearing apart the locomotive and its crew.

ALL ABOARD for VIRGINIA CITY

This busy scene, with the locomotive *Yuba* standing just east of the Cisco depot, was made in late 1867, at the same time as the preceding view. Three stagecoaches loaded with mail and passengers wait for Hart to finish his exposure so they can be off for Virginia City. Two coaches for passengers and one for mail were not uncommon on that run.

The stagecoaches that operated over the Dutch Flat & Donner Lake road from Cisco were those of the Pioneer Stage Company. Pioneer Stage initially operated on the Placerville route and that company had initially opposed the construction of the CP. However, when the CP acquired control of the SVRR in August 1865, Pioneer moved to the Donner route and began connecting with the CP when the end of the line was at Colfax. Wells Fargo contracted with Pioneer to carry their express matter.

Cisco ceased being the end of railroad operations in May 1868, when the winter's snow and ice were cleared off the line east of Cisco and regular trains began running to Summit Valley. One month later, rail service opened all the way to Reno. However, while through passengers no longer used the Cisco depot, mail continued to be transferred between train and stagecoach at Cisco until September 1868, when the government contract was finally altered. By then, Wadsworth was the end-of-train operations. Cisco rapidly declined into near oblivion.

FREIGHT WAGONS AT CISCO

The initial Pacific Railroad Act of 1862 authorized the CP to build to the Nevada state line. In 1864 that limit was extended eastward 150 miles into Nevada. In July 1866, Congress lifted the restriction entirely, freeing the company to build eastward until it met the UP. As government bonds and land—and future revenue from operation—depended upon the length of railroad built, this decision instigated a race between the CP and the UP to build as much railroad as possible before they met. Accordingly, as the track was completed to Cisco in late 1866, the CP's army of workers was immediately moved forward onto the line ahead. Many were assigned to bore the tunnels, but the bulk of the workers were sent beyond the snowline on the eastern slope of the Sierra to carve the roadbed along the Truckee River.

From late fall of 1866 through the spring of 1868, everything needed to supply this advance force, as well as the regular freight for Nevada, Idaho, and Montana, had to be transferred at Cisco from the trains to wagons, or sleds in the winter. By the summer of 1867, 58 carloads of freight were being transferred at Cisco every day.

With his slow emulsion, getting this image of so many wagons and animals without more blurring was a masterful achievement for Hart. It testifies to the cooperation of the teamsters as well.

LOADED TEAMS FROM CISCO

With the track extended to Cisco, virtually all the commerce moving across the Sierra traveled over the Dutch Flat & Donner Lake Wagon Road, and it was continually clogged with animals and wagons. This traffic included the supplies for railroad camps farther east as well as heavy freight for Virginia City, Idaho, and Montana. The superintendent of the road was Robert H. Pratt, and in time he managed the transport of all supplies to the advance railroad camps. He later became superintendent of the CP's Salt Lake division and eventually the assistant general superintendent of the entire railroad.

Everything shipped beyond Cisco moved by animal power. During the two winters that Cisco was the end of train operations, the road was kept open by men with shovels, and teams of oxen pulling heavy sledges compressing the snow into ice. Animals were shod with calk shoes, freight rode on sleds, and stagecoaches were converted into sleighs with runners. In the spring, when the roads became too bare for sleds and sleighs, the patches of icy snow that remained on the road had to be chipped and shoveled off. The dry road was sprinkled with water from tank wagons to limit dust. With snow in shady spots lasting until July, there were several weeks during which sprinkler wagons rolled past deep snowbanks.

This photograph, like several others taken at Cisco, probably dates from late in the summer of 1867.

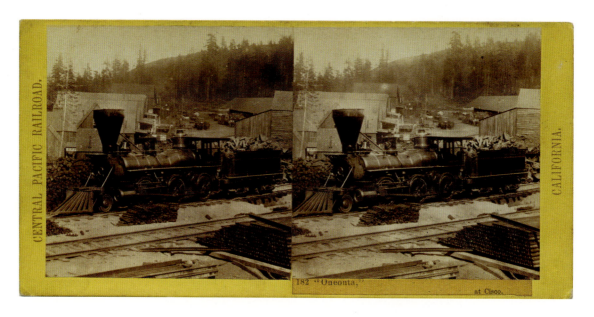

LOCOMOTIVE NO. 14, ONEONTA

By the beginning 1868, the CP had 30 locomotives. Number 14, *Oneonta*, was one of the Danforth 2-6-0s. It had entered service about the time the railroad reached Cisco in late November 1866 and is seen here the following summer, still lacking a headlight.

This image dates from the busy summer of 1867 when rail and other material were being transferred between the cars and wagons at Cisco. In the foreground, a stack of iron rails awaits shipment over the summit. Eventually, enough rail and assorted materials to lay 60 miles of track, along with the rolling stock to operate that much railroad, were carried over the mountain on wagons and sleds before the railroad itself was completed across the summit.

Adjacent to the locomotive's cylinder is a pile of the fish bars that were used to connect rails together. Two "fish joints" are visible in the track in the left foreground. While the use of longer rails connected with fish bars doubled the rate of track production over track laid with the older chair rail, another 47 miles of short chair rail, which had been ordered before the superiority of fish rail was realized, were later laid in Nevada.

Virtually all of Upper Cisco was destroyed by a pair of fires in 1869. Only the freight house and passenger depot survived.

VIEW ABOVE CISCO LOOKING TOWARD THE SUMMIT

From Cisco to Summit Valley the railroad was built high along the ridge above the South Fork of the Yuba River. In the foreground is seen one of the railroad's stone culverts. In the distance is tunnel no. 3 through Trap Spur.

With snow already on the ground when the track reached Cisco in November 1866, no work was attempted on any of the open grade between Cisco and the Truckee River. However, engineers quickly marked the locations of the 11 tunnels in that stretch, and crews were soon put to work at those isolated sites. Once they were underground, where the lack of daylight made no difference, the tunnel crews were divided into shifts and worked around the clock.

Not until the following June, when winter's snow had melted from most of the alignment, did workers begin carving out the open roadbed between the tunnels above Cisco. However, no sooner had they started on this than the Chinese struck for higher wages and reduced hours. This was something of a surprise as wages had just been increased from $30 to $35 per month, and that was $10 more than the mines were paying. However, after just one week, the strike ended as suddenly as it began, and there was no more expression of discontent from the workers. The company managers always believed that the strike had been instigated by agents of the UP sent to delay the CP's entry into Nevada.

TUNNEL NO. 3
92.28 miles from Sacramento

Work on tunnel no. 3 began in late December 1866, soon after the railroad reached Cisco. This tunnel was 280 feet long and required 177 days for crews to connect its headings, working from both ends. It was laid out on a 9° curve. Tunnel no. 4, located just 0.2 mile farther up the line, was carved through Red Spur at the same time. Only 92 feet long, tunnel no. 4 was the shortest on the railroad. The third bore between Cisco and Summit was tunnel no. 5, through Crocker's Spur, 97 miles from Sacramento. Tunnels nos. 4 and 5 were both on 8° right-hand curves.

The hardest rock encountered in constructing the CP was in this area just east of Cisco. Powder charges blasted out of boreholes as if shot from a gun, without breaking up the rock in the slightest. The only recourse was to drill more holes and blast again and again. Meanwhile, the UP was making great progress across the Nebraska prairie. In hopes of lulling the UP into relaxing its effort, the CP publicized its difficulties and predicted it would be another year before they were across the Sierra. It was not far from the truth.

The roadbed as far as Summit was finally ready for the track 12 months after the railroad had reached Cisco. Track laying eastward from Cisco got under way on October 29, 1867.

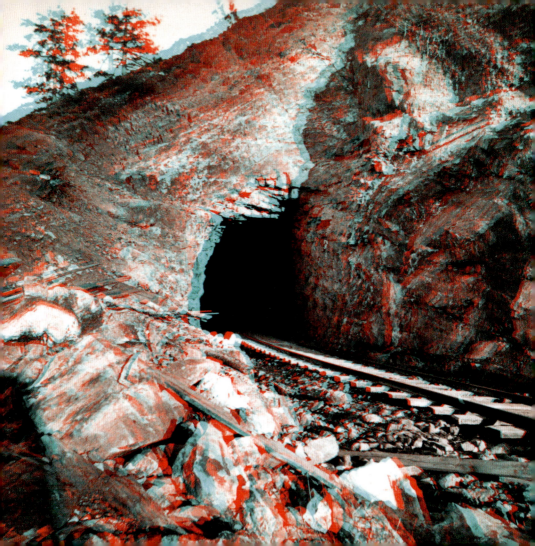

LOWER CASCADE BRIDGE
98.39 miles from Sacramento

Six miles above Cisco, the railroad crosses the outlets of Cascade and Kidd lakes on a pair of bridges within a mile of one another. The CP crossed both of these breaks in the grade with identical single 204-foot Howe trusses strengthened with supplemental arches. As seen in this view from the north, the western Cascade Bridge had two 42-foot straining-beam approach spans on the west end, and a single 80-foot Howe-truss approach on the other. The Upper Cascade Bridge had a single 40-foot straining-beam span on the east approach only.

Timbers for the two bridges were cut by hand at Emigrant Gap during the winter of 1866-67. Because sawmills had yet to be built, logs cut to the proper length were first hewn square, and then ripped in two with whipsaws. The following spring, the pieces were shipped by train to Cisco and then hauled on sleds to the bridge sites. Since snow then covered the country, the timbers were left on the ground while the carpenters moved ahead to build the various bridges down along the Truckee River. Just to prepare a place to store the lumber for the Cascade bridges, 16 feet of snow had to be shoveled aside. Not until October 1867, when the last of the bridges between Truckee and the state line was finished, did the bridge builders return to raise the two Cascades bridges, finishing the bridges just in time for the track.

246. Constructing Snow Cover.
Scene near the Summit.

CONSTRUCTING SNOW COVERING

More than two thousand carpenters were hired in 1868 to build snowsheds. Six trains were devoted to deliver the supplies and material to these crews. Much of the lumber came from sawmills up and down the line, while some was cut and hewn locally by hand. To start the project in the spring, the workers had to shovel six to eight feet of snow from the right-of-way. They worked well into the fall, until they could not keep up with the snowfall. And all the time, the track had to be kept clear for the frequent passage of trains hauling material to the advancing end-of-track far ahead. More than two thousand carloads of rails alone passed over the Sierra that summer.

This scene dates from the summer of 1868. This particular snowshed is near a station, as it is wide enough to cover the mainline and a passing track. It may be located in the curve just west of the station at Summit.

Initially, the snowsheds were built with an inside vertical clearance of 20 feet, high enough to clear an average size brakeman standing on top of one of the small boxcars of the era. Later, however, as freight cars were made larger, brakeman were occasionally knocked from the tops of cars and killed. Derailments in the sheds took on a special danger as they could bring down the shed. That very thing happened in February 1887 when a broken switch near Tamarack sent a doubleheader through the shed wall, causing the roof, along with tons of snow, to collapse onto the train, killing one of the crew.

FRAME of SNOW COVERING

Hart was attracted by the geometric patterns of light and shadow produced by unsheathed bridges and snowsheds.

The first snowsheds were left open on the sides, but snow that drifted in was difficult to remove, so they were soon sheathed completely, though narrow gaps were left between the side boards to allow some light and ventilation. Some roof boards were removed in the summer for the same purpose. The sheds were always gloomy, but in the winter, when snow piled up against the sides, blocking all the gaps, the snowsheds were as dark, cold, and smoky as a tunnel. Passengers despised them for blocking the vistas, and crews were annoyed by the smoke, the inability to see ahead on curves, and the difficulty of signaling. They called it "railroading in a barn."

One adventurer who walked the length of the sheds in the winter of 1884 wrote, "Here is a darkness that can be felt. I have to grope my way forward, inch by inch; afraid to set my foot down until I have felt the place, for fear of blundering into a culvert; at the same time never knowing whether there is room, just where I am, to get out of the way of a train." He had intended to ride his penny-farthing bicycle through the sheds but ended up carrying it the entire way.

SUMMIT STATION
105.21 miles from Sacramento, elevation 6,966 feet

The railroad was completed to Summit on November 30, 1867. A small ceremony and the raising of a flag marked the laying of rails at the highest point on the railroad. Mark Hopkins, who had long wanted to "scream a locomotive whistle on the other side of the summit," along with other directors and reporters attended the event. Although the CP still faced significant obstacles, at last the long, hard climb to the crest of the Sierra was behind it.

Crews worked hard to complete a connection between Summit and the railroad already built and operating down along the Truckee River, and two miles of track were built east of Summit in the course of the following days. But snow soon began to fall faster than men could shovel it aside, and the railroad east of Cisco was abandoned to the elements, leaving Cisco the end of the line for another winter. Trains were not back to the summit until May 1868.

This photograph dates from the summer of 1868, after the entire facility had been enclosed in snowsheds. The tall hexagonal building at the right covers a turntable; two engine houses are attached to it. By the time the weather drove the carpenters out of the mountains in the fall of 1868, 18 miles of railroad had been covered, in addition to the five miles enclosed in 1867. These sheds were continuous from nine miles west of the summit to four miles east of it, with isolated sections of shed beyond.

SUMMIT TUNNEL, EASTERN PORTAL

Just east of Summit, the railroad pierced the crest of the Sierra Nevada through tunnel no. 6, known as "Summit Tunnel." Work was started on this tunnel in the fall of 1865, when the end-of-track was at Colfax. However, winter snows set in before the workers were able to get underground, and the initial effort was abandoned. Then, in August 1866, as men were freed from construction below Cisco, work resumed clearing the approaches, and the headings were started from both ends on September 16. This image places Hart at the tunnel's eastern end only a few days later, when work on the heading had advanced just enough to define the arch-shape of the tunnel's crown. That corresponds closely to the period of Hart's visit to tunnel no. 1 just below Blue Canyon, suggesting that Hart made an excursion from Alta all the way to Donner at that time. Many of Hart's photographs of unfinished work in that district date from this same trip.

To capture this image, Hart set his camera at the side of the Dutch Flat & Donner Lake Wagon Road immediately above its crossing of the railroad's alignment east of the tunnel. The road's summit is to the left, behind Hart and over his left shoulder. Behind the large rock at the lower right, the road turns across the railroad's alignment and, out of view, winds down around the head of the ravine. The tall bare tree trunk, to the left, is a road marker. The direction signs nailed near the top are a graphic indication of the depth of winter snow at this location.

196 Shaft House over Summit Tunnel, American Peak in distance.

SHAFT HOUSE over SUMMIT TUNNEL

Summit Tunnel was the longest on the railroad, extending 1,659 feet from end to end. To hasten construction, a shaft was sunk 73 feet from the surface to the level of the tunnel, allowing crews to work outward from the center as well as inward from the ends. Excavating the shaft began in late August 1866. An old locomotive was acquired from the SVRR to use as a hoisting engine above the center shaft. This happened to be the old *Sacramento*, the first locomotive ever to operate in the West. The stripped locomotive was hauled to the summit on an oversized log-wagon pulled by more than a score of oxen. Its trip over the road began in July from Gold Run, which was then the end-of-track, but not until October 12 was it put to work lifting broken rock from the shaft. On December 19 the shaft reached the level of the floor of the heading and work began driving the center faces outward.

The barn-like shaft house, seen at the right-center of this southward-facing view, housed the hoisting works, firewood, and lodging for its crews. Some kind of blower, such as those used in the mines at Virginia City, must have been used to ventilate the portion of the tunnel being excavated through the shaft, but none was never mentioned in any accounts. Material from the center sections of the tunnel was removed in square "buckets" rolled on light rails, seen here protruding from the shaft house.

197. Summit Tunnel, before completion; Western Summit—altitude 7,042 feet.

INTERIOR of SUMMIT TUNNEL

All CP tunnels were worked in two stages. First opened was the heading—the space directly below the tunnel's crown. This "pioneer tunnel," as it was also called, was made only tall enough for men to work comfortably against the face, but it was made 16 feet wide, the full width of the finished tunnel. The ceiling of the heading was formed into an arch with a radius of eight feet. This arch became the crown of the finished tunnel. After the face of the heading had been driven some distance ahead, the second step was to lower the floor another 12 feet or so to the desired level of the finished grade. The final minimum rail-to-crown height was 19 feet. In the murky distance in this image, one can make out the ledge between the pioneer heading and the bottom portion, or bench, yet to be removed.

John R. Gilliss was the resident engineer responsible for keeping Summit Tunnel's four faces aligned so they would meet perfectly. The initial alignment, as well as the position and depth of the central shaft, was determined by surveying across the top of the ridge and establishing bench marks well outside the tunnel's mouths. Later, the faces were kept in alignment by sighting along a row of tacks hammered into wooden dowels driven into holes drilled into the tunnel ceiling.

Hart produced this remarkable photograph of the east end of tunnel no. 6 by reflecting sunlight into the dark interior with a large mirror during a 15 minute exposure.

LABORERS AND ROCKS

Though compressed-air drills existed at the time, all blasting holes on the CP project were drilled by hand using hammers and bits, the tools held by the drillers in this photograph. The bits were simply steel rods with ends forged into chisel-shaped points. In use, one man would hold and rotate a bit while two others alternately struck it with sledge hammers. Horizontal holes into the faces of the headings—the most difficult to drill—were driven about 18 inches deep, while vertical holes into the bench were drilled up to six feet deep. Once drilled, these holes were filled with black powder, or later with nitroglycerin. After detonation, and time for the smoke and dust to clear, the broken pieces of rock were loaded by hand into carts and removed from the tunnel. In Summit Tunnel, this went on 24 hours a day, seven days a week, for 15 months. From 30 to 40 Chinese worked at each of the four faces, with half drilling and the rest clearing out rubble from previous blasts. Four or five drill teams were used at each face. Laborers worked in eight-hour shifts, while the Caucasian foremen worked 12-hour shifts.

Altogether, the workforce at the summit numbered about four hundred men consisting of laborers, butchers, cooks, bakers, and teamsters. Two crews manned the hoist. Blacksmiths constantly sharpened drills. Strobridge lived at the tunnel, driving the crews.

198. East Portal of Summit Tunnel.
Western Summit. Length 1,600 feet.

EAST PORTAL SUMMIT TUNNEL
105.64 miles from Sacramento

Using black powder, the headings were driven an average of 1.18 feet per day per face. On February 9, 1867 nitroglycerin was first used in Summit Tunnel. With nitro, the daily advance per face was increased to 1.82 feet.

Mindful of the devastating explosion of nitroglycerin being shipped through downtown San Francisco in 1866, the railroad hired chemist James Howden to manufacture nitroglycerin right at the tunnel. The company paid him $300 per month in addition to the $500 paid in royalties for use of the patented formula.

The advantage of nitroglycerin was that, with its greater power, the holes for the charges could be smaller, and thus drilled faster. In working the faces with nitro, holes 1-1/4 inches in diameter were drilled—half the size required for black powder. Furthermore, because nitro broke the rock into smaller pieces, less time was needed to clear the rubble. Nitroglycerin produced less smoke to foul the air, but it caused headaches. At the faces of the headings, nitro was placed in horizontal holes in tin cartridges. In the bottoms, larger vertical holes were drilled six or seven feet deep. Nitro was carefully poured into the vertical holes through a funnel and an iron tube. The tube and cold temperature within the tunnel slowed the flow of the viscous oil. Nitro was detonated with common blasting powder in cartridges. Electrical detonators were tried, but the company continued with conventional powder fuses.

199. East Portal of Summit Tunnel, and Wagon Road from Tunnel No. 7.

EAST PORTAL of SUMMIT TUNNEL

This and the preceding views of the east portal of Summit Tunnel date from the fall of 1867, when the tunnel was nearly complete. This photograph was made looking west from on top of tunnel no. 7. The wagon is heading down the road toward the railroad grade. At the crossing the road turns right to continue down toward Donner Lake.

In early November 1867, a stagecoach traveling from Truckee to Cisco was ascending the road past this portal about two o'clock one morning, just in time for its passengers to witness a blast inside the tunnel. It happened to be the last of three coaches, and perhaps the tunnel crew thought all were past. Because of the steep incline of the road, made slippery by snow, most of the passengers were walking to lighten the load. Just as they came opposite the tunnel mouth, some 20 or 30 Chinese came running out, hollering and gesticulating. Then the foreman appeared, imploring the driver to "whip the horses!" and get clear. This was quickly followed by a flash of light and a loud report from inside the tunnel. Even though the working face was nearly four hundred feet into the mountain, a shower of stones was thrown well beyond the portal. The startled witnesses counted 13 or 14 distinct detonations.

In 1925, a second summit tunnel—10,326-foot long tunnel no. 41—was opened as the last element of the second-tracking of the railroad across the Sierra. The original tunnel remained in use until July 1993, when its track was removed and all traffic directed through the 1925 tunnel.

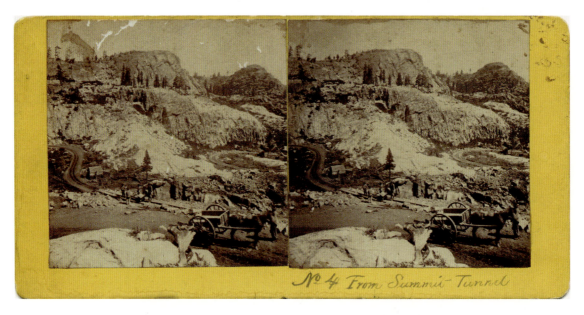

VIEW FROM NEAR SUMMIT TUNNEL

Hart made this seldom seen photograph by pointing his camera north, across the wagon road, from a point between tunnel no. 7 and the road's crossing of the railroad grade. The dirt cart is on the wagon road, while the workmen beyond it are standing on the edge of the railroad grade between tunnels nos. 6 and 7. Far below, the wagon road winds down the ravine toward Donner Lake, which is out of view to the right. The 1926 highway was built on the natural shelf that runs immediately below the two rocky knolls across the ravine.

Of particular interest in this photograph is the mine-type car, seen adjacent to the workers on the railroad grade. The rails on which it sits extend into the west end of tunnel no. 7 (out of view to the right). Though the tunnel itself was only 99.5 feet long, it required 113.5 days to complete the heading because the work was performed only intermittently while men became available from adjacent projects.

Small cars on rails were also used to remove debris from the west and center sections of Summit Tunnel. On the east end, however, an ordinary horse-drawn "stone boat" was used well into spring, so long as snow and ice covered the tunnel floor. Later, when the ice melted, and the face was farther into the mountain, ordinary horse-drawn dump carts—like the one on the road in this image—were used. A track was apparently not used at the east end of Summit Tunnel because the haul was downhill and the dump was close by.

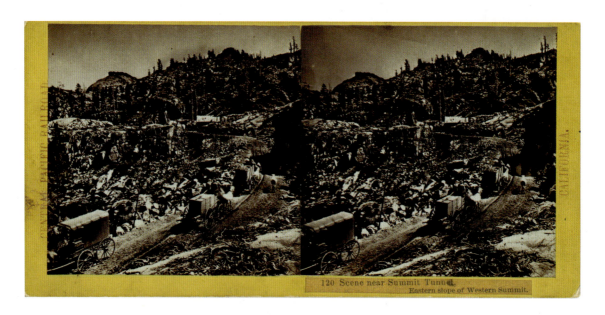

SCENE NEAR SUMMIT TUNNEL

The Dutch Flat & Donner Lake Wagon Road approached Donner Pass from Truckee up this steep grade. The road crossed the railroad between tunnels nos. 6 and 7 near the top, adjacent to the building visible in this view.

Any road-railroad crossing immediately outside a tunnel portal is dangerous because of the difficulty of seeing or hearing a train inside the tunnel. The crossing at Donner Pass was made even more dangerous in 1868 when the railroad was enclosed in a snowshed. Then the wagon road entered the dark shed though large doorways on either side. However, traffic on this road was very light after the opening of the railroad to Truckee in 1868.

With increased traffic after the appearance of the automobile, an underpass was built for this crossing in 1914. By locating it east of tunnel no. 7, the road's path was made longer, reducing the overall gradient. The underpass allowed automobiles to pass safely under the railroad without regard to railroad traffic. The old underpass still exists, but the road through it was abandoned in 1926 with the opening of the Donner Summit Bridge and a new highway route that did not cross the railroad.

Hart's mobile darkroom appears at the lower left while a water wagon sprinkles past it on the road.

DUTCH FLAT & DONNER LAKE WAGON ROAD

Hart made this view of the wagon road somewhere between Donner Pass and Donner Lake in the summer of 1867. The wagons are westbound, heading to Cisco. They all appear to be empty freight wagons. Note that traffic is on the left-hand side of the road. Generally, wagon drivers, with their whip in their right hand, sat on the right-hand side of the seat so their whip would swing clear of their wagon. Because they preferred to meet oncoming wagons on their side of the wagon, they ran to the left of opposing traffic.

This roadway was built by the CP-controlled Dutch Flat & Donner Lake Wagon Road Company. The original trail, used by the Donners and various parties before them, ran up the opposite side of the ravine, crossing the eventual railroad line somewhere between tunnels nos. 7 and 8, near the site of the 1914 underpass. That older wagon route was abandoned several years before the railroad was built for an easier route up Coldstream Valley to Coldstream Pass and Roller Pass.

While a wagon road was not as constrained by limitations of curvature and gradient as railroads, construction still presented challenges. To build this road many gullies had to be filled and many rocks blasted aside.

DONNER LAKE, PEAK, AND PASS FROM WAGON ROAD

Eastbound freight wagons roll past Donner Lake on the Dutch Flat & Donner Lake Wagon Road. The low gap in the distant range is Donner Pass, through which the road and the railroad crossed the Sierra crest. The stream of rolling wagons presented a cacophony of sound, with the creaking of wagon bodies, traces, and leather harnesses, the jangling of harness bells, punctuated with the teamsters' legendary profanity.

"Donner" became fixed to this lake and pass during the period of Judah's surveys, if not by the railroad company itself. Reflecting contemporary usage, Judah called the pass "Lake Pass" and the lake "Truckee Lake" in October 1860, but he was calling it "Donner Lake Pass" just one year later. "Donner Lake" was part of the wagon road title in the fall of 1861.

When the railroad was opened from Sacramento to Truckee and Reno in June of 1868, traffic over the road diminished immediately. Shortly thereafter, the road was deeded to Placer and Nevada counties, though which it passed. However, from that time on, the road carried little traffic and received virtually no maintenance. The old trace was found to be nearly impassable in 1909, when the California Legislature authorized the restoration of the road from Emigrant Gap to Donner Lake as a state highway. Yet, with improvements made, the route was chosen for the Lincoln Highway in 1914 and the Victory Highway nine years later. It became a portion of US 40 in 1928. Interstate 80 was completed across the crest in 1964, following a new course a mile to the north.

DONNER LAKE, TUNNELS NOS. 7 AND 8

This view looks from the Sierra crest above Summit Tunnel down to Donner Lake, more than a thousand feet below. The nearly finished railroad grade runs along the picture's right-hand margin, from the wagon road crossing in the foreground to the mouth of tunnel no. 7. The visitors are standing immediately north of the intersection of the wagon road and the railroad grade. Beyond, the mouth of tunnel no. 8 is just visible at the base of Black Point.

Everyone in the West in the 1860s knew the story of the Donner Party of 1846-47. Most of the adults living in California in the 1860s had come overland, and when they made their trek, the story of the Donners' plight in the snow had made them all anxious to be across the Sierra Nevada before storms blocked the passes. The railroad made crossing the Sierra relatively safe and comfortable, and it also made Donner Lake accessible. Because of the Donner story, the lake was a feature that always attracted the attention of passengers. However, few were as interested as Eliza Houghton, who with her young children rode the first passenger train to cross from Reno to Sacramento in June 1868. She was said to have stared silently and very intently at the lake from the train window. Houghton was the daughter of George and Tamsen Donner. She was only four years old when she had last seen Donner Lake, that terrible winter they were all trapped in the snow.

The 3D effect of this image has been digitally enhanced.

204. Heading of east portal Tunnel No. 8.

HEADING of EAST PORTAL TUNNEL 8
105.97 miles from Sacramento

Hart photographed this water—or perhaps tea—carrier outside the east end of tunnel no. 8 in the summer of 1867. Chief Engineer Montague called this the "finest tunnel entrance" on the entire CP.

Tunnel no. 8 is a 375-foot bore through Black Point. This rock is so hard that the average daily progress was only half that in nearby Summit Tunnel, and it took crews working from both ends seven months to finish it. This was the only tunnel other than Summit Tunnel where nitroglycerin was used, though it was used here only briefly.

Work on this tunnel was not advanced enough before the snow began falling in late 1866 to allow the removal of any of the bottoms, and drifting snow blocked the openings of the shallow headings. However, once the snow had piled deep enough against the sides of Black Point, passages were dug through the snowbanks, providing access to the tunnel faces. Eventually there was so much snow drifted against the west face of the bluff that workers had to walk through a three-hundred foot long snow tunnel just to get to the portal of the rock tunnel. The only way to get to the east end of the tunnel from the camp was by way of a passage carved through the snow mass piled up against the north side of Black Point.

CONSTRUCTING SNOW COVER

Most of the railroad across the crest was enclosed during the summer of 1868. Snow covers with roofs extending all the way to the face of the adjacent bluff were called "galleries." They were designed to carry avalanches harmlessly across the track. This particular view shows the outside of the gallery just east of tunnel no. 8. This is virtually the same location where the water-carrier was standing in the preceding image, taken the year before.

When this photograph was made, the gallery was still under construction. The man standing on the roof is believed to be Arthur Brown, the CP's superintendent of bridges and buildings. In addition to building the snowsheds, Brown supervised the construction of all of the railroad's trestles and bridges from Newcastle east, as well as the shops and probably the depots.

By the end of 1869, the railroad's snow-covering was continuous—except for tunnels—for a distance of 30 miles, from Emigrant Gap to tunnel no. 13. A total of two miles of snowsheds covered double track at stations. In addition, isolated sheds were constructed at troublesome places as far west as Blue Canyon and as far east as Truckee, making a total of 37 miles covered. The advent of the rotary snowplows in 1888 made the sheds less critical, and several miles of sheds were eliminated in connection with double-tracking of the railroad across the Sierra. By 1956 only four miles of snowsheds remained.

SNOW GALLERY AROUND CRESTED PEAK
106.1 miles from Sacramento

This view faces eastward from just outside tunnel no. 8, the point nearly below where the man was standing in the preceding image. The beams of light reveal that the roof has yet to be covered completely.

Much of the responsibility for the protection of life and property on the railroad fell to solitary trackwalkers who were constantly watching for broken rails, loose spikes, or signs of fire. Patrolling the snowsheds always called for steel nerve, as they were perpetually cold and gloomy places, and there was little shelter when a train suddenly appeared.

One lone trackwalker encountered far more than he expected when, near the location of this Hart image, he came face-to-face with a large Bengal tiger on an early morning in May 1904. Unbeknownst to him, a Norris & Rowe circus train had derailed in the snowshed some distance below, and liberated animals were roaming the sheds at will. One tiger was corralled in the waiting room of the depot at Summit, while another was tracked several miles through the snow before being recaptured. A snake charmer had to coax a large boa constrictor back to its cage, but two African lions retreated to their cages on their own after finding the snow outside not to their liking. The monkeys, on the other hand, made themselves quite at home in the snowshed rafters, and it took several weeks to round them all up.

See an alternate Hart view of this scene on p. 479.

CONSTRUCTING SNOW COVER
106.39 miles from Sacramento

This picture, taken at the east end of the gallery that extended about one half mile below tunnel no. 8, reveals the narrow shelf that was blasted into the face of the precipitous cliff to provide a foundation for the railroad. To establish the initial lines for this excavation, surveyors were lowered by ropes over the cliff in several places. Once, one flagman was inadvertently left dangling while the rest of the survey crew broke for lunch.

With the roadbed at this location under construction at all hours of the day and night in the summer and fall of 1867, the bonfires and blasts presented a novel spectacle of light and sound as viewed from the shore of Donner Lake far below. A single charge would be detonated in a hole drilled 12 to 20 feet deep to "spring a seam." The resulting crack was then filled with as much powder as it could hold, from one to 50 kegs, and the resulting explosion would blast a whole mass of rock over the cliff and out of the way. E.B. Crocker wrote, "It makes the earth shake like an earthquake." From three to four hundred kegs of powder were used here every day.

In this photograph from 1868, the railroad is complete and work continues on the construction of the gallery. This is the opposite end of the double "S" curve seen in the preceding view.

CONSTRUCTING SNOW GALLERY

The most troublesome hurdle in completing the railroad between Cisco and Truckee was this stretch of track around the north face of Donner Peak. While underground work in the tunnels continued around-the-clock, generally unhampered by the weather, this work in the open could not be commenced until the summer of 1867, when the snow had finally melted. Because of the late start and tough going, crews were actually pulled from Summit Tunnel, once its headings were connected, and concentrated on this outside section.

The whole time workers chipped and blasted here, other crews were building the railroad westward along the Truckee River from the Nevada state line. As winter grew closer, a race commenced between the weather and the railroad builders, trying to connect the two sections of track before the snow started falling.

This view shows the top of the east end of the Donner Peak snow gallery, seen in the previous three photographs. The outer wall and joists are in place, and workers are preparing to frame the sloping roof. The carpenters in this image provide a scale that conveys the magnitude of these structures. The construction of the snowsheds and galleries required 65 million board-feet of lumber by the end of 1869.

INSIDE VIEW OF SNOW GALLERY AT SUMMIT
BOLTING THE FRAME TO THE ROCKS

To withstand the force of avalanches, the snow galleries were securely anchored to the mountain face with iron rods and bolts.

These photographs of the snow gallery under construction date from 1868, probably August, when Hart was based in Reno.

Fires were a constant threat to the sheds in the summer, especially in the days of wood-burning steam locomotives. To reduce the risk, the roof timbers and boards were covered with a mixture of coal tar and powdered rock, and by 1873 sections of the sheds were sheathed in galvanized corrugated iron.

In addition, fully manned fire trains, with the locomotives under full steam, were stationed at strategic points along the line. Watchmen were on constant patrol, and these trains could be summoned via a fire-alarm telegraph that extended the full length of the sheds by 1874. Twice a week the fire trains sprayed the interior of the sheds with water to keep them from getting too dry. In later years, sections of sheds were built on wheels, so they could be "telescoped" past adjacent sheds in the summer, creating openings to serve as firebreaks. They also helped clear annoying locomotive exhaust smoke from the sheds.

VIEW WEST FROM TUNNEL NO. 9
106.5 miles from Sacramento

This view looks northwestward along the railroad from a point above tunnel no. 9. In the distance is the east end of the snow gallery constructed around Donner Peak. Adjacent to the end of that snow gallery, a massive stone wall is being constructed to protect the track from snow slides. A derrick used for lifting rock into place is visible.

Avalanches were a major problem during the construction of the railroad over Donner Pass. On at least three occasions they swept into camps and buried workmen as they slept. When an avalanche buried 18 men in their cabin on March 2, 1867, Strobridge and 50 workers dug furiously for 12 hours, saving 15 of the trapped men. To minimize the danger, volunteers crept onto the overhanging snow crests and set blasting charges, creating controlled slides when everyone was clear. Still, because of the danger, work on tunnel no. 9 was suspended until well into April.

This location was near the end-of-track in early December 1867, when the CP ran the first public excursion across the summit. A participant wrote, "Unfortunately, for some reasons, the snow was falling thickly, and the fine view of Donner Lake and the surrounding country was very much curtailed." Refreshments ran out, a watch was stolen, and the train stalled for 10 minutes in Summit Tunnel, filling the train with smoke. All in all, it was a memorable 15-hour trip to the summit and back.

LOOKING WEST FROM TUNNEL NO. 10
106.7 miles from Sacramento

Just 700 feet beyond tunnel no. 9, tunnel no. 10 pierces Cement Ridge. This tunnel is 509 feet long and is mostly tangent, though an 8° curve extends a short distance into its west portal, as seen in this view looking back up the grade. Of all the tunnels between Cisco and Coldstream, this was the easiest to work, yielding at an average of 2.51 feet per day in the heading and 3.56 feet per day in the bottom. Work on tunnel no. 10 was started from both directions, but the effort at the uphill end was abandoned due to water accumulation against the face, and it was completed from the east end only. The material is conglomerate, but the tunnel required no lining.

When Hart made this picture in the summer of 1868, workmen were finishing a stone retaining wall just west of the tunnel mouth. The wall was for protection from snow slides.

Hart did not visit Donner during the winter, but his photographs of Cisco in the snow make it easy to visualize the winter scene here. During the cold months, workers wore thick coats, with mittens and scarves. They slept in log cabins and huts made out of shakes. Some cabins had bunks for several men, but others were only four feet high, six feet wide, and eight feet long—little more than wood lined snow caves. Yet another avalanche killed from 15 to 20 workers near tunnel no. 10 in February 1867.

CRESTED PEAK AND TUNNEL NO. 10
107 miles from Sacramento

Hart positioned his camera nearly atop tunnel no. 11 to capture this image. Facing west, the view records the early phase of construction of the snowshed between tunnels nos. 11 and 10. Donner Peak, as it is called today, forms the background. When the railroad was built the mountain was called "Crested Peak"—a descriptive name derived from its unusual volcanic cap-rock.

Tunnel no. 11 is 325 feet long and partly curved. This tunnel was worked from both ends and was the last tunnel to be completed. Tunnels nos. 6 through 12 are all on the segment of track that the SP abandoned in 1993 when it began funneling all traffic through adjacent tunnel no. 41, built in 1925.

Below this point, the railroad makes its way to the Truckee River with a long traverse down and around Schallenberger Ridge. When the railroad was built, this was known as "Lake Ridge," though with macabre humor crews referred to it as "Donner's Backbone." The modern name memorializes Moses Schallenberger, who was left here alone during the winter of 1844-45 because he was too weak to cross the summit. He was 18 years old at the time. Remarkably, he survived the winter by himself at the lake, and lived to revisit the scene in September 1869, after the railroad was completed.

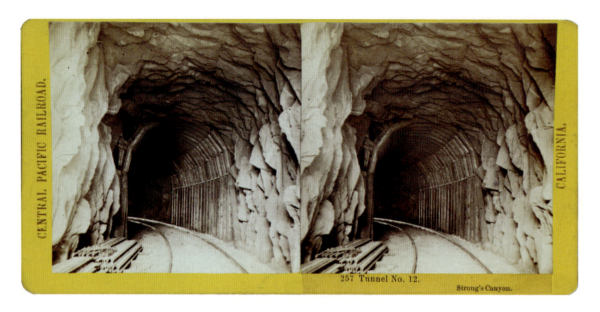

TUNNEL NO. 12
107.37 miles from Sacramento

Tunnel no. 12 is a 262-foot bore through Tunnel Spur, leading the railroad into Strong's Canyon. Soft material in the middle of the tunnel required timbering for 80 feet.

The end-of-track was just downhill from this tunnel on December 17, 1867 when storms brought all work on the mountain to a stop. A six-mile gap separated the railroad west of tunnel no. 12 from the track already built along the Truckee River. When the work stopped, the completed railroad from Cisco to tunnel no. 12 was abandoned to the snow, leaving Cisco the end of rail operations from Sacramento for a second winter.

Late in the spring of 1868, three thousand men using powder and shovels cleared the snow and ice from the railroad between Cisco and tunnel no. 12, and from the unfinished grade between tunnel 12 and Coldstream. Soon the grading between Coldstream and the tunnel was finished, and the track was finally built to close that gap. Adopting track-laying techniques developed by John S. Casement on the UP, those six miles of track were built in just one week, the fastest time yet on the CP. On June 17 foreman David J. Sullivan directed the laying of the last rails and track supervisor Henry Minkler drove a last spike. With the gap closed, the CP had a continuous railroad extending some 175 miles, from Sacramento to a point well beyond Reno.

COLDSTREAM VALLEY
113 miles from Sacramento, elevation 6,214 feet

The isolated railroad that the CP built along the Truckee River during the summer of 1867, extended westward into Coldstream Valley by November 18. That remained the upper end of that track until June 1868, when the gap between it and the line from Sacramento was finally closed.

The railroad climbs 1,147 feet between Truckee and Summit. To hold the rate of ascent to an average 76.5 feet per mile, the engineers found a line for 14 miles of railroad by folding it into a long "S" curve running deep into Coldstream Valley and then out around the nose of Schallenberger Ridge. In this photograph, two legs of the lower horseshoe curve are visible; the curve itself is out of sight to the right.

The sawmill on the far track marks the location of Stanford, a station named for Phillip Stanford, the mill's proprietor and Leland Stanford's brother. While Stanford is long gone, the adjacent horseshoe curve is called "Stanford Curve" to this day. To the engineers, however, it is curve no. 385, of 9°30', through which the railroad turns 172°.

The upper horseshoe of the "S" curve is located some two miles to the left on the near track, where the railroad makes a 140° bend around the point of Schallenberger Ridge. Since part of that curve is inside tunnel no. 13, and cannot therefore be easily straightened, it retains its original 10° curvature.

SCENE AT TRUCKEE

Truckee began its existence in 1863 as Gray's Station, named for Joseph Gray's roadhouse on the trans-Sierra wagon road. Blacksmith Samuel S. Coburn was there almost from the beginning, and by 1866 the locality was known as "Coburn's Station." By then it was an important place, as the eastward development of the railroad and the connecting Dutch Flat & Donner Lake Wagon Road attracted more and more Virginia City traffic from the Placerville route. The CP selected "Truckee" as the name for its railroad station by August 1867.

Truckee flourished even before the railroad arrived. Railroad builders, displaced by Sierra snows, descended upon the Truckee River in late 1866 to begin building the railroad down the canyon. Soon several sawmills were supplying crossties and bridge timbers, and for years thereafter, Truckee was a major lumbering center.

The town of Truckee was described as "one-third of a mile long [and] about two houses deep" across a broad street from the railroad. For years it had a brand-new look, primarily because of a repeating cycle of conflagration and reconstruction. With the convenience of railroad travel and proximity to Donner Lake and Lake Tahoe, Truckee became an early recreation destination. An 1876 guide book proclaimed Truckee, with its many hotels and bars, "the best place in the [Sierra Nevada] to be snowed in."

DEPOT AT TRUCKEE
119.5 miles from Sacramento, elevation 5,819 feet

The railroad grade along the Truckee River was built during the winter of 1866-67 and the following summer. The work was carried out generally east-to-west, starting at the state line, where the railroad would make its second crossing of the river, and advanced uphill as the snow melted. Enough rail and hardware for 24 miles of track and rolling stock for this isolated stretch of railroad were shipped from Cisco to Truckee over the wagon road beginning in July 1867.

Local lumberman George Schaffer, who along with Joseph Gray—of Gray's Station fame—had established the first Truckee area sawmill, took the contract to haul the rail and the first locomotive across the mountain. Schaffer had scores of oxen used to pulling heavy loads. Still unassembled and in crates, the locomotive was transported to Truckee, where it was erected. The ironwork for six flatcars was also delivered across the mountains, and the following winter three additional locomotives were pulled across the snow-covered mountain on sledges. Eventually, a passenger coach was also hauled across on the road.

By the time Hart took this picture toward the east in August 1868, the railroad across the mountain was complete. Truckee became a regular crew change point in January 1869. As long as steam ruled the rails, Truckee was an important facility for locomotive, fire, and snow fighting crews.

TRUCKEE RIVER BELOW TRUCKEE STATION
120.8 miles from Sacramento

In October 1867 Hart visited the brand new—and still isolated—railroad along the Truckee River and made this and several other photographs. While grading on that stretch of railroad began at the state line and worked west as the snow melted, track was built eastward from Truckee, where rail and rolling stock were stockpiled. When Hart made this trip to the Truckee, the rails had yet to be laid all the way to the state line. This view, facing west, was taken about a mile east of town, very close to the bridge that carries modern Highway 267 across the Truckee River. The prominence in the distance is the eastern point of Schallenberger Ridge, which the railroad wound around.

John F. Kidder was the engineer who established the railroad's location down the Truckee. Charles Cadwalader was the supervising engineer who oversaw construction.

As a westbound train was passing near this point one night in August 1887, a lady from Elko, Nevada summoned the conductor to her berth to request that a doctor be sought among the passengers. Soon Dr. Paul Kirby of Virginia City was located, and upon his arrival at her side he recognized that she was laboring in childbirth. Later that night, as the train neared Auburn, a healthy baby girl was born.

FIRST LOCOMOTIVE IN NEVADA
121.2 miles from Sacramento

The first locomotive hauled across the Sierra to Truckee River was the *San Mateo*, seen here standing beside the Truckee River. This photograph was made from nearly the same place as the preceding view, though with Hart's camera facing the opposite direction.

While it and its two classmates exhibit some unique characteristics, such as the cab with the curved front corners, the identification of this locomotive as the *San Mateo* is based on the fact that it was the only locomotive operating on the railroad east of Truckee when Hart made his visit in October 1867. The *San Mateo* belonged to the Western Pacific Railroad, the company that held the franchise to build the section of the Pacific railroad from Sacramento to San Jose, but which the CP absorbed in 1867. Of all the locomotives available, the *San Mateo* was shipped to Truckee because it had yet to be assembled and was still in packing crates.

The presence of ladies in the locomotive gangway suggests that this was an informal Sunday excursion. The *San Mateo*'s regular engineer was identified only as "G. Reilly;" James N. Abboy was fireman. They first ran the *San Mateo* over new track into Nevada (as the boundary was then marked) within a day or two of October 31, the third anniversary of Nevada's statehood.

The 3D effect of this image has been digitally enhanced.

CROSSING OF LITTLE TRUCKEE RIVER AT BOCA
127.72 miles from Sacramento, elevation 5,532 feet

The CP crossed the mouth of the Little Truckee River at Boca on this Howe-truss bridge. The locomotive pulling this train of crossties is a Mason 4-4-0, possibly no. 2 *Pacific*. The image dates from August 1868, and one can only speculate why the train was pointed away from the advancing end-of-track, which was then well into the Humboldt desert.

With financing from Sacramento lumber merchants Joseph Friend and Wallace Terry, Lattimer Doan purchased a small sawmill at Boca in 1868, along with extensive timber holdings nearby. Doan had previously operated a mill at Canyon Creek, near Alta, providing lumber to the CP. Inspired by the heavy ice on the Boca mill pond the following winter, Doan erected a large icehouse and in 1869 organized the Boca Mill & Ice Company for the production and sale of ice. When that company ceased production in 1927, it was the last to harvest ice on the Truckee River.

To further capitalize on his ice, Doan built the Boca Brewery in 1875. At the time, it was the largest brewery on the West Coast, and it produced the West's first commercial lager—which is fermented and conditioned cold. While local loggers and lumbermen were eager customers, the brewery took advantage of the railroad to distribute its product throughout the western US. The frame brewery buildings burned in January 1893. By the time the railroad's fire train arrived from Truckee, nothing was left to save.

See an alternate Hart view of this scene on p. 473.

PROFILE ROCK
131.6 miles from Sacramento

The catalog numbers printed on most of the stereo cards reproduced in this book were assigned, apparently by Hart, as a way to keep tabs of the various images. Generally, the numbers were assigned in geographical order eastward from Sacramento. However, in at least five places in the numbering, the sequence of numbers jumps back to the west, overlapping scenes already numbered. These discontinuities provide a framework for dating the images as each break in the west-to-east sequence is taken to represent the introduction of a new series of photographs to the collection. Known dates of specific scenes and references to Hart's activity in correspondence and newspapers allow general dates to be assigned to each successive group.

Occasionally, however, the west-to-east numbering pattern was ignored. This view of Profile Rock is one such anomaly. While its number follows that of the scenes of the railroad's first crossing of the Truckee, thus creating the impression that it was east of that bridge, various clues in the image reveal that Profile Rock was actually a short distance to the west. Still, we know from the numbers that the photograph dates from Hart's late October 1867 trip to the Truckee.

Profile Rock was destroyed during the double-tracking of the railroad between Lawton, Nevada and Truckee in 1913. The second track was extended westward from Truckee to tunnel no. 13 a decade later.

FIRST CROSSING OF THE TRUCKEE RIVER
132.24 miles from Sacramento

As with its tunnels and curves, the CP numbered its river crossings in sequential order eastward from Sacramento. The first crossing of the Truckee River, where the railroad crossed over to the right-hand bank (as the river flows), was some 12 miles below Truckee.

The bridge in the distance in this image crosses Gray Creek. Early CP reports consistently called this "Juniper Creek," but the accepted name commemorates Joseph Gray, of Gray's Station, who had a sawmill here. During construction days, this was the location of Camp 20. By 1874 this location was named "Cuba." With a relatively wide bottom to the canyon and abundant water, ice ponds were soon developed here. Gray leased land for a pond in 1876 to People's Ice Company, and in time, both the Mountain and Floriston ice companies also had ponds. The station name was changed to "Iceland" in 1897. It lasted as a station until 1939. Truckee River ice found many uses, from cooling home iceboxes and railroad refrigerator cars to cooling Comstock miners.

Below this point, the Truckee River's canyon is quite narrow. Overland pioneers only negotiated the canyon once with wagons, as the steep banks confined their way to the boulder-strewn frigid stream itself. Beginning in 1845 immigrants followed an easier path through Dog Valley, which remained the route of road-vehicle travel until the development of the state highway in 1926.

BRIDGE at FIRST CROSSING TRUCKEE RIVER

A crew of carpenters led by John Haten began framing the bridges along the Truckee River in late July 1867. They first raised the bridge at Boca, then the one at Prosser Creek, and finally this one at the first crossing and the nearby bridge over Gray Creek. The structures were only weeks old when Hart visited in October and made these photographs. The afternoon sun cast the long shadow of Hart and his camera across the foreground. The first-crossing bridge consisted of a single 204-foot Howe truss span with reinforcing arches. The bridge over Gray Creek, seen just beyond, was a 73-foot Howe truss. Both structures were soon sheathed to protect the woodwork from the weather.

After these bridges were constructed, Haten's crew built the four-span bridge at Donner Creek, just west of Truckee. It was finished by the end of September. Donner Creek is the outflow from Donner Lake; it is called Coldstream in some early documents.

While the bridges and trestles west of Cisco were framed with Oregon fir and California redwood, the timbers for the Cascades and Truckee bridges were hewn and sawn locally. The metalwork for these structures—the nuts, bolts, washers, and tie rods—were shipped from New York on steamers by way of Panama and the Panama Railroad. Later, as it became imperative for the CP to beat the UP to Salt Lake Valley, thousands of tons of rail and 18 locomotives were also shipped across Panama.

VIEW NEAR STATE LINE ALONG THE TRUCKEE RIVER
136.28 miles from Sacramento

Just past Iceland, the track turns northward and runs through the narrowest and steepest part of the Truckee River's canyon. This August 1868 view was taken facing northwest at a point approximately one and a half miles downstream from modern Floriston.

The station of Floriston was established in 1887 to serve local ice warehouses. In 1899, Herbert and Mortimer Fleishhacker of San Francisco organized the Truckee River General Electric Company to generate electricity to sell to the Comstock to operate pumps to drain the mines. The company built a seven-foot rock-filled crib dam at Floriston, and a powerhouse at Farad, connected with a wooden flume. A 33-mile transmission line conveyed the electricity from Farad to Virginia City. The Farad plant is located on the opposite side of the river from where Hart made this photograph. The name "Farad" comes from the unit of electrical capacitance, which is itself named for Michael Faraday.

In 1900, the Fleishhackers went on to organize the Floriston Pulp & Paper Company, which built a paper mill at Floriston to make fruit wrapping paper from local wood. Both the pulpwood and the paper were transported by rail. After several changes of ownership and many complaints about the pollution, the paper mill was closed in 1930. The power plant at Farad operated until 1997, when the dam at Floriston was washed out in a flood.

TUNNEL NO. 15
137.7 miles from Sacramento

Tunnel no. 15 was the CP's easternmost tunnel, completed by June 1867. For a few years beginning in 1879, a siding called "Mystic," located just west of the tunnel, served "Elle" Ellen's logging operation.

One unexpected consequence of the transcontinental railroad was the easy communication of disease, and in the early 1880s residents of California were in a panic over smallpox apparently introduced by rail from eastern cities. In January 1882, a medical officer who boarded a westbound train at Reno discovered two cases of smallpox. The train was stopped, and two emigrant cars and the caboose were uncoupled and left in quarantine at Mystic, along with 47 passengers and crew. Two days later, the crew and most of the passengers were vaccinated, fumigated, and allowed to depart. The two sick brothers, however, were left to fend for themselves in the frigid canyon in a boxcar supplied with some food and a stove. Ultimately they recovered, though one of the "healthy" passengers released from quarantine died soon after reaching San Francisco. The immediate consequence of this event was the system wide vaccination of all CP train crews.

A few weeks later yet another car was quarantined at Boca. Fearful residents kept the passengers confined to the car even after their water and provisions ran out. Before they were rescued, two children contracted pneumonia and died.

TUNNEL NO. 15
137.8 miles from Sacramento

Tunnel no. 15 was just 94 feet long, only two feet longer than tunnel 4, the shortest on the railroad.

In composing this August 1868 photograph, Hart placed himself about halfway between tunnel no. 15 and the state line with his camera facing west. The track had been built here at the very end of October 1867.

The California-Nevada boundary north of Lake Tahoe is the 120th Longitude, a line marked in 1863 by surveyors James F. Houghton, Butler Ives, and John F. Kidder. Relying on a chronometer, Houghton's team determined the boundary by finding positions that were directly under the sun's meridian exactly eight hours after it had crossed the Prime Meridian at Greenwich, England. However, the completion of the railroad's telegraph line invited a reexamination of the survey using time signals sent from established observatories. In 1872, George Davidson demonstrated that the 1863 line was about three thousand feet too far west. Soon thereafter, Allexey Von Schmidt marked the new state line that is recognized today.

Given the railroad's nearly north-south orientation along the Truckee, the effect of Von Schmidt's adjustment was to shift about two more miles of railroad into California. This put approximately 8,100 feet of the CP railroad onto Sierra County's tax rolls.

SECOND CROSSING OF THE TRUCKEE RIVER
138.32 miles from Sacramento

This and the following view illustrate the CP's second crossing of the Truckee River, just inside Nevada—as it was then defined. Camp 24 was established at this location late in the fall of 1866 as the easternmost base camp for the construction of the isolated railroad along the Truckee River. Roadbed grading began here in December. The rails laid from Truckee reached the bridge site at the end of October 1867.

In December 1867, when heavy mud closed the Dog Valley wagon road that carried the traffic east of Truckee, the CP began carrying freight and passengers on trains between Truckee and Camp 24. This was while the railroad along the Truckee was still isolated from the rest of the CP, and open flatcars were the only cars available to ride. Thus, for a time that winter, a trip from San Francisco to Virginia City involved a riverboat to Sacramento, a regular passenger train to Cisco, a sleigh to Truckee, a flatcar to Camp 24, and finally a stagecoach on to the Comstock. The celebrated reinsman Hank Monk was one of the stage drivers running between Camp 24 and Virginia City.

Work on the bridge at Camp 24 got underway after the completion of the railroad from Truckee. Each of the bridge's two Howe-truss spans was 150 feet long.

SECOND CROSSING OF THE TRUCKEE RIVER

Not all of Hart's photographs were assigned inventory numbers. Those without numbers may never have been published for sale, and certainly this is a seldom seen view. Someone mistakenly marked the card as "Yuba River," but it is one of several photographs taken near the CP's second crossing of the Truckee River at Camp 24. The bridge was not completed until late March 1868, and the photograph probably dates from the following August, when Hart spent a month in the Reno area. His camera was facing southward from a point just north of the bridge.

Track laying into Nevada began immediately after the bridge was finished. By then, the roadbed was almost completed to the site of Wadsworth, 50 miles ahead, though two unfinished bridges in the first eight miles, and the scarcity of ties, caused some delays. Until the railroad between Coldstream and tunnel no.12 was completed, all of the rails laid east of Camp 24 had to be hauled across the summit on the wagon road from Cisco. As late as June, rails were being hauled at least part of the way to Truckee on sleds over the snowpack.

With the advance of the end-of-track, Camp 24 was abandoned as a construction camp. The name, however, remained in use by Reno fishermen through the end of the century. Like the CP's other wooden bridges, this one was covered. An iron bridge replaced the original structure in 1892.

EAGLE GAP
139.2 miles from Sacramento

"Eagle Gap" is one of the more obscure place names used by Hart, and it seems never to have stuck to the landscape. Another name for this location was "Rattlesnake Cliffs." The scene is located about one mile below the railroad's second crossing of the Truckee River, halfway between the old and the new state lines. Hart's camera faced south. A landslide at this point in April 1868 killed a track layer—one of at least three Irishmen on the CP named Sullivan. Double-tracking and highway construction have changed the topography considerably since then.

In 1905, the Truckee River General Electric Company built the Fleish diversion dam immediately to the left of Hart's camera position. Fleish takes its name from Herbert and Mortimer Fleishhacker, principals in that company. As a first step toward developing hydroelectric power plants on the Truckee River, the Fleishhackers obtained the rights of the old Donner Lumber & Boom Company, which had been organized in 1870 by the CP to facilitate logging along the Truckee River. Its Tahoe City dam and floodgates were originally intended to create artificial freshets to float saw logs to downstream mills. While logs were driven as far as Glendale, east of Reno, in the 1870s, long river drives on the Truckee River were generally uneconomical.

THIRD CROSSING OF THE TRUCKEE RIVER
141.5 miles from Sacramento

The bridge seen in the distance in this view is the CP's third crossing of the Truckee River. This and the following views were made from virtually the same location, facing opposite directions, from the top of a rocky outcropping. This view looks upstream. During construction days, this was the site of Camp 26. Fishermen from Reno called the river narrows here "Manassas Gap." The Fleish hydroelectric powerhouse was located just upstream of this bridge.

The bridge itself was a 204-foot Howe truss with supplemental arches, identical in design and dimensions to the first-crossing bridge, as well as the next bridge four miles below. All of these structures were virtually identical to the two Cascades bridges, though those carried the track on the top chords rather than the bottom chords.

This particular bridge was built in March 1868, and the track was first laid across it in early April. The original bridge burned in August 1883 and was replaced with an iron, three-span deck-girder structure—the first iron bridge on the CP's overland route. That bridge, in turn, was replaced 30 years later as part of the double-tracking of the railroad through the canyon between Truckee and Lawton.

VIEW NEAR VERDI
141.7 miles from Sacramento

Downstream from the railroad's third crossing, the Truckee River's canyon opens into a broad valley. This view looks north from a rocky prominence.

The arrival of the CP opened a period of intense lumbering all along the Truckee River; most of the ties used in building the remaining 550 miles of railroad came from the Truckee area. In 1875 a water-powered sawmill was established in the flat area in the middle distance of this view, a location initially called "Essex." The mill was operated by John P. and George Foulkes until 1882, and by Sylvester A. Hamlin until 1886. Essex stood at the eastern edge of the Sierra forest, and it was an important wood stop for locomotives. A locomotive coaling facility was installed here in 1881 as wood fuel was phased out.

In 1890, the Inyo Marble Company established a water-powered marble dressing works adjacent to Essex, naming its station "Marmol." Stone was delivered from Keeler, California via the Carson & Colorado, Virginia & Truckee, and CP railroads. Marmol was renamed "Fleish" in 1908.

Verdi, located just one mile east of Essex, was the railroad's station for the nearby settlement of Crystal Peak, which had been established in 1864. "Verdi" was selected as the station name by September 1866, months before the track reached the point in April 1868. Verdi replaced Crystal Peak as the post office in 1869.

FOURTH CROSSING OF THE TRUCKEE RIVER
145.6 miles from Sacramento

The track re-crossed to the left bank of the Truckee River just east of Verdi. In this photograph, the bridge at the fourth crossing frames an eastward view downstream toward Reno.

CP bridge carpenter A.P. Partridge reminisced, "Some time in March, we (the gang that I was with at the time, under M.J. Healey) were sent to frame the bridge at the fourth crossing. That bridge was also a 204 ft. span. After we had framed the bridge we were sent back to put the arches on the third crossing. That was seven miles from the fourth crossing and one night about 9 P.M. there came word for us to come to the fourth crossing and help to raise the bridge the next day. We got up at 3 A.M., went out on our bridge, got our tackle and some bars and carried them seven miles, the occasion being a heavy rise in the river, and arrived there before 7 A.M. To make a long story short, we raised that bridge and had it swinging by 5 o'clock that evening, then walked back home; a good day's work for a man."

Partridge's story is hardly diminished by the fact that the seven-mile distance he remembered between the third and fourth crossings is actually the round-trip distance they walked. Trains first reached the fourth crossing on April 23, 1868.

FOURTH CROSSING OF THE TRUCKEE RIVER

The bridge at the fourth crossing was a single Howe-truss span with reinforcing arches, identical to the bridges at the first and third crossings. It was replaced with an iron bridge in 1896. Until new bridges were added east of Reno in 1902-03, the railroad remained on the north side of the river all the way from here to Wadsworth, 42 miles to the east. This view looks toward the northwest.

Newspapers called this crossing point "Hunter's Crossing," but it was actually three miles short of Hunter's itself. The large house in the picture belonged to rancher Warren King. In the 1870s there was a station named "Angora" or "Angora Ranch" just east of the crossing. Angora was renamed "Mogul" in 1907. "Mogul" was the type name for locomotives having a 2-6-0 wheel arrangement, but the term, derived from the name of the Mongol conquerors of India, was in popular usage in the early 1900s to denote anything of superlative power. In that period, various mines, race horses, and prominent political and business leaders were christened "mogul," so it is uncertain how or why this particular location got that name. Mogul was the site of the Mogul hydroelectric power plant, and it is possible the railroad station was named for the plant, not the other way around.

Deposits resembling coal were found in the hillside just south of this crossing, but the much sought coal mine did not materialize. Still, this hillside was marked "Coal Mine Point" on an early CP profile.

281 Reno and Washoe Range in distance.
From Base of Sierra Nevada Mountains.

RENO AND WASHOE RANGE
153 miles from Sacramento

Reno is located in the Truckee Meadows, a place where pioneers heading west often recuperated from their desert crossing. During the early years of the Comstock boom, enterprising farmers settled there to raise produce to sell in nearby Virginia City. By the time the railroad surveyors arrived, several settlements were thriving both along the Truckee River and south along Steamboat Creek. Of these, both Hunter's and Glendale were mentioned as potential locations for the railroad's Truckee Meadows depot. But in March 1868 Glendale was flooded, and the company selected a station site adjacent to Myron Lake's wagon bridge across the Truckee River. CP construction engineer Joseph M. Graham drove the first stake in surveying the new town on April 1, and town lots were auctioned on May 5.

The track arrived at the site of Reno on May 4. As the railroad between Coldstream and tunnel no. 12 was yet to be finished, the first trains to Reno were construction trains running only from Truckee, though passengers were soon being carried. The first train to operate all the way from Sacramento to Reno arrived on June 18.

Hart arrived in Reno for the first time in August and stayed a month. He made several photographs along the railroad from Donner to Granite Point during that period, including this one of the new town from the hill just west of town.

RENO DEPOT
154.47 miles from Sacramento, elevation 4,500 feet

"Argenta" was the name initially proposed for the CP's Truckee Meadows depot. Since this was a name for silver ore, the choice was considered appropriate. Thus, the announcement of "Reno" as the chosen name in April 1868 was met with considerable surprise. Indeed, the selection was so unexpected and apparently unjustified as to puzzle writers for more than a century. A relevant clue in explaining the choice is that Wadsworth, the railroad's next station of significance to the east, was also named at the same time. Both Jesse L. Reno and James S. Wadsworth were rather obscure military officers killed in the Civil War. Though neither had any connection with the West, both were important to General Irvin McDowell, commandant of the Army's Pacific Division, who had served with both Reno and Wadsworth. McDowell was a personal friend of CP President Stanford, and the two important railroad stations apparently were named to please him, though the ulterior motive was probably to gain McDowell's support for the CP's use of Yerba Buena, an island in San Francisco Bay controlled by the military. The CP wanted to use Yerba Buena as a terminal.

This view of the railroad facilities at Reno was taken from the north side of the tracks, adjacent to the freight warehouses. The depot-hotel stands on the other side, closer to town. This was the first of four passenger depots serving Reno for the CP and its successor SP. This particular one was destroyed in the Great Reno Fire of March 2, 1879.

FREIGHT DEPOTS AT RENO

While everyone involved in the CP had their own objectives, which likely changed through time, there is no question that turning a profit from the rich commerce of the Comstock was as much a part of the CP's initial agenda as was forging a rail connection with the eastern United States. As it happened, the railroad company was able to corner the Washoe trade without ever laying a track to Virginia City. Even with the expense and inconvenience of trans-shipping freight between the cars and wagons at Reno, the overall cost of shipping from Sacramento to Virginia City via rail to Reno was less than the cost of shipping the entire way by team and wagon. Initial traffic was so heavy that three freight houses were erected along the north side of the railroad's yard, as seen in the background. The view faces east.

In 1872, the independent Virginia & Truckee Railroad was completed from Reno to Virginia City by way of Carson City. By that time the CP had merged with the Western Pacific, a railroad running from Sacramento to Alameda via Stockton. Thus, with the completion of the V&T, a passenger could at last ride a train all the way from San Francisco Bay to the Comstock.

Reno also became the shipping point for Susanville and northeastern California, as well as for points south.

TRUCKEE MEADOWS
159 miles from Sacramento

East of Reno the railroad skirted the margins of the boggy Truckee Meadows. The prominent hill to the south is Rattlesnake Mountain, with Slide Mountain and Mount Rose looming faintly in the background. The locomotive is a McKay & Aldus 4-6-0, pointing toward the end-of-track though standing still. The smoke stream indicates the direction of the prevailing wind, locally known as the "Washoe Zephyr."

When the track east of Reno was rebuilt beginning in 1902, a new division point to replace Wadsworth was laid out in the wetlands seen beyond this train. Carloads of fill material were hauled from a quarry west of Reno to raise the ground for the new facility. It was named for Nevada Governor John Sparks after UP President Edward H. Harriman declined the honor. (At the time, the UP controlled the SP, which by then owned the CP.) Sparks became the division point in June 1904.

The Pacific Railroad Act of 1862 authorized $48,000 in bonds for each of 150 miles east of the western base of the Sierra Nevada. When Abraham Lincoln set the western base of the mountains just seven miles east of Sacramento, on the flat Rancho del Paso, enemies of the railroad cried "foul!" However, the decision was enacted simply to provide the extra bonds when the CP most needed them and it did not add to the total, as the point where the maximum bonding rate stopped was also shifted west. The 150 miles of maximum bonding ran out just east of Reno.

SCENE near CAMP 37
161.3 miles from Sacramento

At the base of the Pah Rah Range, east of the Truckee Meadows, the original line of the CP turned south, following the foothills until it rejoined the Truckee River, marked in this photograph by the distant line of trees. The new line built through Sparks rejoined the original CP right-of-way near this point, close to the intersection of modern Interstate 80 and Vista Boulevard. This view faces east.

The development of Sparks and the new route were just part of a general rebuilding of the entire railroad. During the original construction, the company forced the pace in an effort to beat the UP to Salt Lake Valley, and the railroad east of here was built as quickly as possible. Commissioners who examined the railroad on behalf of the federal government in the 1860s noted that the railroad's alignment east of here was determined by immediate cost rather than long term economy. Engineers soon developed plans to rebuild much of the line, but the CP was unable to fund the work until the company came under SP ownership and its bonded debt was redeemed.

When the railroad eventually was rebuilt in 1902-03, some 373 of the 589 miles between Reno and Ogden were replaced by 322 miles of straighter and flatter alignments, while relatively fewer changes were made west of Reno.

287. Entering Lower Canyon of Truckee River.

ENTERING LOWER CANYON of TRUCKEE RIVER
162 miles from Sacramento

Camp 37 was a construction base established at the point where the railroad entered the lower canyon of the Truckee River. The rails reached it on May 21, 1868. Camp 37 remained a section maintenance headquarters after the railroad was completed and all the construction forces had moved on. It was renamed "Vista" in 1874.

In this Hart photograph, two trains hauling supplies to the front are awaiting clearance to proceed. Under the bags on each of those flatcars is a layer of iron rail. By August 1868, when Hart made this photograph, the end-of-track had reached the Humboldt River, some one hundred miles eastward. There, on August 25, a few feet more than six miles of track were laid. This was more than double the average daily progress, and it would stand as the CP's one-day track-laying record until the following April.

The amount of track laid in a day was invariably limited by the material on hand, not by the will of the crews or daylight. Some days they were short of spikes, other days they ran out of rails. Some days the supply train simply failed to arrive. Loaded 48 rails to the car, eight cars were required to haul enough rails for a mile of track. To provide a timely supply, rail and track hardware was hurried to California by way of Panama, but the longer the track grew, the more difficult it became to deliver supplies to the front as supply trains clogged the railroad.

293 Crossing of Wagon Road. Lower Canyon of Truckee.

CROSSING OF WAGON ROAD
162.8 miles from Sacramento

Overland pioneers began winding their way up the lower canyon of the Truckee River in 1844 on their way from the Humboldt River to Truckee Pass (which was renamed "Donner Pass" a generation later). The original pioneer trail forded the river 22 times in 30 miles, but it left the canyon some distance east of the Truckee Meadows to bypass the narrowest stretch where the Pah Rah Range and Virginia Range squeeze in upon the river. Hart made this picture in the narrow section, immediately below Vista.

By 1852 the trail had been refined, eliminating 14 crossings, and in 1866 local contractor Abraham O. Savage built the toll road through the canyon that is seen in this view. Both Savage's road and the railroad, which was built two years later, stayed on the north side of the river for the entire length of the canyon. For the railroad, this avoided costly bridges. But in some places, the river forced the road and railroad to crowd in closely upon one another. In this scene, the railroad crossed the wagon road twice within a few yards, and it looks like the railroad graders actually filled in an elbow of the stream to make a bed for the track.

When the railroad through the lower canyon was rebuilt in 1902, its straighter and shorter alignment required nine new river crossings. No changes were made in the crossings in the upper canyon.

COTTONWOOD VALLEY
165 miles from Sacramento

Once through the narrow stretch of canyon directly east of the Truckee Meadows, the lower canyon of the Truckee River opens up into this picturesque valley that Hart called "Cottonwood Valley." It is just three miles below Camp 37 or Vista. The old pioneer road left the Truckee River at this point to ascend Long Valley Creek and cross the northwest tip of the Virginia Range to avoid the narrow portion of the canyon just upstream. The modern Reno suburb of Lockwood is located on the broad flat area on the other side of river, while modern Interstate 80 runs along a shelf carved into the hillside above the railroad. This view looks toward the east.

Around the distant bend, the railroad company established Sheep Ranch station in 1885. In 1888 it was renamed "Hafed," presumably derived from "hay-fed," and a reminder of the ranches that once surrounded Reno. Another attractive valley, seven miles farther to the east, was the location of Clark's, a station established in 1869.

While capturing the Comstock trade was a vital part of the CP's initial plan, by the time the railroad crossed the Sierra, the company was fully motivated to meet the UP as far east as possible. Thus, there was no slack in the pace of construction when the builders reached Nevada.

BASALTIC ROCKS
165.65 miles from Sacramento

Leaving Cottonwood Valley, the railroad runs past this prominent cliff. This view looks back toward the west. While the modernization of the railroad in the early 20th century involved double-tracking the line across the Sierra, the railroad east of Sparks was left single track by the SP. Still, it was entirely rebuilt and considerably realigned. Nevertheless, at this location in the lower Truckee canyon, the modern railroad continues to run on the old CP grade, and except for a fence to protect the railroad from falling rock, the modern scene looks much as it did in Hart's day.

While the SP across Nevada remained single track, the Western Pacific was completed on a generally parallel course in 1908. During the First World War the government forced the rival companies into a "paired track" arrangement for the 183 miles where their lines were side-by-side. Recognizing the benefit of cooperation, the companies made the arrangement permanent in 1924. The UP absorbed the modern Western Pacific in 1982 and the SP in 1996, bringing the two lines across northern Nevada under a single management.

Hart's advertisement in the *Reno Crescent* newspaper places him in the Reno area throughout the month of August 1868, and all of his Reno area views date from that period. While he is believed to have passed through Reno on at least three subsequent occasions, there is no evidence that he ever paused to make additional photographs.

PLEASANT VALLEY
176 miles from Sacramento

Another point where the lower canyon of the Truckee River opens up was called "Pleasant Valley." Nowhere is the lower canyon as confined as the upper canyon, especially as it is near Floriston. The engineers found enough room for the railroad on the left bank of the river through the entire course of the canyon, but a few tight curves nevertheless were required. The distant curve, where the railroad turns right to leave the valley, was the last 10° curve on the CP until it reached Powder Bluff at the west end of Palisade Canyon, 250 miles ahead. Half of the railroad's curves between Sacramento and Promontory Summit were west of Pleasant Valley, though this was just barely one-fourth of the entire distance.

The end-of-track was very close to Pleasant Valley on June 18, 1868, when the railroad was finally completed between Donner and Truckee. All of the iron for the 57 miles of railroad between Truckee and this point had been hauled across the summit from Cisco on the wagon road. With the gap closed, supply trains could run all the way to the front from Sacramento. Even though the CP recognized the superiority of rails connected with fish bars in 1866, delays in getting rail from the East forced the company to revert to using some obsolete chair-connected rail still on hand. Some of that was laid along the lower portion of the Truckee River, from mile 171 through 201.

LOOKING WEST FROM RED BLUFFS
178 miles from Sacramento

This and the following view were photographed from virtually the same location at Red Bluffs, a prominent outcropping of red volcanic rock on the north side of the Truckee River near the lower end of the canyon. Here the railroad ran around the outside of a sweeping bend of the river on a narrow shelf blasted along the base of the bluffs. The track's compound curve ranged from 2° to 9°. This was the last place the graders had to do any extensive blasting until they were past Winnemucca.

Many changes have been made at this location since Hart recorded this scene. The original CP alignment along the base of the bluff was abandoned in 1902 in favor of a new line that cut directly across the river's oxbow on two new bridges, passing close to the hillside on the south side of the canyon. Later, Highway 40 was built on the original CP grade. In 1959, Interstate 80 was built on an alignment running between the old railroad grade and its 1902 alignment. To avoid having to build bridges for the highway, a river itself was moved to a new channel dug between the new highway and the railroad. Five years later, the SP relocated the Truckee River yet again, digging a channel south of the railroad. This allowed the retirement of both of the 1902 railroad bridges. The old scar from the original CP alignment is still visible along the base of Red Bluffs.

This view looks southwest toward Pleasant Valley.

303. Red Bluffs, looking from the West.
Lower Canyon of Truckee River.

RED BLUFFS, LOOKING FROM THE WEST

The Truckee River takes its name from a prominent Paiute Indian. The accepted story, traced back to Truckee's granddaughter, Sarah Winnemucca, is that both the Indian and the river were named by John C. Frémont. However, Frémont called the river the "Salmon-Trout River," and another account holds that the Paiute was called "Trucky" by members of the Stevens Party in 1844 because of his "truckling" behind them for several days along the Humboldt River. That account goes on to credit Truckee for showing those pioneers the way to the Truckee River from the sink of the Humboldt, and claims that they named the river for him.

Regardless of the origin of the name, the Truckee River was as important to the railroad as was the long ridge it ascended on the west side of the Sierra, for the Truckee provided a path first between the Verdi and Carson ranges (the upper canyon), and then between the Pah Rah and Virginia ranges (the lower canyon). From Wadsworth, where the railroad finally left the Truckee, there was generally open access to the Humboldt River, which in turn provided a path through a succession of ranges nearly the rest of the way across Nevada.

During Hart's visit to the Reno area in August, he made several excursions with his buggy darkroom, both up and down the Truckee River. In this view, his darkroom buggy is seen parked by the river.

TRUCKEE RIVER, NEAR WADSWORTH
180.45 miles from Sacramento

This scene faces east near the mouth of the lower canyon of the Truckee River. After a passage of about 18 miles through the canyon, the railroad here enters a broad valley. The green fields along the banks of the Truckee River between the canyon and Wadsworth mark the western fringe of the desert.

By the time track construction resumed at Camp 24 in March 1868, graders were already working in the lower canyon of the Truckee, and in late May the grade was ready for the rails all the way to the site of Wadsworth, eight miles beyond the location of this Hart photograph. Track was laid through here in June, two months before Hart's visit.

Just around the distant bend, in this eastward-facing view, is the location of Salvia, a station established in 1874. Salvia was the point where the 1902 line diverged from the original CP. The railroad's new route runs around the Hot Springs Mountains through Fernley. In 1905 Salvia was renamed "Derby," taking the name from Derby Dam, built in 1903-05 at a location just behind where Hart stood in making this photograph. Derby Dam retains Truckee River water for irrigation as part of the Newlands Project, an effort to extend agriculture into the desert. Derby was the first dam built by the newly formed US Reclamation Service.

FIFTH CROSSING OF THE TRUCKEE, WADSWORTH
188.59 miles from Sacramento

The CP's track followed the Truckee River for 69 miles, all the way from Truckee to Wadsworth. In that distance the railroad descended 1,734 feet. Near Wadsworth, the Truckee River makes its "Big Bend" to the north, following its natural course on to Pyramid Lake. At Wadsworth the railroad crossed the Truckee River for the last time and struck out eastward across the desert toward the Humboldt River.

Hart photographed the railroad's temporary bridge across the Truckee River at Wadsworth with this eastward facing view. This structure was completed by the end of May 1868, and rails were laid across it on July 9. The temporary bridge consisted of three 50-foot spans. In making this image, Hart stood on the embankment already in place for the permanent bridge, which was not built for several more months. The corresponding embankment is visible on the opposite shore. The boat in the foreground was apparently a passenger ferry. The little stone structure with the smokestack, just to the left of the water tank, housed a boiler and pump for lifting water into the cisterns.

The first permanent bridge at Wadsworth burned on November 22, 1889. It was replaced with an iron span.

The 3D effect of this image has been digitally enhanced.

309 Turntable at Wadsworth.
188 miles from Sacramento.

WADSWORTH
188.93 miles from Sacramento, elevation 4,085 feet

This view looks north across the main track of the CP toward the turntable, freight depot, and railroad shops. Town structures are arrayed beyond the turntable, to the left, with their backs toward the river. The railroad's bridge is out of view to the left.

While the CP gave Wadsworth its name, the site had long been important to westbound pioneers as the point where they first tasted the sweet water of the Truckee River. For them, the Truckee River marked the end of a 40-mile trek across a virtually waterless desert, and an even greater distance since the Humboldt River was potable. The lack of water was similarly a problem for the railroad and its thirsty steam locomotives. Soon after the railroad was completed, locomotives operating between Wadsworth and Winnemucca were equipped with extra-large tenders, enabling them to run 70 miles without taking on more water.

When rail operations to Wadsworth commenced on July 15, 1868 the company had 50 locomotives in service, along with 18 passenger, baggage, mail and express cars, and more than seven hundred freight cars. At some 189 miles from Sacramento, and the last place for many miles with a good supply of water, Wadsworth was selected as a railroad operation headquarters and the location of major maintenance and repair shops. These consisted of machine, blacksmith, and car shops, as well as a 20-stall roundhouse, all built of wood.

WADSWORTH
188.95 miles from Sacramento

This photograph was made at a point slightly east of the preceding view. It faces west. The Wadsworth railroad facilities are on the right, while the mainline extends straight past the switch toward the Truckee River and on to Reno and Sacramento.

All the railroad's early locomotives burned wood, but it soon became apparent that an alternative fuel would be needed to power engines operating beyond the easy sources of wood in the Sierra. The CP followed up on every rumor of a coal mine in Nevada, but none was ever found. During construction days, the CP shipped coal from Mount Diablo to Nevada to supplement cordwood. Finally, after the CP and UP connected, coal was imported from Wyoming for the locomotives running east of Wadsworth. In 1880 the district for coal burning engines was extended west to Truckee. Wood was phased out even in the Sierra a decade later.

The switch in the distance was operated with a "harp" switch machine, a simple lever held in a cast iron frame resembling a harp. The switch itself was of a design known as a "stub" switch, in which the running rails were bent to line up with one track or the other. This style remained in general use on the CP well into the 1890s when they were replaced with modern "point" switches.

THE GOLIAH AT WADSWORTH

For many years no. 27, *Goliah*, was the regular switch engine at Wadsworth. It was one of two identical locomotives acquired in 1867 by the CP from Danforth Locomotive & Machine of Paterson, New Jersey. It operated until 1906. Its twin was no. 26, *Sampson*, the Truckee switcher.

Locomotives such as this were called "tank engines" because they carried their water supply in a tank mounted on the locomotive itself, rather than in a separate tender. In this case, the tank was located under the cab and running board. Fuel was carried in a bunker in the cab. With limited capacity for water and fuel, tank engines were not expected to wander far from a water tank or fuel supply. Rather, they were used to move cars around in yards that had enough business to warrant a locomotive dedicated to that purpose. Because they were used only for switching, they had no need to move fast, and so were made without pilot wheels, which were used on road engines to lead them into curves. *Goliah* and *Sampson* each had six drive wheels.

The construction of a new brick roundhouse and shop on the west side of the Truckee River at Wadsworth commenced in November 1883. However, on April 15, 1884, before the new facility was complete, the old complex and most of the old town burned.

CONSTRUCTION TRAIN ON THE ALKALI DESERT
Approximately 210-225 miles from Sacramento

Between Wadsworth and the Humboldt River lies the 40-Mile Desert, so named for the distance between water—a distance that tried the endurance of humans and draft animals alike. The CP followed close by the old wagon road, and the names of the railroad's stations—"Desert," "Hot Springs," "Mirage," and "White Plains"—reinforce the stories the pioneers told of that fearful desert crossing. Several of names predated the railroad. The pioneers' dreadful experience crossing the 40-Mile Desert reinforced the general desire for a transcontinental railroad. Many pioneers never revisited their old homes until after the railroad was built.

This photograph records the earliest appearance of the CP construction train, a complete headquarters with cooking, lodging, and repair facilities, with the mobility necessary to keep up with the now rapidly advancing end-of-track. Due to the desert heat, track laying across the desert was performed in shifts.

In 1902, the section of the original railroad across the 40-Mile Desert was abandoned in favor of a new line to the south of Hot Springs Mountains by way of Fernley. While the new route was longer, it eliminated the need for helper locomotives over White Plains Hill, between Hot Springs and White Plains, and thus made for faster and more efficient operation. At an elevation of 3,894 feet, White Plains was the lowest point on the CP in the Great Basin.

WATER TRAIN OPPOSITE HUMBOLDT LAKE

The lack of water in the desert posed a serious problem for the railroad, and special provisions had to be made for construction crews, and later for steam locomotives. The company sent teams of engineers and dowsers into the desert to find water and dig wells, to no avail. At Hot Springs, at the western base of White Plains Hill, a well more than one thousand feet deep failed to produce water any better than the undrinkable brine that flowed from the namesake spring. To solve the problem, the railroad equipped at least eight flatcars with round tanks, three to a car, to carry water from the Truckee River at Wadsworth to various points out in the desert.

This photograph records one of the CP's water trains, facing the end-of-track, with Humboldt Lake and the West Humboldt Range off in the distance.

Humboldt Lake is the termination of the Humboldt River. It varied in size according to the wetness of the season, but it was always stagnant with poor quality water. Beyond it, to the south, was the Humboldt Sink, separated from the lake by a natural dike of lacustrine deposits.

Railroad graders began working east from Wadsworth early in June 1868, and the rails had crossed the 40-Mile Desert to Humboldt Lake by the end of July.

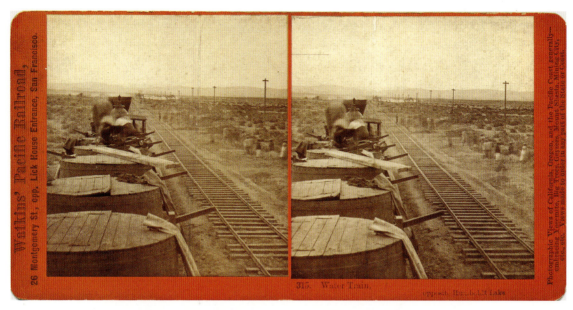

WATER TRAIN opposite HUMBOLDT LAKE

Hart took this view, facing northeastward toward the end-of-track, from the top of the water train seen in the preceding image. In both this and the following photographs, one can see in the distance the framework for the Brown's Station water tank, then under construction.

Due to the lengthy exposure time required by Hart's collodion emulsion, subjects had to stand still for several seconds or they would appear blurred. Because of this limitation, Hart made few photographs that included moving objects. This image, however, is a remarkable exception. Not only do we see the blurry figures of men attending to some task on top of one of the water tanks, but scores of workers can be made out along the east side of the main track. These are actually more apparent in the stereo image than in the "flat" view. They are preparing the roadbed for a siding.

One unexpected discovery in building across 40-Mile Desert was that the alkalinity of the soil acted as a preservative on the railroad's wooden crossties. While most of the railroad's ties lasted only about 10 years, some of the original pine ties laid in the desert in 1868 were still in service 25 years later. On the other hand, the alkali water found in many places in Nevada foamed when heated in the locomotive boilers.

CHINESE CAMP, BROWN'S STATION
234.98 miles from Sacramento, elevation 3,934 feet

Brown's Station was near the site of Sulfur Wells, the point where the old California Trail forked and pioneers had to choose between the Truckee Route, which crossed the 40-Mile Desert westward to the Truckee River, or the Carson Route, which headed south about the same distance across the desert to the Carson River. Joseph B. "Poker" Brown established a station at this point to cater to travelers on the wagon road, and when the railroad arrived, his name was already fixed to the site.

The railroad reached Brown's Station early in the first week of August 1868, and Hart recorded the scene within a day or two of that event. Regular service on the railroad commenced on August 21.

This view faces back toward Wadsworth, in the opposite direction of the preceding photograph. Men idle in the shade of a canvas sheet to the left, in what Hart described as the Chinese camp, while many others are seen in the distance working along the track. Though the main track has been backfilled, it has yet to be leveled to a true surface or aligned. The wooden framework in the distance, with a man standing on top, is the base for the water tank under construction. Humboldt Lake is on the left in the distance.

BROWN'S STATION

Brown's Station had developed considerably by the time Hart revisited the scene in October 1868. A two-story depot is in the final stages of construction on the left, while the overhanging porch of a freight house is evident on the right. Where the earlier photograph showed only a row of crossties, here a sidetrack has been built and is occupied by a trainload of ties and hay awaiting clearance to the end-of-track, then past Iron Point. The boxcar with marker flags mounted on diagonal corners, spotted in front of the depot, serves as a caboose. The water tank is now fully functional, though the water here was so bad it was only used in emergencies. Brown's also had a coaling stage and a turntable for helper engines used on Brown's Hill. A telegraph line ran from Brown's to Unionville.

Most of the CP stations in Nevada served only the railroad, having only a telegraph office, perhaps a water tank and a collection of track-worker shanties. Brown's Station was also home, for a while, to a village of Paiutes, who entertained the passengers of trains that stopped. The agent at Brown's in 1881 was George S. Nixon, who later became a US senator from Nevada.

The 1902 realignment that bypassed Wadsworth and ran around the south side of Hot Springs Mountains rejoined the original railroad at Brown's. In 1910, Brown's Station was renamed "Toy," perhaps for W.J. Toy, the division's road foreman of engines.

END-OF-TRACK, NEAR HUMBOLDT LAKE

On Hart's first visit to Brown's Station in August 1868, he went on to the end-of-track, then some seven miles beyond, at Granite Point. He made several photographs there before returning to Reno. Granite Point was the farthest east that Hart went until the following October. Indeed, Hart never ventured beyond the end-of-track after it was at Alta.

This photograph, facing northwest, captures the essence of the end-of-track construction camp. The outfit train sits on the railroad, while tents are pitched randomly nearby. The horses and wagons in the background are but a small portion of those used by the railroad. Many teams were used to supply the laborers who were working up to two or three hundred miles ahead, preparing the roadbed for the rails, while others were used to carry crossties from the supply trains to the roadbed just ahead of the rail layers. By August 1868 the CP work force had been reduced to some eight thousand men, down by about one-third from the number employed while working in the Sierra.

At this location, the modern railroad still runs on the original CP alignment. Except for the absence of train and tents, and Interstate 80, which runs between the track and the bluffs, the scene is virtually unchanged today. Even the wagon ruts of the old California Trail, which cross the foreground of Hart's photograph, remain.

END-OF-TRACK on HUMBOLDT PLAINS
242 miles from Sacramento

Another photograph, made at Granite Point, shows workers loading rails onto track-laying cars. These small, four-wheeled cars were used to distribute the rails to the advancing end-of-track. The cars were pulled by horses hitched to a ring on the car's side so they could trot alongside the track clear of the ties. Kegs of spikes and fish bars were carried loose atop the carload of rails. A crew of men also rode the car. At the end-of-track, this crew pushed the car forward onto each new pair of rails as they were set in place in front of the car by the "iron crew." Returning for another load, the car's crew had to stop the empty car and tip it off the track every time they met a loaded car heading forward. This way, the loaded cars passed forward uninterrupted.

At about the time the end-of-track passed Granite Point, 30-foot long rails were introduced. This, along with specialization of workers to specific tasks, increased the average rate of construction to more than 11 miles of track per week. Speed of construction was all important. To lessen the burden of hauling ties beyond the track, only every other tie was set in place before the rails were laid, as seen here. When spikes were scarce, only every other tie was spiked.

This picture was made from the top of the camp cars, which had been pulled back by the departing supply train to clear the rail piles. The youngsters are the two children adopted by Strobridge in 1866.

LOWER CROSSING HUMBOLDT RIVER
255.19 miles from Sacramento

Just five miles northeast of Lovelock, the railroad made its first crossing of the Humboldt River.

The water tower here had four cisterns or tanks with a total capacity of 14,000 gallons. As at Wadsworth, a semi-conical structure next to the tank houses a boiler and pump to lift water from the river into the tanks. Steam locomotives require a lot of water. The CP built 54 water tanks between Sacramento and Promontory Summit, Utah. West of Reno the average spacing between tanks was 6.5 miles; east of Reno they averaged 17.3 miles apart, with the greatest distance between tanks being the 33 miles immediately east of Wadsworth.

Just beyond the water tank, the railroad crossed the Humboldt River on a temporary bridge. As at Wadsworth, Hart made the photograph from the embankment on the line of the permanent bridge.

In the distance, across the river, are workmen's tents. But the workers themselves can be seen lounging in the shade of the water tank. With summertime high temperatures well over 90° in this part of Nevada, the cooling effect of the water dripping through the tank floor must have been refreshing. Data recorded at the railroad's telegraph offices provides a continuous meteorological record stretching back into the 1870s.

FIRST CROSSING OF THE HUMBOLDT RIVER
255.2 miles from Sacramento, elevation 4,015 feet

These water-filled holes are the excavations for the piers to support the railroad's permanent bridge across the Humboldt River. To the right is the temporary bridge with the workers' camps in the background.

The track reached this point on August 12, 1868, approximately one week after Hart had visited the end-of-track at Granite Point. Hart may have come out here to take pictures before returning to Sacramento from Reno in late August, but the completed water tanks and the amount of progress on the embankment and footings for the permanent bridge suggest that these photographs date from his next trip, in October, when the end-of-track was well ahead, beyond Iron Point. The tents may belong to the workers building the permanent bridge, or to crews lining and surfacing the track to bring it into full service condition. The permanent bridge built here was finished sometime before January 1869. It was a 160-foot Howe-truss structure.

Smith's Ford and Cooper's Ferry were two places nearby where pioneers on the old California Trail could cross the Humboldt River. The CP initially called its crossing "Bridge," but by 1890 the name had evolved into "Humbridge." In 1902 it was given its modern name "Kodak."

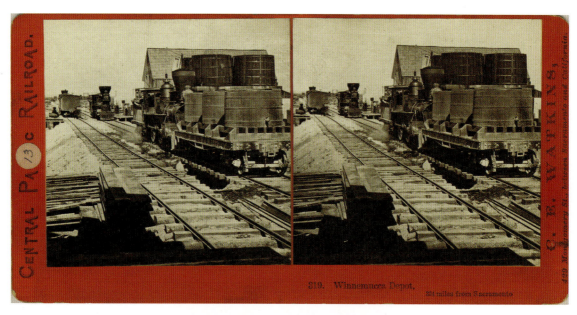

WINNEMUCCA DEPOT
324 miles from Sacramento, elevation 4,336 feet

Rails reached Winnemucca on September 15, 1868, with service commencing October 1. The station took its name from the nearby post office, which had been established in February 1866.

The closest locomotive in this photograph is one of the Western Pacific's three Baldwins. It may be the *San Mateo*, the first locomotive in Nevada.

Visible on the near end of the flatcar is a link-and-pin drawhead. Coupling with link and pins was reliable, but it was dangerous, because the crewman had to work between the cars, often hidden from the locomotive engineer. To connect cars, the trainman guided the link extending from one drawhead into the pocket of the adjacent car's drawhead while the locomotive pushed the cars together. At the instant the link entered the second drawhead, the trainman had to pull his hand back to avoid having his fingers crushed. At the same time he had to drop the pin through the top of the drawhead, thus hooking the link and coupling the cars. Disconnecting was less dangerous, unless it was attempted while the train was moving. The CP began installing automatic couplers in the 1880s, though link-pin coupling was not outlawed on interchange cars until the end of the century.

The last of the company's chair rail was laid through here, and two of the distinctive chairs can be seen in the foreground on the near track.

ADVANCE OF CIVILIZATION
359.92 miles from Sacramento

On October 8, 1868 the end-of-track was in Pumpernickel Valley, between Iron Point and Stone House, when Hart visited and made this and the following photographs of construction activity. The railroad was relocated in 1903, but the site of this view is established with reference to Lone Tree Hill, faintly visible in the distance.

To the left in this view, workers can be seen stringing the telegraph wire along the newly placed pole line. Though the construction of the telegraph line fulfilled a requirement of the Pacific Railroad Act, it aided construction by allowing continuous communication between Sacramento and construction forces at the front. Every time the outfit cars were shifted to the new end-of-track, at noon and in the evening, the wire was connected to a key and sounder in Strobridge's office. This enabled progress reports and supply orders to be transmitted, and also kept Strobridge appraised of events and decisions made at headquarters in Sacramento. Additionally, the telegraph allowed some control of trains over the single-track railroad.

The general foreman of telegraph construction was Amos L. Bowsher. He was 28 years old in 1869 when the railroad was completed.

ADVANCE OF CIVILIZATION
360.5 miles from Sacramento

East of Donner, the track was built in a carefully choreographed sequence of steps developed to involve as many workers as possible without them getting in each other's way. First, graders built a roadbed along a line of center stakes using material dug from two parallel drainage ditches. Once this bed was smoothed, crossties were distributed by wagons, spaced, and lined up against a string stretched along the side of the roadbed, four feet to one side of the center stakes. The even tie-ends seen in this photo indicate that the "tie line" was on the right. Ties were set far enough ahead to not impede the progress of the rail layers.

Rails were delivered to the end-of-track on the track-laying cars seen in the foreground. Rollers at the cars' corners facilitated unloading the rails nearly to gauge. Because the rail joints were kept directly opposite each other, the rails on either side of the track were laid simultaneously. Four brawny men handled each 560-pound rail, rolling them off the car and setting them down against the last rails laid. While a worker held the loose rails to gauge with a clamp, the car crew pushed the car forward so the process could be repeated. It required as much time to get the empty car tipped out of the way and a new one advanced as it did to unload. More special teams followed behind the car, splicing the rails together and spiking them to the ties. Behind them, even more men adding the missing ties and backfilled, and finally surfaced and lined the track. It was a mobile assembly line, advancing at the speed of a walk.

TRAIN AT ARGENTA
395.88 miles from Sacramento, elevation 4,552 feet

Argenta is located near the confluence of the Reese and Humboldt rivers, about half way across Nevada. Silver had been discovered some 90 miles to the south in 1862, and the Reese River mines had been booming ever since. In 1865, other mines were developed in the White Pine District some 120 miles farther east. As the railroad extended eastward, it began to carry more and more of the commerce of these districts, and Argenta was established as a station on the railroad to serve this trade.

The end-of-track reached this site on October 27, and regular trains began running to Argenta the following month. As long as the overland stagecoaches connected here with the trains, Argenta was a lively place. But it faded once the railroad was opened for traffic to Carlin. Reese River Siding, some 12 miles to the west, proved more convenient for the Reese River trade, while Elko provided a better connection with White Pine when the CP opened to that point in early 1869. Only four frame structures were ever built at Argenta. The settlement was abandoned by year's end, though the place name persists. Reese River Siding became Battle Mountain.

This eastbound train appears to be the same one we see in photographs taken at Carlin and Elko. The locomotive is Rogers-built no. 108, *Stager*.

SHOSHONE INDIANS LOOKING AT LOCOMOTIVE

Locomotive no. 50, *Champion*, was delivered by McKay & Aldus early in 1868. Upon completion of the railroad, the company's roster of 166 locomotives was a mismatched collection of five different wheel arrangements from 11 different builders. Much of this lack of standardization was a consequence of inexperience upon the part of the CP's managers—they just did not know what to buy. However, when they finally figured out what worked best on their railroad, locomotive builders were unable to meet the high demand, and orders had to be split among several factories. Altogether, McKay & Aldus provided 41 locomotives, of which no. 50 was one of 12 built to the same plan. Despite the CP's willingness to order from McKay, it was not very happy with those machines, complaining that they were not well-built and required considerable refitting to get them assembled.

Building across Nevada, the CP was constantly short of equipment. In order to get more use out of the locomotives it had, the CP began running them around the clock, with crews operating in shifts. Locomotives were only allowed to cool when they went into the shop. Yet the high use only increased the demand for fuel. Even before the CP reached Winnemucca, it required 30 carloads of firewood per day just to fuel the locomotives working east of Reno. Until the track reached Wells, where wood was cut locally, all of that wood had to be hauled from the Sierra, adding to the congestion on the railroad. By fall, all of the dry wood had been used up and crews were left with only poor-burning green wood.

327 Chinese Camp. At end of track.

CHINESE CAMP AT END-OF-TRACK
427.41 miles from Sacramento

The Humboldt River was important to the CP as it provided an easy path through a succession of mountain ranges for 290 miles, from Brown's to Wells, climbing 1,699 feet. Without that watercourse across Nevada, the first Pacific railroad would certainly have taken a much different and more difficult route. Indeed, while pioneers had been following the Humboldt River since the 1840s, those contemplating the Pacific railroad ignored that route until Edward G. Beckwith demonstrated in 1853 that it could be utilized by a railroad running around the north end of the Sierra Nevada via the Madeline Plains. Before Beckwith's exploration, planners envisioned that a Pacific railroad on the central route would run from Salt Lake Valley to Tehachapi Pass along the Spanish Trail. The Comstock excitement inspired Judah to draw a shortcut directly from Sacramento to the route Beckwith had recommended along the Humboldt River.

Palisade Canyon provides the path through the Tuscarora Mountains for the Humboldt River. Because it was impractical for the wagon road, few other than Indians visited the canyon before the railroad. In late May or early June 1868, before the CP was even completed across the Sierra, some three thousand men were sent ahead to begin carving the roadbed through the canyon. The track finally arrived in November 1868, when Hart visited the scene. This view toward the east records the railroad's entrance into Palisade Canyon, nine miles east of Beowawe.

CAR OF SUPERINTENDENT OF CONSTRUCTION

The second car from the left in the preceding view of the construction train was the living quarters of James H. Strobridge and family. The car had a porch along part of its side, which was often covered with a canvas sheet to block out the sun. It was described as having all the amenities of a San Francisco hotel and was probably as comfortable as the cabin they had lived in at Alta in 1866. It had the added advantage of portability, enabling Strobridge to keep up with the rapidly advancing end-of-track.

Strobridge had a reputation for quick temper and firmness, and he was known for his sharp tongue and liberal use of profanity. But those who knew him considered it all to be an act to motivate the workers under his charge. Indeed, this was apparently the common management style of that era. One witness claimed that Irish navvies generally interpreted haranguing by their foremen as encouragement and an indication of good work. As the Chinese worked beside the Irish on the CP, they probably shrugged the shouting off as part of the strange culture.

As the photograph shows there were indeed women at the end-of-track. One was Hannah Marie Strobridge, whose presence no doubt played a positive role. But there were also Chinese women. Within weeks of the scenes recorded in these views in Palisade Canyon, the railroad construction camp was struck by smallpox. Hannah Strobridge nursed those affected until she caught it herself. It is only by a newspaper's mention of their graves that we know of the Chinese women.

POWDER BLUFF
427.6 miles from Sacramento

The locomotive in this view is standing just around the bend from the construction train two views ago. The locomotive is facing away from Sacramento; Hart's camera was facing north.

This curve was the first 10° bend on the railroad east of the lower canyon of the Truckee River (three 9° curves were located in Pioneer Canyon, between Golconda and Iron Point). This sharp reverse curve was straightened considerably with the general realignment of the railroad in 1903, although, to accomplish that, two bridges were built to carry the track across the meandering river. In August 1939, the westbound *City of San Francisco* streamliner derailed just east of the easternmost of these two 1903 bridges, destroying the bridge and killing 24 passengers and crew members. The derailed diesel locomotives came to rest at a point on the new alignment adjacent to the location Hart chose for this photograph.

Hart called Palisade Canyon "10-Mile Canyon." That was just one of its names. Others called it "12-Mile Canyon" or "Humboldt Canyon." It was one of three canyons through which both the Humboldt River and the railroad pass. In addition to Pioneer Canyon, mentioned above, Carlin Canyon is between Carlin and Moleen. Carlin Canyon was sometimes called "Frémont" or "Five-Mile Canyon."

330 Commencement of a Snow Storm.
Scene east of Second crossing of Humboldt.

SCENE WEST OF SECOND CROSSING OF HUMBOLDT
428.25 miles from Sacramento

Fresh snow covered the ground in November 1868 when Hart recorded this scene near the railroad's second crossing of the Humboldt River. While heat had been a problem only months before, the shorter daylight hours of fall signaled the arrival of cold weather. In the Great Basin, that cold can be bitter, indeed.

The partially erected framework of the bridge can be seen just beyond the deep cut. The Humboldt River is not very wide at this point, and it was bridged with a 150-foot Howe-truss main span and a 50-foot straining-beam approach span. Unlike the practice followed at Wadsworth and the first Humboldt crossing, no temporary bridge was built here. Rather, the permanent structure was erected before the track was laid. It was shipped as a kit and assembled on November 16 through 18, the three days shown in the construction record when this was the end-of-track. This photograph dates from that narrow period of time. Hart's camera faced east.

As the railroad was originally built, this was the only crossing of the river in Palisade Canyon. However, when the line was rebuilt in 1902, several new crossings provided a more direct alignment. This bridge site was then renumbered as the sixth crossing.

SCENE EAST OF SECOND CROSSING OF HUMBOLDT
429 miles from Sacramento

This is another photograph made with fresh snow covering the ground. It looks back toward the second crossing of the Humboldt River from the east. The bridge itself is out of sight around the distant bend. This picture dates from shortly after November 19 when rails crossed the bridge. Hart apparently stayed several days with the construction crews in Palisade Canyon.

As grading through the canyons of the Humboldt was completed, the workforce was incrementally reduced. Strobridge recalled many years later that the average number working in Nevada was about five thousand men, less than half the number that built the railroad across the Sierra. However, no one knows how many men were actually employed. Most of the figures we have are those published in contemporary newspapers, and even if those numbers came from the railroad itself, there is a strong hint that the numbers were inflated. Partly to sell bonds, and partly out of pure braggadocio, the CP promoted the impression that it had the means to complete the project despite any and all obstacles. At the very time of peak activity in the summer of 1867, E.B. Crocker confided to Huntington that, while the "general impression" was that there were 12,000 laborers, there were not more than 3,000, plus teamsters and foremen, actually at work on the line.

EVENING VIEW of TRAIN CAMP
429.87 miles from Sacramento

As adjacent views illustrate, the western end of Palisade Canyon was generally an open valley. However, in places, rock outcroppings present interesting features, such as Sentinel Rock, seen here. This view looks south across the Humboldt River, with the mobile construction camp in the foreground. It appears that the horses have just been fed, and the workers are doubtless enjoying their evening meal, warm inside the mess cars. Water cars, such as the one seen here behind the locomotive, were used as auxiliary tenders until water tanks were erected. Where local water of good quality was unavailable, water was hauled for men and animals as well.

Once the heavy grading in Palisade Canyon, and Carlin Canyon to the east, was completed, some of the force was moved ahead to the Pequop Mountains beyond Wells. Others were moved back to California to complete the Western Pacific between Sacramento and Alameda (by way of Stockton and Livermore). Also about this time, crews built a new track between Front Street and the American River in Sacramento.

The station of Barth was established in 1904 near Sentinel Rock, and iron ore was mined here for several years.

The 3D effect of this image has been digitally enhanced.

THANKSGIVING in 10-MILE CANYON

The western end of the Palisade Canyon was the only place Hart is known to have photographed the outfit cars in topography like that seen in this unlabeled view. All of the scenes made in that area date from the last two weeks of November 1868, when the end-of-track advanced through the canyon. This photograph may merely record a clergyman's visit to the construction camp during that time, or it may be a special visit, perhaps for Thanksgiving itself. In 1868, Thanksgiving fell on November 26, when the end-of-track was just west of Pine Creek. Abraham Lincoln made Thanksgiving a national holiday in 1863.

Strobridge and his wife, with their adopted son Sam, stand to the right. While Hannah Maria Strobridge was continuously at the front with her husband, she often had visitors, including the wife of construction engineer Joseph M. Graham. Perhaps the Grahams are one of the other couples.

The present whereabouts of this particular stereo card is unknown, if it even still exists. This presentation is made from a high-resolution digital scan of a color photocopy made from the only known original card, taken shortly before it disappeared in the mail. Hart did not publish this view; it was not assigned a catalog number, nor was it captioned. The card belonged to a Strobridge family member.

The 3D effect of this image has been digitally enhanced.

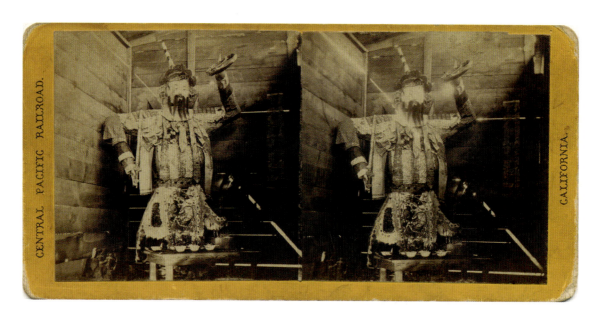

GUAN YU

The Chinese also observed elements of their culture in the Nevada hinterlands. This figure of Guan Yu may have been installed in the corner of one of the construction train cars. Guan Yu, a traditional protective deity, was widely worshiped by the Cantonese who made up the bulk of the CP's work force. The small cups visible at the figure's feet probably contained wine or tea as a drink offering. Some food was undoubtedly offered as well. We also know from newspaper references that the Chinese railroad workers observed their culture's New Year celebration.

Provision was always made for the return of Chinese workers to their ancestral home, even if they had died. However, the number who died in the course of construction of the CP is unknown. Fewer than one hundred deaths due to construction accidents are recorded in newspapers, and the newspapers seem to have been eager to report accidents and deaths. On the other hand, after the railroad was completed, several cars were set aside to convey the bones of the deceased from trackside graves to San Francisco for their return to China, suggesting a larger number. It is likely that most of the workers' deaths were caused by the smallpox epidemic in the winter of 1868-69. Furthermore, not all the dead were railroad workers, as many Chinese also found employment in area mines.

CURVING IRON
431.42 miles from Sacramento, elevation 4,824 feet

Following standard track-laying practice of the day, the CP bent the rails of all curves sharper than a few degrees before they were laid. To curve rail, a piece was laid on its side with its ends resting on timbers set across finished railroad track. The suspended rail was then forced into an arc by means of levers hooked to one of the track's fixed rails, bearing down on the loose rail. Tables of ordinates published in track-layers' handbooks told exactly how much deflection was required for curves of various dimensions. While the men with levers held the rail to its desired deflection, others struck it several times with sledge hammers to set the bend. In this view, the men pushing down on the levers are kneeling on the left side of the track, with their levers hooked to the right-hand track rail. The workers with hammers are on the right.

There were 1,013 curves in the 690 miles of railroad between Sacramento and Promontory Summit; they totaled nearly 278 miles and made the equivalent of 125 complete circles, with an average curvature of about 3°. Of these, rails for about 150 miles of track had to be bent. In time, railroads found that steel rail in longer lengths, laid with staggered joints, could be sprung into shape as it was laid, eliminating the need for time-consuming pre-curving. The SP did not adopt staggered joints and cease curving rails until about 1900.

HUMBOLDT GATE
433.9 miles from Sacramento

About two-thirds of the way through Palisade Canyon, the gorge opens into a valley where Pine Creek joins the Humboldt River from the south. Hart called the narrow gap just west of this open valley "Humboldt Gate." This view looks eastward through the "gate" toward the mouth of Pine Creek. The outfit cars of the construction train can be seen in the distance, just at the narrows, where the track disappears into a cut. The track was laid here on November 26.

The end of a stone culvert can be seen in the face of the embankment in the foreground. Culverts were built wherever a natural drainage was crossed to prevent the embankment from acting like a dam. Stone culverts were preferred, though at many places in Nevada and Utah temporary trestles were initially built, and the stone culverts came later.

Another way the company sped construction was to set only every other crosstie before laying rail. Once the rails were spiked, the remaining ties were distributed from a slow-moving train, and then pushed into place. Here we see the new ties awaiting installation, lying on the side of the embankment where they have been dropped. The CP learned most of its time-saving tricks from a worker who came over from the UP, but they were taught to lay every other tie by a track layer named Ned Hussey. He had seen it done on the Freeport Railroad, south of Sacramento. All the ties needed to be installed before regular operation.

BUILDING A WATER TANK
435.13 miles from Sacramento, elevation 4,846 feet

Hart made this picture of carpenters building a water tank between the mouth of Pine Creek and Palisade station. Hart called Pine Creek "Trout Creek."

Between the track in the foreground and the bluff on the right, where a locomotive is nearly hidden in the shadows, the railroad made a 14° bend. This was curve no. 737, the tightest mainline curve on the original railroad. While it just barely complied with the limit set by the Pacific Railroad Act, it was considerably sharper than the company's adopted standard of 10°. This curve was temporary, and within six months it was replaced with a 7° bend that ran on an embankment thrown across the low ground beyond the workers' tent. This change shortened the railroad by 1,200 feet, though it required relocating the water tank. The more extensive rebuilding of the railroad in 1902 reduced the total mileage in Palisade Canyon by nearly a mile and eliminated almost three miles of curves. However, accomplishing those improvements required the construction of 10 new river crossings, one of which, at this point, led into a new eight-hundred foot tunnel directly through the hillside across the river on the left.

The "square" rail joints adopted by the CP, with the joints opposite each other, are apparent in this photograph.

ENTERING THE PALISADES
436.27 miles from Sacramento

Rails were laid past the future site of Palisade on November 27, 1868, and train service to that point commenced about six weeks later. Immediately east of Palisade, the railroad enters the most spectacular portion of Palisade Canyon, the "palisades" that give the entire canyon its name. These towering cliffs rise some five hundred feet above the railroad, though various guidebooks credited them with even greater height.

In the summer, when daylight hours were long, crews worked in two shifts between 4 A.M. and 8 P.M., with no work on Sundays. However, in the winter the working hours were reduced. The farther the railroad extended from Sacramento, the more difficult were the problems of getting supplies to the front. Often, 24 hours were required to move a trainload of supplies merely one hundred miles. Many of the delays were related to derailments on the hurriedly-built track. Locomotives were often stalled for lack of good water or wood. There was often only enough rail on hand to lay one mile of track per day. By the fall of 1868, with track laying a well-honed drill, that much railroad could be built in three or four hours.

The 3D effect of this image has been digitally enhanced

INDIAN VIEWING RAILROAD from PALISADES
436.61 miles from Sacramento

Hart was a painter before he was a photographer, and he approached photography as an artist. His photographs do not merely record the railroad and its equipment; they portray the railroad in its environment. To make this image, Hart packed his camera, plates, and tripod to the top of the round-topped bluff visible beyond the track in the preceding image. The views are virtually the reverse of one another.

The town of Palisade subsequently sprang up around the railroad's station at Palisade. It was located just out of view behind the bluff to the left, where the gorge begins to open up in the distance. The Indian in his rabbit robe is probably a Shoshone from their settlement near the mouth of Pine Creek.

While the UP required military escorts for surveyors and builders alike to ward off Indian attack, the CP did not. After a single incident, the CP negotiated a treaty with the Indians granting free transport on the trains in exchange for unmolested passage of railroad workers and trains across Indian land, and there was no subsequent trouble.

See an alternate Hart view of this scene on p. 468.

ALCOVE IN PALISADES
436.62 miles from Sacramento

Railroad passengers thrilled at the passage through Palisade Canyon, and its stark beauty was extolled in travel guides to the Pacific railroad. The guidebooks called this cave near the east end of the palisades "Maggie's Bower." By the 1880s, enterprising salesmen had painted large, glaring signs on the canyon walls, advertising various patent medicines.

The first car of the eastbound train of this Hart photograph is one of the CP water cars, here being used as an auxiliary tender for the locomotive. The auxiliary tenders were necessary until water tanks were built.

The last step in building a railroad is to backfill around the ties with ballast as the track is lined and leveled. The ballast holds the track true, and the voids in good stone ballast enable water to quickly drain away from the wooden ties. However, well into the late 1880s, much of the railroad in Nevada had yet to be fully ballasted with stone. Eventually, an extensive quarry, providing fill material and ballast that was used all across the Salt Lake Division, was established at the location of this photograph. In time, most of the bluff on the right was removed by quarrying. This was the bluff where Hart and the Indian had stood for the preceding view.

FIRST CONSTRUCTION TRAIN PASSING THE PALISADES
436.65 miles from Sacramento

The track was laid to this point in Palisade Canyon on November 30, 1868. Hart's caption, and the direction of shadows, suggests that this photograph was made the following morning. The widely spaced, un-ballasted ties are characteristic of brand-new construction. Regular train service would not commence until the missing crossties had been set, and the railroad lined and surfaced. But construction material and supplies were carried on to the front as soon as trains could pass. Still, until the track was fully prepared, train movements were slow and hazardous. Derailments and delays were frequent.

By the end of November 1868, the company had 82 locomotives in service, but that number was insufficient to handle all the construction, supply, and regular trains operating on the rapidly lengthening railroad. Various clues, such as the peaked cab roof and steam chest covers, identify this locomotive as a Mason-built 4-4-0. The peculiar, flat smokebox front suggests this was the no. 11, *Arctic*, which had suffered a head-on collision with no. 24 near Summit on the last day of August 1868. It apparently had received a temporary repair to get it back into service as quickly as possible.

This view marks the easternmost extent of Hart's November trip to the end-of-track. It was also his last construction-related photograph until he went to Promontory Summit six months later.

MACHINE SHOP AT CARLIN
444.48 miles from Sacramento, elevation 4,901 feet

Rails reached Carlin on December 4, 1868. Carlin was selected as the site for the first repair facilities east of Wadsworth. The shop was under construction in January 1869, well before the date of this photograph.

Like Reno and Wadsworth, Carlin was named for a Civil War general. However, unlike Reno and Wadsworth, Carlin's namesake, William Passmore Carlin, had a connection with the area, having been stationed near here during the Utah Expedition of 1858. Also, General Carlin was still very much alive when the station was named in his honor.

Compared to the number of photographs Hart made of the CP in the Sierra, there are relatively few taken in Nevada. For Hart, Nevada was far from home, and after five years of construction the novelty was wearing off. Most of Hart's Nevada photographs were made on short excursions from Reno in August 1868. Hart's latter photograph at Brown's, the two images at the first crossing of the Humboldt, and the one taken at Winnemucca were made while he was en route to the end-of-track near Iron Point. Others views were made within a short distance of the outfit cars on his visits to the end-of-track in October and November. All of the views from Palisades Canyon date from his trip there in November. Hart apparently made only two trips east of Palisade.

CARLIN FROM THE WATER TANKS

One of Hart's two trips east of Palisade was made on this train, seen also in photographs taken at Argenta and Elko. The train was pulled by locomotive no. 108. The last car on the train happens to be the CP's first business car. After it went into service in November 1868 it was used to convey government commissioners and railroad officials over the line. The adjacent car was its "tender," which carried provisions. Its known in-service date makes February 1869 the earliest possible date for this trip into eastern Nevada.

One of the men watching Hart make this photograph wears a linen duster to protect his clothes. Until the days of closed, air conditioned cars, dust stirred up by the passing train was a constant nuisance. In the distance of the west-facing view are the Tuscarora Mountains, through which Palisade Canyon cuts. At Carlin, the old wagon road split, with branches detouring around the canyon to the north and south, to rejoin at Gravelly Ford, a few miles west of the canyon. Just east of Carlin the South Fork of the Humboldt River joins the main stem of the river.

In later years the CP built large ponds at Carlin for the production of ice, and Carlin became a regular stop for eastbound produce trains, where the ice bunkers of refrigerator cars were topped off.

ELKO FROM THE WEST
467.94 miles from Sacramento, elevation 5,063 feet

Explorers and travelers alike had camped at the site of Elko since the 1840s, and it was already a freighting point before the railroad arrived, serving mining districts to the north, east, and south. The town of Elko was established by George F. Paddleford in December 1868 in anticipation of the arrival of the railroad; the name was apparently selected by Charles Crocker. Regular trains began running to Elko in mid-January 1869. Elko became the seat of Elko County, established in March 1869, and it continues to serve as the commercial center for northeastern Nevada.

When the railroad was built through eastern Nevada and northwest Utah, the ground was frozen as much as three feet deep, and to build the roadbed workers had to use blasting powder to break up the frozen ground. Adding to the misery, a smallpox epidemic raged through the railroad camps and surrounding mining settlements that winter. Charles Crocker wrote: "The smallpox completely demoralized our track-laying force . . . very nearly all the white men left the work and most of our best foremen also . . . Strobridge sick with a very bad cold and afraid it was the smallpox as the symptoms were very similar . . . men running off scared out of their senses—thermometer 10° below zero."

DEPOT AT ELKO

The eastbound locomotive in this view at Elko is no. 108, *Stager*. It was one of 10 identical 4-4-0s delivered by the Rogers Locomotive Works of Paterson, New Jersey, in August, September, and October 1868. *Stager* was among the 18 engines shipped across Panama, rather than around Cape Horn—a great expense and a lot of trouble just to get them into service as quickly as possible.

Locomotive *Stager* entered service in late December 1868 and was one of the locomotives that pulled the train that met Huntington when he arrived from New York on his first overland journey. At that time the track extended only 11 miles beyond Elko.

However, this appears to be the same train seen at Argenta and Carlin, dating the photograph to late February 1869 at the earliest. The crewman in shirtsleeves and the completed state of the depot-hotel suggest a date well into spring. Regardless of the occasion, it appears that entire population of the district has crowded onto the station platform.

A passenger on the first train west after the railroad was completed recorded, "The dust was stifling. There was very little air and the alkali came into the car in *clouds* filling eyes, nose, mouth and ears. With all this we ran like lightning at a frightful speed.... Oh this alkali and sage brush! We are sick and tired of it."

WATER TANK AT PEKO
488.15 miles from Sacramento, elevation 5,204 feet

An eastbound train is the focus of this photograph at Peko, Nevada. The North Fork of the Humboldt River joins the primary stream a short distance west of Peko. In this image, the East Humboldt Range is faintly visible in the distance. The water tower is fully enclosed to protect the water from freezing. The railroad had only few facilities here: the water tower, a sidetrack, and section house.

As an inducement to build the Pacific railroad, the federal government granted to the various railroad companies involved every other section of land for 20 miles on each side of the track. Potentially, this amounted to 9.5 million acres for the CP's 742 miles. However, the grant was for 20 sections of land for each section through which the railroad ran, not for each mile of track, and mineral land and land already occupied was excluded. The actual grant to the CP was about seven million acres. While subsequent land-grant railroads (including the SP and the CP line to Portland) were required to carry government freight, mail, and personnel at significantly reduced rates, the CP and UP were not so restricted. However, the Pacific Railroad Act of 1862 required that all compensation for services rendered to the government, plus 5% of the road's net earnings, had to be set aside toward the eventual repayment of the federal bonds. Even though the amount to be set aside was reduced by half by the revised law of 1864, this provision severely restricted the cash available to the CP to offset operating expenses.

SCENE NEAR DEETH
504.4 miles from Sacramento, elevation 5,343 feet

Rails reached Deeth on January 26, 1869. The locomotive in this view is Schenectady-built no. 63, *Leviathan*, which entered service just prior to April 6, 1869. This may be Stanford's train heading to Promontory Summit on May 6 for the gold spike ceremony, though this apparently is not the train seen at Argenta, Carlin, and Elko.

The completed railroad was expected to give value to land adjacent to the track by the access it provided. The subsequent sale of the railroad's land was expected to reimburse the expense of building the road, while the sale of adjacent federal land was expected to generate an equivalent income for the government. However, little of the land in Nevada and Utah proved attractive to settlers, and by 1880 the CP had sold only 295,886 acres. At an average sale price of $3.77 per acre, this yielded barely enough to pay for 18 miles of railroad at the average cost of $64,000 per mile. Most of the unsold railroad land eventually was leased for livestock grazing or mining.

While the CP was disappointed with the land grant, the railroad nevertheless had a huge fiscal impact on Nevada. Until about 1900, property taxes paid by the CP on its land and railroad provided more than 60% of the income of the state's rural counties. To this day, roughly half of the taxable land in Nevada was originally part of the CP land grant.

SCENE AT MONUMENT POINT
666 miles from Sacramento, elevation 4,227 feet

The CP's track was completed to the Utah state line, 590 miles from Sacramento, in late March 1869, and it reached the northwest corner of Great Salt Lake at Monument Point on April 17. Stanford and his guests arrived at Promontory Summit from Sacramento on May 7 for the culminating ceremony, scheduled for the following day. When the UP delegation failed to arrive, the party made an excursion back to Monument Point on May 9 for some hunting. Hart took advantage of the opportunity to make this and the following photographs.

Titled "Poetry and Prose," this image is often presented as a contrast between the modern railroad train and the wagons it made obsolete. While none of the traditional pioneer trails crossed the Promontory Range, the railroad did alter the location of roads as travelers preferred to follow the track between the towns that developed along the line. So it is possible that pioneers who had wintered in the Salt Lake Valley were indeed passing by Monument Point in May 1869. But this scene may also have been staged for Hart using idle CP supply wagons.

While overland immigrants began to ride the train following the completion of the Pacific railroad, some continued to travel in wagons, just as some travelers continued to take the steamers between San Francisco and New York via Panama for many years to come.

GREAT SALT LAKE from MONUMENT POINT

Number 60, *Jupiter*, was the locomotive that took Stanford's party to Monument Point, and it subsequently played a role at the ceremony of the last spikes. It was a Schenectady product, placed in service in March 1869. The car behind the *Jupiter* is one of the CP's late-model water cars, here being used as an auxiliary tender.

With both companies jealous of commercial territory, it was a struggle for them to agree on a junction for the two railroads. Routes around both ends of the Great Salt Lake were examined before the northerly route, surveyed by Butler Ives in 1866-67, was finally adopted in May 1868. Even then, crews from the rival railroads graded sections of roadbed nearly side by side in several locations between Wells, Nevada and Echo Summit, Utah, including a stretch near Monument Point. Finally, at an all-night conference in Washington, D.C. in early April 1869, the companies agreed to connect their tracks at Promontory Summit.

In 1876, the Jarrett & Palmer theatrical company made a record-setting special run from New York to San Francisco. Its fastest time on the CP was over the 14 miles between Monument and Kelton, running at 55.4 miles per hour. The elapsed time for the entire run was 82 hours and 15 minutes. That record stood until 1906, when UP President Harriman traveled from San Francisco to New York in 71 hours and 21 minutes.

The 3D effect of this image has been digitally enhanced.

RAILROAD CAMP NEAR VICTORY
682.5 miles from Sacramento

On a single day, April 28, 1869, an army of CP workmen laid 10 miles plus 56 feet of track. The feat was undertaken only for bragging rights, as the junction point of the two railroads had already been determined. They were able to do it because of the deliberate staging of material and the diligent training and organization of crews. While credit goes to the teamwork of hundreds of men delivering supplies, setting ties, and splicing and spiking rail, the iron gang that unloaded and placed each of at least 3,520 rails laid that day consisted of only eight Irishmen—George Elliott, Edward Kelleen, Thomas Daley, Mike Shaw, Mike Sullivan, Mike Kennedy, Patrick Joyce, and Fred McNamara, under foreman George Coley. For the six hours and 42 minutes worked before lunch, they unloaded on average one track-laying car every three minutes. The unloading of each carload of 16 rails, and setting them in place, was done in only 80 seconds. The rest of the time was spent catching their breath while others tipped the empty car aside and brought a loaded car to the front. Tie layers, splicers, and spikers matched this pace. Progress was slower in the afternoon while rails were bent for curves. The CP's 10-miles-in-a-day record has never been broken.

"Victory" station was where track layers stopped for lunch on their record-setting day. The photograph was certainly made a few days later, after sidetracks had been laid. Strobridge and track-laying superintendent Henry Minkler stand together on the flatcar.

THE FIRST GREETING OF THE IRON HORSE
Promontory Summit, 690.28 miles from Sacramento, elevation 4,905 feet

Three photographers were on hand to document the activities pertaining to the joining of the rails. Of them, Hart is credited with making both the first and last photographs—this being the first. Despite his dating on the card as May 9, the heavy weather and the absence of many of the tents that appeared before May 10 strongly suggests that this photograph was made on the afternoon of May 7, shortly after Stanford's special arrived from Sacramento. The event itself, the very first approach of CP and UP locomotives within whistling distance of one another, was reported in the press as having occurred on that date.

CP locomotives no. 60, *Jupiter*, and no. 62, *Whirlwind*, were both on hand. The locomotive in the foreground is believed to be the *Jupiter*, though both were identical Schenectady products. The firewood in the tender appears to be sagebrush trunks. The UP locomotive on the opposite track was variously reported as no. 60 or no. 66. The UP did not name its engines.

The two railroads did not approach one another end-to-end but were laid on parallel grades. Subsequent to this photograph, a connecting track was built curving between them, leaving a gap to be closed on May 10.

On May 9 an eastbound traveler walked from a CP train to a UP train, making what is believed to be the first transcontinental trip by train without recourse to a connecting stagecoach.

THE INVOCATION, FIXING THE WIRE

The ceremony marking the joining of the rails was not planned very far in advance. Even on the morning of May 10, representatives of the two companies were arguing about who would drive the last spike. In mid-morning, with only a few spectators on hand, Irish track layers from the UP completed the curving connection from the east, followed soon thereafter by Chinese, directed by CP rail-laying boss David Sullivan, who laid the last two rails to close the final gap. A space was left under the joints between the CP rails and the UP rails for a polished laurel tie that would later be slipped into place.

Meanwhile, a crowd of perhaps a thousand people gathered, made up of local settlers, railroad workers, and the curious from distant towns who arrived by UP train. Some wagons were drawn up on the north side of the track to provide a makeshift viewing platform. Stanford's spike maul and a spike were wired to the telegraph circuit so that they could transmit a signal when struck together. CP telegraph construction foreman Amos Bowsher was still on the telegraph pole completing that connection when Edgar Mills, a banker from Sacramento, opened the proceedings. Rev. John Todd of Pittsfield, Massachusetts then offered an invocation. The telegraph operator tapped out the message: ALMOST READY HATS OFF PRAYER IS BEING OFFERED.

THE LAST RAIL IS LAID

After the speeches, the crowd was moved aside for the photographers to make pictures. Hart placed himself on the left-hand side of the *Jupiter*'s pilot deck, and at his word, the crowd stood still for the exposure. Leland Stanford holds his silver-plated spike maul high, while UP Vice President Thomas Durant's maul rests on his shoulder. Another UP vice president at the ceremony was Silas Seymour who, in 1851, had driven the last spike on the Erie Railroad. Seymour had been instrumental in sending Theodore Judah to California in 1854 as the chief engineer of the Sacramento Valley Railroad.

After this photograph was made, the two construction superintendents, James Strobridge and Samuel Reed of the UP, slid the laurel tie into the space provided. In this image, the vacant space for the last tie is evident in front of young Sam Strobridge. With the tie in place, the commemorative spikes were set in their holes. The telegrapher transmitted, ALL READY NOW THE SPIKE WILL SOON BE DRIVEN.

The controversy over who was to drive the last spike was settled with both Durant and Stanford to tap their spikes home simultaneously. According to Durant, both missed on their first attempts, but the job was completed. Just 20 minutes after it began, the ceremony was over. The operator tapped out: DONE.

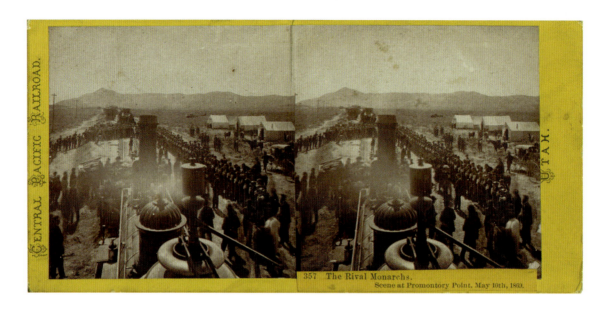

THE RIVAL MONARCHS

Of the four ceremonial spikes used at Promontory Summit, two came from Nevada. One, of Comstock silver, was presented by Frederick A. Tritle, manager of the Yellow Jacket Mine in Virginia City. At the time of the ceremony, he was also a candidate for governor of Nevada. Each of one hundred miners struck a blow to forge this spike. As used at the ceremony, it was only roughly made, not being finished and engraved until sometime later.

Another spike, made of gold, silver, and iron, was presented by Anson P.K. Safford, surveyor-general of Nevada. Shortly before the last-spike ceremony, Safford had been appointed governor of Arizona Territory, and his spike was presented on behalf of Arizona; however its gold and silver undoubtedly came from Nevada mines, and Safford had yet to move to Arizona.

San Francisco contractor David Hewes, and Frank Marriott, editor of the *San Francisco News Letter* each donated gold spikes that were used at the ceremony.

About the time the last spikes were tapped home, a train arrived from the east carrying about 250 troops of the 21st Infantry Regiment, bound for San Francisco. Too late for the ceremony, they lined up on the north side of the track to present a guard, its band provided music "until they had taken too much ardent spirit."

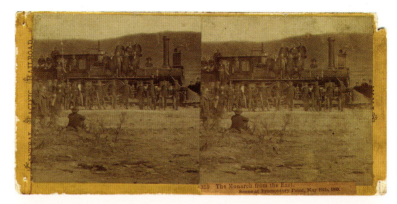

MONARCHS FROM THE EAST AND THE WEST

The CP locomotive at the ceremony was no. 60, *Jupiter*, built by Schenectady. Like many Schenectady products of the period, *Jupiter* was painted in crimson and Caledonian blue. The UP engine was no. 119, a product of the Rogers Locomotive Works of Paterson, New Jersey. Other than it being set up as a coal-burner, it was very much like the Rogers-built 4-4-0s purchased by the CP.

Hart photographed the locomotives in two separate images, as seen here. They have been merged into the single composite image, seen opposite. The 3D effect has been digitally added. The *Jupiter* is on the right.

360 The Last Act—690 Miles from Sacramento.
Scene at Promontory Point, May 10th, 1869.

THE LAST ACT

Following the ceremony, officials and guests of the railroads retired to their cars for meals, though participants circulated among the various parties. Strobridge invited the eight Chinese who had laid the last rails to the gathering he hosted. He saw to it that they were recognized on behalf of the contributions of all the Chinese who aided in the construction of the CP railroad. Capt. John C. Currier of the 21st Regiment observed: "Much nonsense was got off but we had a jolly day. . . . Thus is the greatest accomplishment of the 19th century accomplished."

Completed, the Pacific railroad provided a continuous rail connection between the Missouri River and Pacific tidewater. For those who needed to make that journey, or for those who merely sent mail or packages across the continent, the completion of the railroad alone was cause for celebration. But for America as a whole, the completion of a transcontinental railroad in 1869 was far more than just a road of iron—it was the fulfillment of Manifest Destiny, the marriage of the continent's two shores, the symbolic unification of a nation recently torn by civil war. The national celebration that greeted the driving of the last spikes at Promontory Summit was a response to the broader significance of the event.

The celebrations in most cities were actually held on May 8, the date originally scheduled for the event at Promontory.

RAILROAD AT OGDEN
743.45 miles from Sacramento, elevation 4,300 feet

Having connected with the UP, the CP immediately shifted its attention to completing the Western Pacific between Sacramento and San Francisco Bay. That line was finished to Alameda by way of Stockton, Livermore, and Niles on September 5, 1869. The track was extended to Oakland at the end of October. A connection with San Francisco was made via San Jose and the San Francisco & San Jose Railroad.

Hart made the above view on May 8, 1869, when a UP train took Stanford's party on a tour of the UP track to Ogden. In November the UP sold 48.5 miles of railroad east of Promontory Summit to the CP and leased them another 5.5 miles, thereby allowing the CP to operate trains directly into Ogden. On December 6, Ogden replaced Promontory Summit as the junction of the two railroads. Early in 1870, the CP finally built the railroad it had surveyed down the east side of the Promontory Range, replacing some 10 miles of the original UP line with its steep grades and tight curves.

In 1903, the original railroad around the north side of the Great Salt Lake was bypassed with a new cutoff, running directly across the lake. However, the old line remained in service as a branch until World War II. One of those present at a ceremony at Promontory Summit marking the abandonment of that branch in 1942 was 85-year-old Mary Ipsen, who had witnessed the driving of the last spikes 73 years before.

DINING CAR INTERNATIONAL

The completion of the Pacific railroad cemented the bond between America's Pacific and Atlantic shores and forever changed the way goods and people moved across the country. Nevertheless, for many years steamships continued to carry passengers between the coasts via Panama and the Panama Railroad. Bulk freight, such as California wheat, coal, and even rail for railroads, was carried by sail around Cape Horn until the opening of the Panama Canal. On the other hand, merchandise and mail now crossed the continent by rail, and most immigrants were quick to abandon the covered wagons. During the 1870s, the CP carried more than twice as many people westbound as eastward.

The completion of the Pacific railroad allowed rail cars to be hauled all the way across the continent. Freight cars from East Coast railroads began appearing on the CP, while carloads of West Coast produce were carried overland to the East. Within weeks of the Gold Spike Ceremony, George M. Pullman travelled to California with some of his cars in the hope of securing a franchise to operate them on CP trains. Hart photographed the Pullman cars in Sacramento in June 1869 before they returned east. In this image, we see the dining car *International* spotted on the wharf (then under expansion) at Sacramento, with an assortment of hardware in the foreground. The car was 60 feet long, 10 feet wide, and rode on 16 wheels arranged in double trucks. This and the related images are the last railroad photographs Hart is known to have made.

INTERIOR of DINING CAR INTERNATIONAL

This companion view of the dining car *International* shows its interior arrangement. Unlike the design that subsequently became standard, with the kitchen at one end and tables at the other, the kitchen of the *International* was located in the center, with six dining tables at either end of the car. When Pullman's train returned to the East, the kitchen was stocked with all kinds of California produce.

Despite Pullman's persuasion and opulent cars, not until 1883 did the CP contract to run Pullman cars over its railroad. As a consequence, the appearance of dining cars such as this on the CP was limited to special trains on special occasions. For many years, passenger trains continued to stop at meal times to allow passengers to detrain and eat in depot dining rooms.

Upon the connection of the CP with the UP in May 1869, the CP was operating with 143 locomotives, 14 passenger cars, two combines, 18 baggage-mail-express combines, 480 boxcars, and 1,293 flatcars. Several cars and locomotives were still on order and arrived over the following months—several still by sea. Stock cars and fruit cars were soon added for specialized freight while new passenger cars, including 13 Silver Palace sleepers, were also acquired.

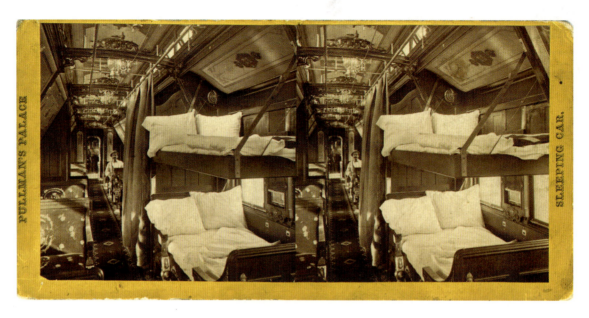

SLEEPING CAR

This is the interior of one of the sleepers that was in Pullman's train returning east in June 1869. It illustrates the way the lower seats folded together to make a bed, while an upper berth folded down from above. Washrooms were located at the ends of the car.

The railroad train and the sleeping car made travel for recreation available to almost everyone. For most early settlers, their initial trip west was a one-way journey. But in September 1869, the month the railroad was opened all the way from San Francisco to Omaha, a special train carried about two hundred of them east to revisit their old homes, families, and friends. No longer did moving west mean being isolated on the far side of the world. Also in September 1869, the Cincinnati Red Stockings—America's first professional baseball team—traveled to California by train to play some local clubs. Railroads even changed the way Americans played.

While the first-class railroad sleeping car provided luxury for travelers who could afford the price, most immigrants rode in far more basic accommodations. The plain wooden seats of the emigrant cars folded together into beds, but the travelers had to provide their own bedding. Others rode in common boxcars with all of their belongings. Still, by rail, the overland journey lasted only a matter of days and was a far more bearable crossing than it had been for those who went west in ox-drawn wagons.

SILVER PALACE CAR

Leland Stanford, sitting closest to the camera, and various companions are here enjoying the luxury of a new sleeping car. This car is one of Thomas T. Woodruff's Silver Palace cars, not a Pullman. Until the CP contracted with Pullman in 1883, the railroad company operated its own cars built to Woodruff's pattern.

As a business venture, the CP was not particularly successful. The Suez Canal opened within months of the completion of the Pacific railroad, diverting much of the Asian commerce that had been expected to follow the railroad across North America to Europe. Furthermore, the CP always had to share the revenue of its cross-country traffic with connecting railroads, notably the UP. However, while the extent of that traffic increased as the West matured, the CP's share of it diminished with the opening of the second transcontinental railroad in 1881. And that was only the first of several competing cross-country lines eventually built. While it continued to exist as a corporate entity until 1959, the CP all but disappeared after 1899, when its stockholders traded their shared for SP stock and the funds necessary to pay creditors the cost of the railroad's construction. But while the CP was eclipsed by the SP, it will always hold its place a part of the first Pacific railroad. As such, it fulfilled the public's expectations. The Central Pacific linked the Pacific Coast to the East, integrating the two regions into a vibrant, single nation spanning the continent.

Cut through Dixie Spur
See p. 110.

NOTES

As a rule, information about events mentioned in this book and not otherwise attributed in the notes are from local newspaper reports published within a day or two of the event. Also, all letters from Hopkins, E.B. Crocker, or C. Crocker were addressed to Huntington, unless noted otherwise. The notes refer to material presented on specific pages.

12. FRONT STREET, SACRAMENTO. The image dates from between October 1864, when the flag staff was added to the north end of the California Steam Navigation Company shed (*Sacramento Union* October 28), and June 1865, when a steam engine was installed at the foot of K street to pull trucks up from the wharf (*Sacramento Bee* June 20). The bare trees and water standing in the street narrow the timeframe to winter or early spring.

All of the photographs included in this book are believed to be the work of Alfred A. Hart. However, one may legitimately question the origins of cards without a "Hart number" or Hart's imprint. In fact, William Dickman is known to have sold photographs to the CP about this time. Nevertheless, this and the following card bear the imprint of Lawrence & Houseworth, who were publishing Hart views as early as March 1865, and they are believed to be Hart images.

14. CENTRAL PACIFIC DEPOT, SACRAMENTO. Most of the elevation figures used in this work are from the 1941 SP *List of Officers, Agencies and Stations*. While this source postdates construction by nearly 80 years, it is assumed the later figures are most accurate and that the rail elevations had not been changed appreciably. Where stations were abandoned before the later surveys, elevations are taken from Williams.

16 and 18. SACRAMENTO WATERFRONT FROM RIVERBOAT. The other locomotives with semicircular saddle tanks were nos. 46 and 47, *Unicorn* and *Griffin*, which arrived from McKay & Aldus in March 1868. All the saddle-tank locomotives were 0-6-0Ts. The *Capital* is described in detail in the *Bee*, March 5, 1866.

20. RAILROAD WHARVES AT SACRAMENTO CITY. E.B. Crocker first requested that C.P. Huntington hurry rail via Panama on May 25, 1868. Most of the rail that came via Panama was shipped the following July through September (Huntington letters to Hopkins, September 23, and to E.B. Crocker, October 12, 1868).

Most CP rail weighed 56 pounds per yard. Generally, 110 long tons of rail and 5,200 pounds of spikes were ordered for a mile of track. This included some extra for sidings. Data on rail comes from

the reports of the commissioners who certified sections of the railroad on behalf of the Department of the Interior before the issuance of bonds and land; Huntington's letters, particularly those of December 25 and 29, 1867 and April 16, 1868; and *Bee*, August 27, 1868. Still, the reports of the commissioners miss entirely the introduction of 30-foot rail in August 1868, which is documented in Huntington's letter of August 15, 1868 and C. Crocker's letter of August 22, 1868. Huntington's quote is from his letter of August 17, 1868 to C. Crocker.

22. J STREET, SACRAMENTO, FROM THE LEVEE. Sargent introduced the matter of Judah's route across the Sierra as a potential course for a central Pacific railroad to congress in January 1862. He was also instrumental in securing Judah's appointment as secretary of the House's special subcommittee on the Pacific railroad. This is remarkable in that Judah was in Washington as a lobbyist representing the CP. Even more remarkable, Judah was also made secretary of the Senate's Pacific railroad committee. The proper name of the "Pacific Railroad Act" is: *An Act to aid in the construction of a railroad and telegraph line from the Missouri river to the Pacific Ocean, and to secure to the government the use of the same for postal, military, and other purposes.* Later, Huntington, who

lobbied in Washington D.C. after Judah's death, complained about Sargent (Huntington to Hopkins, January 9, 1868).

Locomotive no. 7's arrival in Sacramento was reported in the *Bee* and *Union*, December 14 and 15, 1865. Hopkins explained in a letter of January 7, 1867 that California factories expected payment in gold.

24. LOCOMOTIVE NO. 1 *GOV. STANFORD.* Hopkins's letter regarding the *Gov. Stanford* dates from February 5, 1867. Hart's photographs were published by Lawrence & Houseworth, the CP itself, as well as by Hart. By 1870, Huntington's friend Carleton E. Watkins was publishing Hart's views as if they were his own.

26. NORTH OF CENTRAL PACIFIC DEPOT. The *Union* reported the "City" dropped from the post office name on March 6, 1883.

28. LOCOMOTIVE NO. 6 *CONNESS*, ON AMERICAN RIVER TRESTLE. The *Bee* of March 16, 1865 reported that the image was made "by a special artist who had recently been a justice of the Supreme Court," a clear reference to E.B. Crocker. The issue of naming locomotives was discussed by E.B. Crocker in a letter dated February 11, 1868.

30. AMERICAN RIVER BRIDGE. The *Union* of January 1, 1863 identified the contractors and stated that piles were being driven. The covering and painting of the bridge was recorded in Montague's report of December 1865, while the raising and lengthening of the bridge was reported in Sacramento newspapers in September, November, and December of 1868. The *Union* of March 25, 1870 documents the burning of the bridge.

Earlier in his career, contractor Hubbard had built the telegraph line between Sacramento and Salt Lake City as a section of the first transcontinental telegraph. The telegraph associated with the Pacific railroad was the second cross-country line.

32. TWELVE-MILE TANGENT. The Sacramento Placer & Nevada was incorporated in 1859 to build from Folsom to Auburn with the expectation that it would eventually reach Nevada City (the "Nevada" of its corporate name). With the discovery of the Comstock Lode, the company planned an extension to Nevada Territory via Henness Pass. By the fall of 1862, the SP&N was operating 14 miles from Folsom to a point immediately east of the intersection of Whiskey Bar and Auburn-Folsom roads, six miles short of Auburn. Operated by the SVRR, the SP&N is a generally forgotten rival to the CP for the cross-Sierra traffic.

Two tangents longer than this on the CPRR were an 18-mile

stretch west of Battle Mountain and one of 24 miles immediately east of Lucin. The report that 10 miles of track were laid by January 8, 1864 comes from the *Bee* of that date.

34. DRY CREEK BRIDGE. Information on the bridge is from Montague's 1864 report.

36 and 38. ROCKLIN. The quote is from Stevens's "Across America on a Bicycle," 47. Rocklin was called "Rockville" in the *Bee*, March 20, 1865; *Mining & Scientific Press*, August 3, 1867, called the place "Rockland." The *Bee* of February 6, 1865 noted authority for the track on Sixth Street.

40. ROUNDHOUSE AND TRAIN, ROCKLIN and 16. ENGINE HOUSE AND TURNTABLE. An incline of 25 feet to the mile is roughly equivalent to .5%. An early profile indicates five short sections of that gradient between Sacramento and Roseville, the first of which was immediately east of the crossing of Antelope Creek. This was apparently the justification for designating that as the point where the CP would begin to draw the maximum number of federal bonds per mile.

The installation of the water pipe to Loomis was reported in the *Annual Report of the Commissioner of Railroads* (1888-89, 74).

42. ENGINE HOUSE AND TURNTABLE. The *Union* of September 25, 1866 reported that the

town was being laid out and that the construction of the roundhouse had commenced. The *Bee* of the following May 24 told of locomotives being moved to Rocklin from Sacramento, and the *Union* of 16 May 1868 reported the structure completed. That it took so long to complete the roundhouse suggests that not all stalls were built at once. Employee statistics are from the *Centennial Spirit of the Times* (July 4, 1876). The May 9, 1913 *Bee* reported the old roundhouse being torn down to make room for a baseball diamond.

The *Bee* of October 2, 1886 reported the installation of coaling facilities at Rocklin and Colfax, while the company annual report of 1887 indicates a coal platform was built at Gold Run soon thereafter. Wood apparently remained an option for locomotive fuel into 1892. The last mention found of the CP contracting for firewood was published in the *Daily Nevada State Journal*, November 28, 1891, though the woodshed at Shady Run was enlarged that same year.

In addition to its vulnerability to loss by fire, wood was expensive as a fuel because it had to be handled one piece at a time every time it was moved. Coal stocks still caught fire, and like wood piles, they were subject to pilfering, but coal could be handled mechanically. Oil was suggested as a fuel for locomotives before the CP was even completed (*Alta* November 7, 1867), but not until 1901, after years of experimenting, was it introduced on a wide

scale. Locomotives were being converted at Sparks to burn oil in 1909, though apparently the Sacramento-Ogden line was not wholly converted to oil until 1913. For more on locomotive fuel, see Menke and Mullaly.

44. TANGENT BELOW PINO. The arrangement for using local innkeepers to provide depots was discussed by Jones in "Rough and Ready was the Early Day Motto," 24. The Pino-Loomis station name change took place on February 18, 1884, as reported in the *Union*, February 22. J.J. Morrison was listed as the station agent in the October 1885 *Official List of Officers, Stations, Agents*. While Loomis still operated a hotel, it is not clear whether the hotel he operated was connected with the depot. The post office name remained Pino for some time.

46. GRIFFITH'S QUARRY AT PENRYN. This image (like the one on page 56) dates from the March 26, 1865 excursion to Newcastle. The story of the SP&N and the "Placer County Railroad War" is pieced together from reports in the Sacramento and Auburn papers throughout 1864, but primarily from July of that year.

E.B. Crocker had a degree in civil engineering; yet, his profession was that of an attorney, and he served as the CP's legal counsel and strategist until sidelined by a stroke in June 1869. Crocker died in 1875, before the sobriquet "Big Four" was coined, and thus he was not counted. Accordingly, it is anachronistic to use "Big Four" in connection with the construction of the CP. Griffith's first and last names were indeed the same.

48. ANTELOPE RIDGE, NEAR NEWCASTLE. C.

Crocker resigned as a director prior to the annual election of July 1863, while E.B. Crocker does not appear as director until the election of October 1864. The various contractors are identified in Montague's report of October 8, 1864. The problems with the independent contractors were recounted by C. Crocker and Clement before the United States Pacific Railway Commission in 1887. Their testimony is printed on pages 3224 and 3640 of the commission's published reports (hereafter noted as USPRC). See also Kraus.

50. NEWCASTLE. The resump-

tion of Sunday train service was announced in the Bee, May 21 and 24, 1869.

52. LOCOMOTIVE NO. 5 AT-

LANTIC. The race between the CP and the SVRR commenced shortly before midnight on August 22, 1865, when the riverboat Chrysopolis docked at Freeport, from which point the SVRR ran to Latrobe. While the CP train did not depart Sacramento until newspapers had been delivered by pony courier from Freeport, both trains reached their respective destinations of Latrobe and New-castle at about 1 o'clock the fol-

lowing morning. The stagecoach carrying the newspapers delivered by the CP arrived at Virginia City 12 hours later, nine hours before the stagecoach from Latrobe. The details of the event were reported in the local papers over the following days. The quote about the bar maids is from a Hopkins letter, February 16, 1866.

While there is no report that the CP used camels in Nevada, the SP did so while building across Arizona. The SP's camels were shipped to Australia when the railroad was through with them (New York Times, January 8, 1884).

54. TRESTLE UNDER CON-

STRUCTION, NEWCASTLE. There is frustratingly little consistency among the sources with regard to the dimensions of the CP trestles. These sources include the report of R.S. Williamson (January 1869) and annual reports by CP chief engineer Montague, particularly those of 1865, 1869, and 1877, and tables of bridges and trestles he prepared in 1869. The reports of the commissioners who examined the various sections of the railroad upon completion on behalf of the Department of the Interior are of marginal use as they describe the trestles in terms of the number of bents, and there is no agreement among sources whether the bents were 15 feet, 16 feet, or one rod apart. Furthermore, the reports fail to tell us whether the outer abutments were counted as bents or ignored

entirely. Most troubling, the number of bents reported disagrees in some cases with what we can count in photographs. That said, in the single case of the Newcastle trestle, the sources do agree that it was 528 feet long by 63 feet high. Even the 33-bent count recorded by the 1865 commissioners conforms if we assume a one-rod bent spacing and count the end abutments as bents.

The paucity of the company treasury in this period was recounted by newspaper publisher Marcus D. Boruck (USPRC, 3421-2), and is referred to in the Bee obituary of Benjamin R. Crocker on December 12, 1900 (see page 168 for more on B.R. Crocker).

56. LOCOMOTIVE CONNESS

AT NEWCASTLE. The CP's financial woes have been recounted by various authors, such as Bain, Daggett, Griswold, and Kraus.

58. RAILROAD ABOVE NEW-

CASTLE. The numbers of workers given here are from the Union January 7 and 21, April 3, and May 1, 1865, and Bee March 18, 1865. Hopkins's statement regarding the Chinese is from his letter of May 31, 1865. Before accepting any value for the number for workers, note E.B. Crocker's comment quoted on page 386.

60. EMBANKMENT IN

DUTCH RAVINE. The embankment dimensions come from the commissioners' reports. The

Union of May 1, 1865 recounted the difficulty of obtaining enough fill material. The Bee, November 22, 1865 and Placer Herald three days later reported embankments washed out.

62. APPROACHING BLOOM-

ER CUT. Dimensions of the cut are from Montague's report of October 1864, 11, and "Summit of the Sierras," 797. Montague's report stated the excavation was "fully complete." Track was laid through it soon after May 1, 1865 (on which date the Union reported the end-of-track 1.5 miles above Newcastle). The Bee of January 25, 1865 reported a photographer taking pictures at Bloomer, but no photographs of Bloomer without tracks have come to light. Douglas Judah's role is revealed in the November 8, 1862 Placer Herald. His full name was Edward Douglas Judah. The identification of the other engineers is from various company reports and the Mining & Scientific Press, November 21, 1868.

64. BLOOMER CUT. The Placer

Herald April 16, 1864 reported the blasting accident. Russell's effort to preserve Bloomer Cut in its original form was recounted by Lynn D. Farrar, the last SP valuation engineer, posted to cprr.org on June 26, 2005.

66. BLOOMER CUT AND

EMBANKMENT. Hopkins lamented the problems with "chair rail" in letters on May 5, 1866 and

December 8, 1867. Rail on the inside of curves has to be shortened roughly one inch per one hundred feet per degree of curvature to keep the joints even.

68. AUBURN STATION. The *Bee* of May 14, 1865 reported the first passenger train to Auburn. The receipt of the first federal bonds was reported by the same paper on May 18. Mrs. George Willment was listed as the Auburn station agent in 1879, the first year for which a published list of company officers, stations, and agents is known.

The matter of the redemption of the United States bonds was at the heart of the United States Pacific Railway Commission hearing in 1887, and the railroad's position is outlined in Conkling's summary. The values of the bonds cited are from Conkling, 124–25. The final settlement was reported in the *Annual Report of the Commissioner of Railroads* (1899). The SP gave the CP the funds to pay this obligation in exchange for CP stock, which is how the CP ultimately became an SP property. CP stockholders were given SP stock as part of the exchange. This (and the date of the final payment to the government) is recounted in Myrick's "Refinancing and Rebuilding the Central Pacific," and summarized in his *Railroads of Nevada*, 29.

70. RAILROAD EAST OF AUBURN STATION. Warning signs were mentioned in "Things as they are in America," 131. The number of CP road crossings was reported in the commissioners' reports. The rule for the use of the bell at crossings is from C. Crocker's "Rules and Regulations for Employees." (This undated list of rules originated before September 1869, when Crocker finally found someone else to superintend the railroad.) The new policy of whistling for crossings was reported in the Sacramento *Record-Union* February 8 1882. The tax assessment was reported in the *Placer Herald* November 18, 1865.

74. TRESTLE AT LOVELL'S RANCH. The two trestles at Lovell's ranch were located at 40.05 miles and 40.33 miles from Sacramento. The trestle in this photograph is the easternmost of the two, which Heuer documented as having a left-handed curve at its western end, as we see here. (Curves were described as "right" or "left" as oriented to someone facing away from Sacramento.) Hart card no. 27 (not included in this work) is of the westernmost Lovell's Ranch trestle. Montague reported in June 1877 that both trestles had been eliminated with line changes.

76. CLIPPER GAP. Construction of the toll road from Nevada City to Clipper Gap was reported in the *Bee* of March 25, 1865, quoting the *Nevada [City] Transcript*. Generally, statements relating to the location and dimensions of early woodsheds, water tanks, and other facilities are from an unpublished 1869 company inventory of railroad structures found in the National Archives.

78. CLIPPER RAVINE TRESTLE. The commissioners reported that the Clipper Gap trestle had 30 bents and rose 46 feet high. Length figures vary among the reports from four hundred feet to five hundred feet. The trestle was eliminated by a line change in the year covered by Montague's June 1877 report. The Clipper Ravine trestle was reported to have had 26 bents, the same as the first one at Lovell's ranch, but its length is consistently reported to have been over one hundred feet shorter. Montague's table of trestles has it as only three hundred feet in length. Sources do agree that it was 50 feet tall, however. Because it was filled in 1873 Heuer missed it entirely, and so we are left with only the vague indication that it was within the same mile as the truss-trestle structure at Deep Gulch. It was always listed before Deep Gulch, so it was likely to the west.

The Chinese in California were primarily from the Guangdong Province. See Choy, 17–19.

80. DEEP GULCH TRESTLE. Because of its design, combining elements of trestlework and bridge spans, the Deep Gulch trestle is easy to identify in photographs. Montague listed its respective elements in both his 1869 table of bridges and his table of trestles. His report of June 1873 stated that this was the "highest structure of its kind" on the railroad.

The speed limit on bridges and trestles was rule no. 22 of Crocker's "Rules and Regulations for Employees." Rule no. 31 provided a general speed limit of 25 miles per hour for passenger trains, and 10 miles per hour for freight trains east of Junction and 12 miles per hour west of Junction. (See page 422 for later speed limits.)

Montague's report of June 1874 stated that trains first began to use Tunnel no. 0 on July 24, 1873. The explanation of tunnel no. 0's substandard width is from Stevens, 49. Signor, *Donner Pass* (253), gives 1942 as the date for the eventual bypass of Tunnel no. 0, stating that the tunnel was eliminated because it was too narrow to accommodate Navy landing craft being carried to West Coast embarkation ports. An annotation on a SP right of way and track map states that operation through Tunnel no. 0 ended in January 1944.

82. CUT NEAR NEW ENGLAND MILLS. The data on cuts and fills between Clipper Gap and Colfax are from the *Union* of September 4, 1865. The *Union* of May 1, 1865 reported a sawmill cutting timber for trestles and crossties, though the sawmill at New England Mills apparently predated the railroad. John Starbuck's information is from the 1870 census, while the identification of the namesake of George's Cut comes from Williams, 241.

84. DEPOT AT COLFAX. Hopkins immediately wrote of the railroad's arrival at Colfax. The *Bee* of July 18 and 19, 1865 report the townsite being laid out, while the dimensions of the freight depot are from the 1869 structures inventory. The quote is from the *Alta* November 17, 1867. Colfax itself was established by the CP just north of the older community of Illinoistown. The station was named for Schuyler Colfax, a congressman from Indiana who was then speaker of the U.S. House of Representatives. When he toured the railroad works in July 1865, when the line was in operation only to Clipper Gap, Colfax was the highest ranking government official yet to visit California. He later became Ulysses Grant's vice president. Four years later, Colfax rode the finished railroad through Colfax (*Truckee Tribune* August 17, 1869). Colfax eventually was disgraced by his involvement in the UP's Credit Mobilier scandal.

86. LOCOMOTIVE NO. 8 *NEVADA* AT COLFAX. Locomotive costs were included in the commissioners' reports and are also in Huntington's invoice ledgers. Complaints about the Danforth moguls were penned by Hopkins on February 5, 1867 and by C. Crocker on April 25, 1867. The turntable and engine house at Colfax were counted in the 1869 inventory.

88. LONG RAVINE BRIDGE. The confusion between Long Ravine and Rice's Ravine was clarified by Williams, 238. Most sources (Montague, 1869 table, and June 1877 report; and Williamson's January 1869 report agree that the Long Ravine trestle was 450 feet long by 70 feet tall. However, in 1865 Montague reported that it was five hundred feet long by 60 feet high. Sources agree on the dimensions of the adjacent Howe-truss bridge spans (except Montage, in 1865, made one of the spans 120 rather than 128 feet). In October 1876 the trestle was filled in (*Union*, October 24). That workmen were being shifting forward was reported in the *Placer Herald*, August 19, 1865. Montague remarked on the difficulty of moving workers in his report of December 1865, 17. The figure of four thousand workers and the status of the work to Dutch Flat are from the *Placer Herald*, September 30. E.B. Crocker wrote that the grade was nearly finished to Dutch Flat in a letter dated January 9, 1866.

90. LONG RAVINE BRIDGE FROM BELOW. The Long Ravine structure was completed between a report in the *Union*, March 21, 1866, and another in the *Placer Herald*, April 14. A company annual report (1873, 49) stated that the Long Ravine bridge was covered with corrugated galvanized iron.

Bridge inspection reports make the iron viaduct at Long Ravine 439 feet long. The company's 1899 bridge index states that it was built in 1889 and "remodeled" in 1897; the bridge inspection reports carry 1897 as the construction date and provide the 1914 date for the second structure. The completion dates of various segments of I-80 used in this work come from Duncan.

The artistic considerations of Hart's works are discussed by Willumson, who is preparing a new work, expected in 2013, on the stereo railroad photographs.

92. ROUNDING CAPE HORN. The original line at Cape Horn was composed of four distinct curves. The modern eastbound track on the original grade turns through almost 207° in a single compound curve.

94. CANYON OF THE NORTH FORK OF THE AMERICAN RIVER. The story of the drunk's ride is found in the *Union*, November 13, 1866, copied from the *Grass Valley National* of November 10.

96. EXCURSION TRAIN AT CAPE HORN. The track was laid five miles beyond Colfax by April 21, 1866, when the *Bee* reported the first excursion to Cape Horn. Excursions of July 21 and September 16 were pulled by Danforth 2-6-0s, such as the one in this photograph.

One of the enduring legends of Cape Horn is that workmen were suspended over the bluff in baskets. The primary objection to this is that the original slope would not permit a basket to do anything but drag on the ground. Baskets aside, surveyors and perhaps even drillers *may* have used ropes to provide some semblance of security, probably with bosun's chairs. We do know, for instance, that surveyors were let over bluffs on ropes in the section east of Donner Summit. And, men were indeed suspended by ropes tied to overhanging trees to prepare the foundation for the iron bridge built at Cape Horn (*Sacramento Record-Union* January 29, 1885). In those cases, we have contemporary accounts; something that is lacking entirely for the initial construction at Cape Horn. The iron bridge built at Cape Horn in 1885 spanned a section of roadbed that fell away. It was located near the position of the train in this view.

98. SAWMILL AND CUT EAST OF CAPE HORN. CP annual reports through 1886 give figures which average 28.44 miles per cord of wood. Jones, "Days when hand brake setting was an art," 230, said it took seven cords to fill a tender, and that an eastbound freight train between Rocklin and Truckee would stop five or six times, taking from three to five cords at each stop. That works out to anywhere from 15 to 30 cords for the uphill trip plus the full load at the start.

A transient working as a wood passer was killed in 1868 in the explosion of *Yuba* (see page 214). Another, shoveling coal, was killed in a collision near Verdi in 1904 (*Reno Evening Gazette*, September 13, 1904). For a time, the CP hired wood passers, but in 1883 head-end brakemen were assigned to that task (*Union* December 7, 1883).

100. SECRET RAVINE. See Huffman's "Unanswered Questions About the *T. D. Judah.*" The *Huntington* is at the California State Railroad Museum, Sacramento (as is the *Gov. Stanford*). Stanford's store was in "Michigan Bluff." The name had been changed to "Michigan City" by the time the CP was built.

102. SECRET TOWN. The *Union* of May 9, 1866 commented on the lack of a freight depot. The *Dutch Flat Enquirer* of May 12 reported the turntable. The source of the rail from Colfax to Secret Town was reported in the *Union*, January 12, 1866, and the *Placer Herald* the following day. By the summer of 1868, when the CP principals were trying to figure out how much rail was still on hand, they seem to have forgotten where this rail came from.

104. SECRET TOWN TRESTLE. The *Placer Herald*, June 23, 1866, reported the completion of the Secret Town trestle. The *Union's* report of June 14, 1876 that the trestle was being filled in was confirmed by that year's annual report. All sources agree that the Secret Town structure had seven 40-foot straining-beam trusses, but the stated length of the trestlework varies from source

to source. Williamson (January 1869) reported that it was 660 feet long, while Montague's table gives 688 feet, making an overall length of 968 feet. This last number is close to the one thousand-foot overall length Montague reported in 1865, but quite different from the 1,100 feet ascribed in 1877 when he reported the structure filled in. In 1865 Montague said it was 90 feet high. The report of the commissioners for this section recorded 44 trestle bents, but 47 bents can be counted on the west end alone in other Hart images (not included in this work).

106. TUNNEL HILL. Montague (1865, 6) indicated that a small line change was made in addition to making an excavation rather than a tunnel. Hopkins (May 5, 1866) and E.B. Crocker (June 14, 1866) described the frustrations at Tunnel Hill and Dixie Cut and the nature of the local soil. The *Dutch Flat Enquirer* of March 3, 1866 reported that water was being used to sluice the cut.

108. BEAR RIVER VALLEY. The term "Dutch Flat Divide" is found in the *Nevada City Morning Transcript* of October 4, 1860 in a discussion of Judah's planned exploration of "Truckee Pass."

110. TRAIN IN DIXIE CUT. The *Bee* of August 8 and 12, 1865 describe the work at Dixie Cut. The excavation was reported nearly completed by the *Placer Herald* of June 23, 1866. The problems

with the cut were reported by E.B. Crocker on June 14 and December 22, 1866, and in the *Union* on November 22, 1866. Reports of the explosion appear in the *Bee* (April 18, 1866), *Dutch Flat Enquirer* (April 21, 1866), and *Placer Herald* (April 24, 1866).

112. GOLD RUN. Hopkins's complaint about Bradley and the "water sharks" was expressed in letters of February 10, 21, and 24, 1866. The story of the stagecoach being stuck in the street in Gold Hill is from Strobridge (USPRC, 2580).

114. DUTCH FLAT STATION. The two primary sources of information about Strong and Judah's visit to Donner Pass are Strong's testimony to the USPRC, especially page 2839, and Judah's notebook. E.B. Crocker reported the date of the railroad's arrival at Dutch Flat Station in a postscript to his July 9, 1866 letter.

116. SANDSTONE CUT NEAR ALTA. The powder car is described in the *Union* (August 3, 1865) and *Bee* (August 28, 1865). Powder consumption was reported in a *Scientific American* article reprinted by the *Bee*, January 4, 1867. The quote is from E.B. Crocker, August 13, 1867.

120. ALTA. In reporting the first train to Alta, the *Bee* of July 10, 1866 stated that only the railroad at Santiago, Chile was higher. Though the 8.5 mile Mt. Cenis

Tunnel, between France and Italy, was being built in 1866, that 4,000-foot high railroad did not open until 1871.

Huntington's comment to E.B. Crocker that "the *Alta* seems as mean as ever" (November 26, 1867) tends to discredit the *Nevada City Gazette's* claim (as repeated in the July 17, 1866 *Folsom Telegraph*) that Alta was named to flatter the San Francisco newspaper. Marcus Boruck, publisher of the *Spirit of the Age*, stated years later that his paper was the only one in San Francisco which was friendly to the CP (USPRC, 3421 and 3423).

A long article in the *Union* of July 25, 1866 describes the decline in business on the Placerville route to Virginia City. The relocation of the Alta turntable and snow plow house was reported in the *Annual Report of the Commissioner of Railroads* (1892, 83).

122. CUT ABOVE ALTA. The number of ties per mile was recorded in the various reports of the commissioners who examined completed sections of the railroad.

124. BLASTING AT CHALK BLUFFS ABOVE ALTA. The *Bee* of April 10, 1866 reported the activity on the grade between Dutch Flat and Emigrant Gap. The *Union*, September 21, 1866, reported that rail had been laid four miles above Alta. The use of a monitor to remove material here was reported in the *Union*, April 24, 1880.

126. CULVERT AT CANYON CREEK. Overall dimensions of this structure are from the *Union* January 25, 1867. The inside dimensions are from Hart's stereo card caption.

130. HOG'S BACK CUT. The change in the railroad's line between Dutch Flat and Emigrant Gap from the north to the south side of the divide was discussed at some length in Montague's report of December, 1865. An incline of 116 feet to the mile is equivalent to 2.2%.

132. AMERICAN RIVER FROM GREEN BLUFFS. Giant Gap was originally named "Jehovah Gap." Deemed offensive, the name was changed (*Gold Hill Daily News*, August 26, 1867). The dates of the establishment of Gorge and subsequent name changes, as well as dates for other station name events, are from various CP and SP *List[s] of Officers, Agencies and Stations.*

136. VIEW WEST OF PROSPECT HILL. The introduction of "fish rail" is documented in the reports of the commissioners, and mentioned in E.B. Crocker letters of June 14, 1866 and February 12, 1867. The rate of track laying is derived from various newspaper reports of commencement and completion of particular sections of track. Shady Run's origin as a construction camp is documented in Williams, 233, as is the fact that it was named by construction engineer Guppy.

138. PROSPECT HILL. Montague's 1865 report discussed the adoption of the steeper grade to overcome the obstacles at Prospect Hill and Blue Canyon. The use of water to flush this cut is described in the *Alta California* of July 15, 1866. Lewis M. Clement's account of the work appears in USPRC, 3209.

140. PROSPECT HILL CUT. The number of workers comes from Strobridge (USPRC, 3139).

142. PROSPECT HILL CUT FROM EAST. The arrival of 20 dump cars on the *Ne Plus Ultra* from New York was reported in the *Union*, November 15, 1865. A description of Bradley's water ditch, including the tunnel at Prospect Hill, is found in Williams, 235.

144. CHINA RANCH. Coleman is the source of PG&E history.

146. FORT POINT CUT. Much about the early waterworks of Placer County was researched and posted to the internet by Russell Towle, particularly his "North Fork of the American River" blog. He recounted the origin of Fort Point. See also *Placer Herald*, May 9, 1857, and *Union*, July 6, 1857 and October 15, 1859.

148. VIEW NORTH OF FORT POINT CUT. For more on flumes and ditches, see Bowie, particularly pages 139-41, and 143.

150. HORSE RAVINE WALL AND GRIZZLY HILL TUN-NEL. The report that stone walls were as much as one hundred feet high is from "Summit of the Sierras," 797.

152. WEST PORTAL TUNNEL NO. 1 and 72. GRIZZLY HILL TUNNEL FROM THE NORTH. Dates and data on the tunnel come from Montague's 1869 engineering report and Gilliss.

154. GRIZZLY HILL TUNNEL. The *Union* of December 2, 1867 identifies Ayres, Herrick, and Madden. A.D. Patterson identified Hussey in Willis, 309. And Hopkins identified McWade in a letter of December 8, 1867.

156. LOOKING EAST ACROSS BLUE CANYON. The most accessible evidence for the color of CP passenger cars is an oil painting by Joseph Becker owned by the Gilcrease Museum, Tulsa, Oklahoma. E.B. Crocker wrote on June 14, 1866 of the experiments on wood strength. The May 2 1868 *Bee* described the CP flat cars as brown.

158. BLUE CANYON EMBANKMENT. The embankment dimensions are from the *Union*, December 9, 1867. Engineers describe curves in terms of degrees of deflection between adjacent centerline chords rather than in terms of radii. While the exact equivalents between degree and radius vary with length of chord adopted, generally a 10° curve has

a radius of 573 feet, an 8° curve has a radius of 717 feet, and a 3° curve has a radius of 1910 feet. The limits to grade and curves were set by Section 12 of the Pacific Railway Act of July 1, 1862, which adopted the standards developed on the Baltimore & Ohio Railroad. Thus the CP legally could have made curves as tight as 14.25° (400-foot radius). While the Pacific Railroad Act never gave the specifics of the Baltimore & Ohio's grades and curves, they can be found in Darby, 452. The CP's reduction of gradient on curves is described in Vose, 53-54.

CP track profiles predating the Harriman-era rebuilding show transition easements as modifications of original circular curves, though without indicating when those modifications were made. Heuer recorded gaps between curves 546 and 547 and the intervening tangent which appear to represent transition easements. This is the only hint of transitions in his field notebooks of 1876, which record the locations of the beginnings and ends of most curves between Sacramento and Battle Mountain.

160. BLUE CANYON. The *Bee*, October 12, 1866, reported that rails were across Blue Canyon. The dates for the completion of double-tracking for various sections come from company records maintained by Lynn Farrar. The Blue Cañon fire was reported in the San Francisco *Call*, March 18, 1900. For curves nos. 235 and 238,

data are from the right of way and track map.

162. LOOKING WEST ACROSS BLUE CANYON. Both versions of the naming of Blue Canyon are presented by Gudde. The fact that the name predates the first known sawmill by at least two years suggests that Jim Blue had more to do with it than the smoke. The changes made to the snowsheds here are recorded in CP annual reports.

164. LOST CAMP SPUR. The change in rate of ascent was reported by Montague (1865, 8). The account of Towle brothers establishing a sawmill here in 1859 comes from Towel's posting to the Internet, while Lost Camp is described in the November 13, 1862 *Dutch Flat Enquirer*.

166. BANK AND CUT AT SAILOR RAVINE. Rails were 82 miles from Sacramento according to the *Placer Herald*, October 20, 1866. The balloon track replaced the turntable between the July publications of the 1952 and 1953 *List[s] of Officers, Agencies and Stations*, which record turning facilities system wide.

168. OWL GAP CUT. The story of B.R. Crocker is from his obituary in the December 12, 1900 *Bee*. By their paternal lines, B.R. and Charles were sixth cousins, though there may have been a closer maternal connection.

170 and 172. EMIGRANT GAP RIDGE. Judah and Strong's breakfast at Wilson's ranch is noted in Judah's journal. The name and post office changes are from Durham, 482. The *Union* of November 5, 1866 records the extension of the railroad to this point. Information on road development is from Duncan. That Judah recognized that the long divide between the American and Bear rivers would prove useful for a railroad—specifically because it was not cut by any canyons—is revealed in his interview with the editor of the *Nevada City Morning Transcript*, October 4, 1860—before Judah visited Dutch Flat. This is an important clue in revealing the evolution of Judah's understanding of Sierra topography. Just weeks before, Judah had explored routes via Georgetown Divide and Henness Pass, both of which were unsuitable because of deep canyons. Had he initially understood the importance of the continuous ridge, he likely would not have bothered with either of those other routes.

174. EMIGRANT GAP TUNNEL. The completion of tunnel no. 2 was reported in the *Union*, September 21, 1866.

176. EMIGRANT GAP TUNNEL, WALL AND SNOW COVERING. Judah's snowfall estimates are in his report of October 1861. Montague anticipated snowsheds in his 1865 report, E.B. Crocker warned Huntington as early as January 31, 1867 that they

had to be built, and the *Union* made the matter public on May 14, 1867.

178 and 180. BEAR VALLEY and LOOKING EAST FROM EMIGRANT GAP. The technical details of Hart's photography are described in Kibbey, 79-109.

182. CEMENT RIDGE. The "lava cement" at this location was described by the *Mining & Scientific Press*, August 3, 1867. The date for the establishment of the Birce & Smart spur comes from the *List of Officers, Agencies and Stations*. The date for the application of air brakes to freight equipment is from the annual report of 1883. CP passengers cars were equipped with air brakes in 1872 (*Annual Report*).

184. VALLEY OF THE SOUTH FORK OF THE YUBA RIVER. The lack of a conventional back wall to the cab may be a McKay feature; there appears to be no back wall on the locomotive on page 376, and that certainly is a McKay. Information on the wreck in which Law died is found in the *Reno Evening Gazette*, October 20, 1904, and the *San Francisco Call* of the following day.

186. MILLER'S BLUFF. While Hart identified this as Miller's Bluff, the establishment of its location, as well as that of adjacent Hopkins' Bluff, comes from Williams, 233.

188. ECHO POINT. The *Bee* of May 23, 1866 reported consideration of Henness Pass. *Placer Herald* August 4, 1866 reported Chinese walking off the job.

190. ECHO POINT AND RATTLESNAKE MOUNTAIN. The *Reno Evening Gazette* (September 1) and *Nevada State Journal* (August 25 and November 16) disclose that the lookout was established in the late summer of 1877. The *Commissioner of Railroads* annual report (1882-3, 92) noted the establishment of the telephone connection between the Red Mountain lookout and Cisco. A dedicated telegraph-alarm system within the sheds had been installed in 1874 (*Gold Hill News*—from *Truckee Republican*—August 7, 1874, and CP annual report [1874, 46].) Signor (*Donner Pass*, 107) stated the lookout was abandoned in 1934.

Towne reported (*Railway Mail Transportation*, 67) that cars without brakes on both trucks were not permitted. *Railway Age* (October 11, 1877) speaks of the inspection of foreign cars at Ogden.

192. THE RAILROAD BETWEEN CISCO AND CRYSTAL LAKE. The report that graders were working all the way to Heaton's (Cisco) comes from the *Bee*, May 23, 1866. The *Bee* of January 4, 1867 remarked on the consumption of steel.

194. FOOT OF BLACK BUTTE. As with other trestles,

sources do not agree on dimensions; these figures come from the commissioners' report for this section of railroad. Dates and the account of the washout come from the unpublished reminiscence of A.P. Partridge. The four-span Howe-truss deck bridge which replaced the trestle is reported by Williamson in January 1869 and Montague that same year.

196. SNOW COVERING BELOW CISCO. Initially snowsheds were contemplated only for the six miles nearest the summit (E.B. Crocker, January 31, 1867 and Hopkins, May 14, 1868). Apparently the severity of the winter of 1866-67 impressed the need for greater coverage. Montague's report of July 1869 records that 4.75 miles of shed were built the first year between Lost Camp Spur and Cisco. By October 1868, 25 miles of snowsheds had been built (E.B. Crocker, October 26, 1868).

198. FRAME OF SNOW COVERING. The *Nevada State Journal* of July 20, 1877 records the passenger's death by asphyxiation.

200. LOWER CISCO. Montage's report of 1869 states that the railroad was opened to Cisco on November 24, 1866; however, the *Union* of November 28 indicates that the opening of the line would not take place until the following day. The naming of Cisco was reported in the *Bee*, June 25, 1866.

There are few CP employment records for the period of the railroad's construction, and nearly all figures ever cited come from newspaper reports. The *Bee* of 23 May 1866 reported 9,000 to 11,000 Chinese working on the grade between Secret Town and Cisco. This figure corresponds closely with what Strobridge told the USPRC 20 years later. On that occasion, after a night to look up the answer to the question, he stated that 11,000 Chinese and from 2,500 to 3,000 whites were employed in 1866 (USPRC, 3140). While this sounds like independent corroboration, it is possible that Strobridge merely looked at old newspaper clippings in a scrapbook. As noted on page 386, there is reason to believe that the numbers reported in newspapers were inflated.

202. CISCO. The *Union* May 23, 1867 and *Mining & Scientific Press*, August 10, 1867, describe Cisco and provide dimensions of the freight house. The fires were reported in the *Union*, July 1, and the *Truckee Tribune*, June 30 and November 3. The woodshed was apparently consumed in the first fire, since it is omitted from the September 1869 inventory of structures.

204 and 206. WINTER VIEW IN UPPER CISCO. C. Crocker's letter of April 25, 1867 said the snow on April 15 was deeper than any time the preceding winter. E.B. Crocker referred to these photographs from Cisco in a letter on May 3, 1867, saying they "shall not of course have any printed but

thought it safe to send you specimen copies." The collapse of the roundhouse roof was reported in the *Bee* and *Union* of March 5, 1868 and the *Daily Alta California* of the following day.

208. BUCKER SNOWPLOW. The construction of the snow plows was reported in the *Bee* on September 22 and December 3, 1866 and in the *Union* on October 24. E.B. Crocker mentioned the plows in a letter of January 31, 1867, and he referred to photographs taken of the plow at Cisco in his letter of May 3, 1867.

Crofutt (26) relays that a bucker snowplow was "once propelled by ten locomotives, at a rate of 60 miles an hour, into a snow drift on the Sierra Nevada Mountains, resulting—in a big hole in the snow." Montague reported the use of up to 12 locomotives behind a bucker snowplow in his 1869 report.

210 and 212. LOCOMOTIVES BEHIND SNOWPLOW. The problem of "throwing fire" was discussed by Jones, "Days when hand brake setting was an art," 23. Reports of the train stranded at Cisco can be found in the *Alta*, February 17 and 18, 1887.

214. LOCOMOTIVE NO. 25, *Yuba*. News relating to the *Yuba*'s explosion appears in the *Bee* of October 9, 1868, and the *Union* of October 10 and 12.

216. ALL ABOARD FOR VIRGINIA CITY. The *Mining & Scientific Press* of August 3, 1867 remarked on the number of stagecoaches meeting the trains at Cisco, while the *Virginia Daily Trespass* of May 16, 1868 reported the opening of service to Summit Valley. E.B. Crocker wrote of the change in mail service east of Cisco in his letter of September 3, 1868.

218. FREIGHT WAGONS AT CISCO. The three relevant Pacific railway laws are those of July 1, 1862 section 10, July 2, 1864 section 16, and July 3, 1866 section 2. The statement that 58 carloads were shipped each day from Cisco comes from an E.B. Crocker letter of July 23, 1867.

The transport of locomotives, rolling stock, and rail via team from Cisco to Truckee was reported in various newspapers, such as the *Virginia Daily Trespass* of July 19, 1867, and a number of letters, such as E.B. Crocker's of February 11, 1868 and Hopkins's of April 23 and May 20, 1868. See also the testimony of William Hood, Strobridge, and C. Crocker in USPRC, 2579, 2580, 3150, and 3646.

222. LOCOMOTIVE NO. 14, *Oneonta*. E.B. Crocker's letter of June 28, 1867 states that the rail being sent east of Cisco was connected with splice bars.

224. VIEW ABOVE CISCO. The *Union*, July 1, 1867, reported the

strike, and E.B. Crocker wrote of it on June 28 and July 6 and 10. C. Crocker stated his belief that the strike was incited by emissaries from the "other side" in his testimony recorded in the *Report of the Joint Special Committee to Investigate Chinese Emigration*, 669.

226. TUNNEL NO.3 Tunnel data are from Gilliss and Montague. C. Crocker wrote on October 30, 1867 that the grade was completed to tunnel no. 12 and that rail laying had resumed.

228. LOWER CASCADE BRIDGE. Bridge dimensions are from Montague's 1869 table of bridges. The account of construction comes from Partridge.

230. CONSTRUCTING SNOW COVERING. The primary source for information on building snowsheds comes from Arthur Brown (USPRC, 2581-82 and 3602-05). The *Mining & Scientific Press* of August 10, 1867 gives the inside dimensions of single-track sheds as 14 feet wide by 20 high. Brakeman Samuel P. Milligan was knocked from the roof of a Chicago & Milwaukee furniture car by a shed beam (*Bee*, September 21, and December 8, 1886). The wreck was reported in the February 17, 1887 *Alta California*.

232. FRAME OF SNOW COVERING. The account of walking through the sheds is from Stevens.

234. SUMMIT STATION. "Scream a locomotive whistle" is from Hopkins letter to Huntington February 21, 1866. E.B. Crocker wrote of the summit ceremony on December 5. An account appears in the *Union* of December 2. The *Virginia Daily Trespass* of May 15, 1868 reported the return of trains to Summit the following spring.

236. SUMMIT TUNNEL, EASTERN PORTAL. The *Placer Herald* of October 14, 1865 and the *Union* of October 21 reported the commencement of work on Summit Tunnel in the fall of 1865. Gilliss provided the dates for the resumption of work the following fall.

238. SHAFT HOUSE OVER SUMMIT TUNNEL. Gilliss (161-2) provided data relating to the shaft and its operation. Wilder told the story of hauling the *Sacramento* to the summit; see also Joslyn. Hopkins (February 7 and 15, 1867), E.B. Crocker (April 23, 1867), and the *Bee* (June 14, 1867) discussed air-drills.

240. INTERIOR OF SUMMIT TUNNEL. Gilliss (161-3) described details of Summit Tunnel. John R. Gilliss was the son of James Melville Gilliss, founder of the U.S. Naval Observatory. *The Illustrated Photographer*, May 29, 1868, 202 reported how the tunnel was illuminated for the photograph. Our website (www.waitingforthecars.com) features a

virtual-reality tour of the Summit Tunnel and shaft.

242. LABORERS AND ROCKS. E.B. Crocker (on January 7 and 14, and February 15, 1867), Hopkins (on February 7, 1867), and *Mining & Scientific Press* (August 10, 1867) described the work at tunnel no. 6. Hopkins enumerated the composition of the tunnel forces.

244. EAST PORTAL SUMMIT TUNNEL. The description of using nitroglycerin in the Summit tunnel is from Gilliss, the *Mining & Scientific Press* of August 10, 1867, and the 1873 *Report of the California Board of Health* (143-145). E.B. Crocker remarked that the electrical detonators were too delicate for the Irish foremen (August 15, 1867).

246. EAST PORTAL OF SUMMIT TUNNEL. The stagecoach's narrow escape is reported in the Grass Valley *Union* as reprinted in the *Alta* November 16, 1867. The *Union* of November 30, 1867 reported that rails had reached the summit the previous evening and implies that the track was to be extended through the tunnel during that night. Dates for tunnel no. 27, and for abandonment of tunnel no. 6 are from Lynn Farrar.

248. VIEW FROM NEAR SUMMIT TUNNEL. The means of removing material from the tunnels was described by E.B. Crocker in his letter to Hun-

tington of February 17, 1867. A "Stone boat" (the term used by Crocker) is a low sled for moving heavy objects.

250 and 252. SCENE NEAR SUMMIT TUNNEL. The evolution of the roads at Donner Pass is presented in Duncan.

254. DUTCH FLAT AND DONNER LAKE WAGON ROAD. Judah's terms for the lake and pass are found in his reports. Stanford, Huntington, and C. Crocker themselves may have coined "Donner Lake" as a way to distinguish their Dutch Flat & Donner Lake Wagon Road from its antecedent, the Lake Pass Wagon Road. The Lake Pass road was organized in March 1861, the DF&DL in the fall of 1861.

256. DONNER LAKE, TUNNELS 7 AND 8. Eliza Houghton's story is found in the *Alta* of June 27, 1868 and the Reno *Weekly Gazette Stockman* of May 21, 1896. The *Alta* is very specific that Houghton rode the first train from Reno to Sacramento, leaving us to wonder how and when she got to Reno. Houghton, whose husband was a congressman, is credited with maintaining contact with various Donner survivors and preserving accounts of the tragedy.

258. HEADING OF EAST PORTAL TUNNEL 8. Montague's appreciation of this tunnel portal is expressed in his 1869 report. The description of the snow

tunnels comes from Gilliss (158-9) as well as from E.B. Crocker's letter of January 31, 1867. Harris (245), a member of the railroad's engineer corps, described the workers' clothes and lodgings. Some account of the eating-drinking habits of the Chinese can be found in Spier.

260. CONSTRUCTING SNOW COVER. Brown is identified by Kibbey, p. 36. Statistics on snowsheds come from Brown (USPRC, 2581-2 and 3602-5), and Montague's 1869 report.

262. SNOW GALLERY AROUND CRESTED PEAK. The story of the circus train wreck is from the *Reno Evening Gazette*, May 2, 1904, *Nevada State Journal*, and *San Francisco Call* of May 3.

264. CONSTRUCTING SNOW COVER. Harris (248) described survey-crew members being lowered over the cliff on ropes. E.B. Crocker described blasting in his letter of August 10, 1867.

268. INSIDE VIEW OF SNOW GALLERY AT SUMMIT. CP annual reports provide information as follows: iron sheathing (1873, 49), telegraph-alarm system (1874, 46), and periodic sprinkling (1875, 22). Frederick mentions the telescopic sections.

270. VIEW WEST FROM TUNNEL 9. The *Virginia Trespass*, April 9, 1868, described the wall. The name "Snow Slide Ra-

vine" appears on Gilliss's profile, included in his report (157-8). Strobridge (USPRC, 2580, 3150), the *Bee* (December 27, 1866, February 28, March 4 and 11, 1867), and the *Union* (March 11, 1867) all mention man-killing avalanches. The excursion train was reported by the *Bee*, December 7 and 8, *Union*, December 9 (the source of the quote), and *Virginia City Trespass*, December 9.

272. LOOKING WEST FROM TUNNEL NO. 10. Gilliss and the newspaper accounts make clear that the avalanche that killed 15-20 Chinese near tunnel no. 10 was different than the one discussed on the previous page. It may be the one reported by the *Bee* of March 4, 1867 as having crushed a house on the night of February 22. Initially it was reported that 30 died.

274. CRESTED PEAK AND TUNNEL 10. The unidentified author of "Summit of the Sierras," 816, described walking through all of the tunnels in early November 1867 when 100 feet of the "core" remained in tunnel no. 11. As he used the term, the core was the mass that remained below the heading and between the side excavations in which the shoring was erected. It invited comment as he had to squeeze through that narrow space. It is possible other tunnels he walked through were only completed in the headings. Schallenberger's story is recounted in Stewart, 8-14. "Donner's Back-

bone" is found in Harris (249).

276. TUNNEL NO. 12. E.B. Crocker letters of December 11 and 21, 1867 describe the storm which closed the mountain work and the effort to move the men down to the Truckee. The unfinished gap extended from the east end of tunnel no. 12 to a point .5 mile above the crossing of Coldstream. The *Virginia Trespass* of April 27, 1868 and the *Territorial Enterprise* of June 14 reported on the work clearing the grade of ice and snow in the spring of 1868. The *Alta* of June 17 and *Territorial Enterprise* of June 18, 1868 tell of the closing of that gap. David J. Sullivan was probably the tracklayer C. Crocker said had just arrived from the UP and showed the CP how Casement built track fast (March 29, 1868). Sullivan's involvement at tunnel no. 12 and Promontory is from his obituary in the *Reno Evening Gazette*, January 28, 1918, as well as the *Nevada State Journal*, September 14, 1941 (though the "gap" is confused with Emigrant Gap).

278. COLDSTREAM VALLEY. A gradient of 76.5 feet to the mile is equivalent to 1.44%. A.P. Stanford was operating the Coldstream sawmill in 1868, during which year he shipped 6 million feet of lumber (*Nevada State Journal*, January 20, 1878.) The business was insolvent the following year ("Lawrence v. Neff" *Reports of Cases determined in the Supreme Court of the State of California* 1906, 566). Curve and

grade data for this location are from company track charts, profiles, and the right of way and track map.

280. SCENE AT TRUCKEE. A report of the naming of Truckee appeared in the *Bee*, August 3, 1867, though for some reason the name came as a surprise to the *Union* the following spring (April 11, 1868). The descriptive quotes come from Harris, 248, and Williams, 225.

282. DEPOT AT TRUCKEE. E.B. Crocker's letters of July 15 and 23, 1867 speak of the locomotive being shipped to Truckee. George Schaffer is identified as the man who brought the first locomotive across the summit by Knowles, 16 (citing W.F. Edwards *Tourist' Guide and Directory of the Truckee Basin*, 13-14). The *Virginia Trespass* July 19, 1867 reported the locomotive being set up, while the *Union* of August 30 said it was then in running order.

The *San Mateo* was carried to Truckee in pieces in wagons in the summer of 1867. William Hood and Strobridge (USPRC, 2579 and 2580) stated that three locomotives were taken across on sleds along with rail for 40 miles of track. In as much as over 60 miles of railroad was built along the Truckee before the connection was made across the summit, the 40 miles of rail referred to by Hood and Strobridge must be in addition to the rail hauled across on wagons in the summer of 1867. The implication is that the three locomotives they mention are also in addition to the *San Mateo*, hauled across on wagons in 1867.

284. TRUCKEE RIVER BELOW TRUCKEE STATION. E.B. Crocker sent Huntington copies of the "views just taken" along the Truckee with his letter of November 24, 1867. The eastern-most in this sequence of Hart photographs is at tunnel no. 14, suggesting that Hart made his Truckee visit before the track was laid all the way to the state line, which was accomplished about the end of October. The story of the baby born on the train appeared in the *Alta* of August 8, 1887 and the *Weekly Nevada State Journal* of August 20. While the mother called for the doctor while the train was just east of Truckee, the child was born near Clipper Gap.

286. FIRST LOCOMOTIVE IN NEVADA. The first locomotive taken across the mountains and erected at Truckee was identified as the *San Mateo* in the *Union* of July 13, 1867. Reilly was identified by the *Virginia Trespass*, April 17, 1868; Abboy was identified in his obituary in the *San Francisco Call*, December 29, 1910.

288. BOCA. The story of Doan's activity at Boca is found in Winfield Davis, 345, and *History of San Joaquin County*, 1391. Sources for information on Boca Beer include Richards, and the *Nevada State Journal*, September 4, 1875 and January 13, 1893. The

bridge at Boca and the four-span Howe-truss crossing at Donner Creek were the last of the original wooden CP bridges still in service as of 1899, though in both cases supplementary bents had been installed to shorten the spans and increase the bridges' carrying capacity (1899 bridge index).

290. PROFILE ROCK. With Profile Rock itself long gone, the only clues to its location are found in this image. The determination that it was west of the first crossing of the Truckee is based on the direction of the sun in the photograph, a close study of right-of-way and track maps, and comparison with present-day background terrain. It is believed it to have been in curve no. 425.

292. FIRST CROSSING OF THE TRUCKEE RIVER. Station name changes are from company *List[s] of Officers, Agencies and Stations*. The wagon road-highway history is from Duncan. While engineers considered using rubble-filled cribs for piers for the Truckee River bridges for the sake of expediency (E.B. Crocker, January 31, 1867), this photograph and commissioner reports make clear that masonry piers were built.

294. BRIDGE AT FIRST CROSSING TRUCKEE RIVER. Partridge mentions hewing and whipsawing timbers, though that referred specifically to the Cascade bridges. C. Crocker reported to Huntington (April 25,

1867) that timbers for the Truckee bridges were being prepared. Hopkins ordered iron parts for the Truckee bridges in his letter to Huntington of January 21, 1867. The *Bee* of August 3, 1867 reported five hundred carpenters working on bridges, cars, etc. east of the summit.

296. VIEW NEAR STATE LINE. Information on the Fleishhackers and the development of hydroelectric power on the Truckee River can be found in McGlashan, 19-20; Finlay, 445-456; and the report of the *Truckee-Carson-Lake Tahoe Project*, 57-58. The two McCauley sources tell of Floriston, while the SP-owned *Sunset* of August 1900, 201, mentions the water-powered Floriston paper mill.

298. TUNNEL 15. The story of the train quarantined at Mystic is from the California State Board of Health (1882), 55-57, and the *Reno Evening Gazette* of January 10, 11, and 18, 1882. The *Reno Evening Gazette* of March 10, 1882 reported the car quarantined at Boca.

300. TUNNEL 15. The account of the state line comes from the works of Hulse and Uzes. Surveyor James F. Houghton was distantly related to Eliza Donner's husband Sherman Otis Houghton.

302. SECOND CROSSING OF THE TRUCKEE RIVER. A broader discussion of the

construction of the isolated railroad along the Truckee and the entrance of the CP into Nevada can be found in Huffman's, "Iron Horses along the Truckee." The *Union* of December 22, 1866 reported grading westward from Camp 24. E.B. Crocker wrote on October 29, 1867 that the railroad from Truckee to the 138th mile would be completed in two days, suggesting that the railroad entered Nevada on the anniversary of Nevada's admission day.

The December commencement of commercial traffic on the railroad between Truckee and Camp 24 is documented in the *Territorial Enterprise* and *Gold Hill News* of December 6, 1867, and in an E.B. Crocker letter of December 11. On the other hand, the reports of stagecoaches meeting trains at Camp 24 in the *Virginia Trespass* of March 27, 1868 and the *Territorial Enterprise* of March 31 and April 2 suggest that the initial activity was not sustained. The *Territorial Enterprise* of March 31, 1868 place Monk on the Camp 24 run. A report in the *Union*, June 3, 1868, suggests that a passenger coach was then in operation east of Truckee—before the railroad had been connected with Sacramento.

304. SECOND CROSSING OF THE TRUCKEE RIVER. Hopkins wrote on April 23, 1868 that the grade was nearly finished to Wadsworth before the crews were returned to Truckee to complete the gap below tunnel no. 12. He wrote on March 30, 1868 that track laying eastward from Camp 24 had commenced, though it was not reported in the in press until April 11, 1868 (*Territorial Enterprise*). The *Nevada State Journal*, April 24, 1891, reported the arrival of material for the new bridge, though actual construction was not reported by that same paper until December 9, 1892. The Commissioner of Railroads reported the iron replacement bridge (1891-92, 84.)

306. EAGLE GAP. The "Eagle Gap" name comes from Hart's card. "Rattlesnake Cliffs" was written on an early CP engineering profile. Sources on Truckee River power plants are identified in the note to page 296. Information on Truckee River log drives is from Wilson, 37-9, 72.

308. THIRD CROSSING OF THE TRUCKEE RIVER. Newspaper reports on the August 1, 1883 fire and replacement bridge are found in the *Reno Evening Gazette*, August 2 and 6, October 30, 1883 and February 19, 1884. It is also recorded in the report of the Commissioner of Railroads (1883-4, 86.) The statement that this was the first iron bridge on the CP is based on a comparison of bridge erection dates given in the 1899 bridge index. The 1913 bridge date comes from the 1986 bridge inspection report.

310. ESSEX. Sawmill information is from Wilson, 69-70, and from

the *Nevada State Journal*, June 26, 1875. Foulks's father-in-law was Robert Nixon, the first conductor on the Albany & Schenectady Railroad, March 1831 (*Nevada State Journal* October 17, 1878). The establishment of the coaling facility at Essex is from the *Reno Evening Gazette*, June 7, 1880, and May 3 and December 22, 1881. Marmol information is from *List[s] of Officers, Agencies and Stations*. The first mention found of the name "Verdi" is in a letter in the Huntington collection dated September 14, 1866. The letter is a handwritten copy, without note as to authorship or the original.

316. RENO AND WASHOE RANGE. The *Territorial Enterprise* issues of March 28 and May 10, 1868 reported on the selection of land at Lake's bridge and the sale of lots. Graham's activity was recounted in Heath "First & Last," 11. Glendale's flood is in Townley, 59. The arrival of track and telegraph is documented in the *Bee* of May 5, 1868 and Thompson & West's *History of Nevada*, 275. The first train from Sacramento to Reno was reported in the *Bee* of June 18 and the *Alta* of June 20. What Hart termed the "Washoe Range" today is called the Pah Rah Range north of the Truckee River, and the Virginia Range to the south. The evidence for a 60-passenger coach in use on the Truckee before the gap was closed is the *Union* of June 3, 1868.

318. RENO DEPOT. The history

of the naming of Reno is presented by Flaherty, though the association of that selection with the CP's effort to acquire Yerba Buena Island is original. The burning of the first Reno depot is reported in the *Reno Evening Gazette*, March 3, 1879. The second depot burned on May 26, 1889 and was replaced with a single-story brick structure, as reported in the *Annual Report of the Commissioner of Railroads* (1890, 194). The present depot was dedicated February 8, 1926. In a project completed in November 2005, the station was significantly modified to conform with the new level of the track, lowered to eliminate grade crossings in the downtown area.

320. FREIGHT DEPOTS AT RENO. Only one 30 foot by 130 foot freight house was included in a September 1869 inventory of CP structures at Reno. The other two in the photograph were apparently not owned by the CP. The Western Pacific Railroad that was consolidated with the CP in 1870 was in no way related to the company of the same name built across Nevada in the early 20th century.

322. TRUCKEE MEADOWS. The 1902 date for the construction of the new line is derived from the erection dates (from bridge inspection reports) of bridges in the lower Truckee canyon, as well as in Palisade Canyon.

324. SCENE NEAR CAMP 37. Huntington instructed his partners

to build cheap—to "push forward the track with all possible speed and let the paint and putty man come afterwards" (Huntington to E.B. Crocker, February 3, 1868). The critical comment on the construction of the CP east of the Sierra is from Williamson's May 1869 report (42).

326. ENTERING LOWER CANYON OF TRUCKEE RIVER. E.B. Crocker reported track laid to the upper end of the lower canyon in his letter of May 21, 1868. The *Territorial Enterprise* of May 22 announced that cars were operating to this point. The primary evidence for the amount of track laid on any particular date are annotations on a pre-Harriman track profile held by the Nevada State Historical Society and a sheet of figures dating from November 1868 preserved by Huntington. On August 31, C. Crocker bragged, "We have track laying reduced now to one of the exact sciences & can beat the world at it." The amount of rail needed to build a mile of track, and to fill a flat car, was stated in the *Bee* of August 27, 1868. Sources on the transport of rail via Panama are provided in the note to page 20.

328. CROSSING OF WAGON ROAD. A history of the roads through the lower canyon is given by Dodd. "Pioneer days in Sparks and vicinity," 292, identifies Abraham Savage as the builder of the toll road. He was a second cousin to Leonard Savage, of the Com-

stock's Savage Mine.

330. COTTONWOOD VAL-
LEY. Clark's Station was originally the location of the toll house on
the Savage road. Information about
the pioneer trail is from Dodd.

334. PLEASANT VALLEY. The
Carson Daily Appeal of June 13,
1868 reported that cars were running to Clark's, just two miles west
of the scene in this photograph.
On June 27, the *Territorial Enterprise* reported the end-of-track
two miles east of this point. Williamson reported on rail chair laid
here (May 1869, 50).

336. LOOKING WEST FROM
RED BLUFFS. The SP 1961
bridge inspection report provides the 1902 dates for the 11th
and 12th Truckee crossings, a
single *Reno Evening Gazette*
from August 4, 1959 documents
the relocation of the Truckee
for I-80, while a packet of dated
photographs from the camera of
Ronald H. Hancock provides the
date of the railroad's relocation of
the river.

338. RED BLUFFS, LOOK-
ING FROM THE WEST.
Sarah Winnemucca's account of
the naming of the river is found
on page 9 of her *Life Among the
Piutes*. The alternative story of the
naming by the Stevens party apparently comes from Moses Schallenberger, who was a member of
that party. It is recorded in the *San
Jose Mercury*, September 22, 1869.

340. TRUCKEE RIVER NEAR
WADSWORTH. E.B. Crocker
wrote on May 21, 1868 that the
grade was ready for track to the
Big Bend of Truckee.

342. FOURTH CROSSING
OF THE TRUCKEE, WAD-
SWORTH. The *Territorial Enterprise* of May 30, 1868 reported
the temporary bridge completed.
The permanent bridge was a single
Howe truss span of 204 feet with
supplemental arch. Its burning was
reported in the *Alta* of November
24, 1889. Two days later the *Alta*
reported that the temporary span
was completed. The permanent
iron Pratt-truss replacement
bridge had a span of 208 feet (CP
annual report, 1891, 92).

344. WADSWORTH. The nam-
ing of Wadsworth went hand-in-
hand with the naming of Reno,
and the history is told by Flaherty.
Construction of the shops apparently did not begin until 1869
(*Alta*, December 20, 1868). The
Centennial Spirit of the Times (July
4, 1876) reported 125 employees.
The facilities and commerce are
described in Williams, 200-2.

346. WADSWORTH. The large
tenders of the CP locomotives
running between Wadsworth and
Winnemucca were mentioned in
the *Daily Nevada State Journal* of
July 16, 1876, and in *The Monthly
Journal of the Brotherhood of Locomotive Engineers* (March 1877, 108).
No documentation has been
found dating the introduction of

Wyoming coal on the CP in Utah
and Nevada, but it was no doubt
very soon after the completion of
the railroad. Williams, 200, in 1876,
stated that coal was used east of
Wadsworth, with wood used to the
west. In 1880 the range of coal-
burning locomotives was extended
to Truckee with a coaling station
erected at Essex (*Reno Evening Gazette*, May 8 and June 7, 1880).
While Wharton and Lorenz
switches were installed on the railroad as early as 1879, stub switches
predominated as late as 1894 (*Annual Report[s] of the Commissioner
of Railroads*: 1879, 65; 1880, 73;
1893, 120).

348. THE *GOLIAH* AT WAD-
SWOTH. *Sampson* and *Goliah*
were invoiced in late January and
early February of 1867. They arrived in San Francisco in December 1867 and went into service
early the following year.

350. CONSTRUCTION TRAIN
ON THE ALKALI DESERT.
Details of the desert crossing are
in Curran, 144-54 and 177-84.
The tale of how Mirage got its
name is found in Strobridge, 6.
The *Bee* of July 17, 1868 reported
the double shifts.
According to *Sacramento Record-Union* of February 14, 1902,
the CP originally intended to
build on the longer route around
Hot Springs Mountains but followed the more direct route from
Wadsworth to Brown's because it
saved eight miles of track and they
had just lost a shipload of rail. In

fact, the company was desperately
short of rail in the spring and early
summer of 1868, and they did lose
rail with the burning of the *Hornet*. But, the *Hornet* carried to the
bottom rail for only three miles
when it burned, and that was in
July 1866. Furthermore, nothing
is found in the Huntington correspondence to substantiate the
Record-Union's allegation.

352. WATER TRAIN OPPO-
SITE HUMBOLDT LAKE.
E.B. Crocker wrote of well drillers on July 31, 1868. Accounts of
wells are in Williams, 199, and
*Annual Report of the Commissioner
of Railroads* (1884, 86). Construction of the water cars was mentioned in the *Bee* of June 18, 1868,
the *Alta* of June 19, 1868, and the
Union of August 21, 1868 and
February 17, 1869. E.B. Crocker
mentioned them in a letter dated
July 31, 1868.

354. WATER TRAIN OPPO-
SITE HUMBOLDT LAKE.
*Annual Report[s] of the Com-
missioner of Railroads* (as late as
1893, 120) comment on the long
service of the wooden ties at Hot
Springs. Notes pasted into an old
engineering profile record a long-
running experiment of tie longev-
ity conducted just west of Rose
Creek. Ties of 20 different species
of wood were laid beginning in
1876 and observed as late as 1890.

356. CHINESE CAMP,
BROWN'S STATION. A nota-
tion on the early CP profile places

the end-of-track immediately past Brown's on August 3, 1868.

358. BROWN'S STATION. Williams, 198, remarked on the poor water. The little information about Brown's, including the Paiute village, comes from Basso. Nixon's biography appears in Davis. W.J. Toy is identified in the *Engineers Monthly Journal*, February 1900, 134 as well as various *List[s] of Officers, Agencies and Stations*.

360. END-OF-TRACK ON HUMBOLDT PLAINS. The count of workers is from the *Bee*, August 27, 1868.

362. END-OF-TRACK ON HUMBOLDT PLAINS. Articles published in the *Bee*, August 13, 1868, and the *Alta*, September 21 and November 16, 1868, describe the means of track construction. The boy in the photograph was Samuel, born the son of Samuel Hooker Whitmarsh, the Pioneer Stage Company's agent in Auburn. Sam and his half-sister, Julia Conover, were adopted by Strobridge in 1865 after Whitmarsh's death. In 1884 Sam Strobridge married Idah Meacham, the daughter of George Washington Meacham, who immigrated to California with J.H. Strobridge in 1849, and whose homestead became the noted Humboldt House on the CP. It is possible that Sam and Idah first met three weeks after this photograph was made, when the railhead passed

the Meacham homestead. Idah Meacham Strobridge wrote *Sagebrush Trilogy*.

364 and 366. FIRST CROSSING OF THE HUMBOLDT RIVER. The 1869 inventory of structures is the source of information on the facilities here, while Montague and Williamson's reports fill in information on the bridge. Various *List[s] of Officers, Agencies and Stations* provide the sequence and dates of station names. Basso provided background.

368. WINNEMUCCA DEPOT. The name "Winnemucca" commemorates Poito, a prominent Paiute called "Old Winnemucca." Before that name was applied, the settlement was called "French Bridge" for a crossing of the Humboldt River dating back into the early 1850s (see Carlson). Williamson's May 1869 report (50) documents chair rail between Rose Creek and Tule.

370. ADVANCE OF CIVILIZATION. Credit for identifying this location goes to Lawrence K. Hersh. His book presents a modern photograph taken from the same site. The dating of the end-of-track at this location is from the CP profile; the photograph places Hart here on that date. Amos Bowsher's reminiscence was recorded in Heath's "Eye Witness Tells of 'Last Spike' Driving." An article in the February 4, 1869 *San Francisco Chronicle* (lifted from the *Santa Clara Union*) said that the

telegraph wire was connected to Strobridge's car every noon and night.

372. ADVANCE OF CIVILIZATION. Track laying was described in the *Bee*, August 13, 1868, and the *Alta*, September 21 and November 16, 1868. The *Alta* of September 21 states specifically that the "spikers follow behind the car," and track-laying manuals emphasize that splicing proceeded spiking. The two-wheeled cart on the left is distributing telegraph wire; the spool of wire is mounted horizontally, just as described in the *Alta* of November 16.

374. TRAIN AT ARGENTA. E.B. Crocker mentioned service to Argenta in his letter of November 2, 1868 to Huntington. The *Alta* of December 20, 1868 described stagecoaches meeting trains at this point. Williams, 186, states that hay was shipped from Argenta in later years.

376. SHOSHONE INDIANS LOOKING AT LOCOMOTIVE. C. Crocker expressed dissatisfaction with the McKay locomotives on December 1, 1868. On August 31, 1868, he wrote that crews were beginning to operate locomotives in shifts, confirmed in a letter of October 29. Both Hopkins and C. Crocker lamented the green wood on December 15, 1868.

378. CHINESE CAMP AT END-OF-TRACK. For more on

the development of the central route for a Pacific railroad, see Huffman's "How the Comstock determined the course of the Central Pacific Railroad." The route from the Truckee River to Wells, Nevada was surveyed by the CP during 1866 (*Bee*, May 11, 1867), but grading through Palisade Canyon did not begin until after the Crockers, Montague, and Strobridge visited the location in May 1868 (E.B. Crocker, May 21, 1868). See testimony of Hood, Stanford, and Strobridge (US-PRC, 2523, 2579, and 2580).

Beowawe is adjacent to Gravely Ford, where the pioneer trail crossed the Humboldt River. It is the location of the famous "Maiden's Grave" of Lucinda Duncan. The track reached Beowawe November 12, 1868 (C. Crocker, November 13, 1868). See also LaSalle, 378.

380. CAR OF SUPERINTENDENT OF CONSTRUCTION. The February 4, 1869 *San Francisco Chronicle* described Strobridge's car. The reference to the Irish navvies and their "gangers" may be found in Buckley, 181-82. The only known reference connecting Chinese women with the construction of the CP is in the *Elko Independent* of January 5, 1870 which, in reporting the exhumation of bodies for return to China, noted that "the remains of the females are left to rot in shallow graves while every defunct male is carefully preserved for shipment to the Occident."

382. POWDER BLUFF. Information on the wreck of the *City of San Francisco* is from the research of Steve VanDenburgh.

384. SCENE WEST OF SECOND CROSSING OF HUMBOLDT. In his letter of November 13, 1868, C. Crocker anticipated that the end-of-track would stop here for two days while the bridge was built, implying the bridge was not built in advance of the track. E.B. Crocker remarked on November 24, 1868 that this was the permanent bridge. This bridge was replaced with a 152-foot iron Pratt-truss through bridge in 1889 (1899 bridge index).

386. SCENE EAST OF SECOND CROSSING OF HUMBOLDT. The E.B. Crocker quote regarding the inflation of numbers of workers is from his letter of July 2, 1867 to Huntington.

388. TRAIN CAMP. A comment that good water was provided for men and animals is found in the November 16, 1868 *Alta*. The dates of establishment of Barth are from the *List[s] of Officers, Agencies and Stations*.

390. THANKSGIVING IN TEN-MILE CANYON? Graham information is found in unpublished biographical notes and Heath, *"First and Last,"* 11.

392. GUAN YU. Dr. Sue Fawn Chung, Professor of Asian History at the University of Nevada, Las Vegas, identified the shrine and provided relevant information. The *Oakland Daily News*, February 25, 1869, reported work stopped for Chinese New Year.

Reports of only 47 construction-related deaths have been found by Huffman in newspapers and correspondence. This number includes those killed in avalanches and three killed of heat prostration while casting wheels for the CP in Springfield, Massachusetts. Not counted are the vague "several" reported killed in a rock slide. There certainly were deaths not reported in the papers. "Summit of the Sierras," 815, states 22 deaths in total from avalanches for the winter of 1866-67, while only eight deaths from that cause were reported in the papers during that season. And, these numbers do not include deaths relating to train operation. Still, the numbers of construction-related deaths are apparently not remarkably high for that era. For comparison, there averaged two hundred deaths per year in English coal mines during that period (*Bee*, February 28, 1867).

On the other hand, two reports from 1870 imply a much larger number of deaths among the Chinese. The *Elko Independent* of January 5 reports six cars being loaded with bones, and the *Sacramento Reporter* of June 20 says the bones of 1,200 Chinese were being returned to China. Any number of explanations can be advanced for the discrepancy between the number of deaths reported and the apparent numbers of bodies, but the small pox epidemic which swept the scene in the winter of 1868-69 must be included among them. That disease rather than accident was the primary cause is consistent with near-contemporary Civil War mortality experience.

394. CURVING IRON. The *Union* of October 14, 1863 described the process of curving iron for the railroad's very first curve, at the corner of Front and I Streets in Sacramento. The very same process is described in Huntington, 162-65. When it was still a SP publication, *Sunset* (1898, 78) related that rail was still being pre-bent. The statement that there was the equivalent of 125 complete circles of curves comes from CP superintendent Towne (USPRC, 2545). The figure for the length of curved track is the sum of the figures given in reports of the commissioners appointed to examine the Central Pacific Railroad for the various sections of track.

396. HUMBOLDT GATE. The statement that culverts were omitted at some locations along the Truckee and Humboldt rivers is from Williamson's May 1869 report (54-5). The description of track building in the November 16, 1868 *Alta* mentioned that only every other tie was placed before the rail was laid. A.D. Patterson related that Hussey—his former employee on the Freeport—told the CP how to lay track that way, in Willis, 309.

398. BUILDING WATER TANK. The only record of this short-lived 14° curve is found in the appendix to Montague's July 1869 engineering report. However, it and the 7° replacement curve can be traced on the ground and in aerial images.

400. ENTERING THE PALISADES. The *Alta* of December 20, 1868 speaks of the shortage of rail at the front.

402. INDIAN VIEWING RAILROAD FROM PALISADES. Williams, 182, remarked on the Indian settlement at Palisade. The story of the CP's treaty with the Indians is from Phillips, 56.

404. ALCOVE IN PALISADES. Stevens complained about the advertising signs. The physical condition of the railroad, including the ballast, was described in the *Annual Report[s] of the Commissioner of Railroads*, as well as in USPRC, 4464. Photographs of the quarry appear in Signor's *Southern Pacific Salt Lake Division*, 164.

406. FIRST CONSTRUCTION TRAIN PASSING THE PALISADES. The *Arctic's* wreck was reported in the *Union* of September 1, 1868. Both E.B. Crocker and Hopkins expressed frustration in not having enough locomotives on November 2, 1868.

408. MACHINE SHOP AT CARLIN. The *Truckee Tribune* of January 9, 1869 reported the Carlin shop under construction. In addition to the machine, car repair, and blacksmith shops, Carlin had a 16-stall roundhouse by the end of 1869 (structure inventory).

410. CARLIN FROM THE WATER TANKS. E.B. Crocker reported the CP "commissioners" car in service on November 24, 1868. The *Union*, February 12, 1869 reported the supply car completed.

412. ELKO FROM THE WEST. Clement, Hood, and Strobridge testified about the frozen ground (USPRC 2577, 2579, and 2581, respectively). Small pox was reported in the *Truckee Tribune* December 27, 1868 and May 8, 1869. The *Bee* of December 28, 1869 repeated from the *Elko Independent* that C. Crocker had named Elko, without giving an explanation for the selection. Crocker's account of the small pox is in his letter of January 20, 1869.

414. DEPOT AT ELKO. More about shipping railroad material can be found in Huffman's "Railroads Shipped by Sea." The *Union* of December 31, 1868 places *Stager* on the train bound east to receive Huntington when it departed Sacramento. The quote is from Currier. While eastern railroads required crew members of passenger trains to wear uniforms as early as 1856, uniforms were not mandated on the CP until 1883

(*Union* November 26, 1856 and *Record-Union* June 29, 1883).

Elko was a regular breakfast and supper stop for CP trains (Williams, 177). The dining room was kept by James Clark, who was the namesake of Clark's station in the lower Truckee canyon. Clark married the daughter of CP track-laying supervisor Henry Minkler (according to descendant James Barkley).

416. WATER TANK AT PEKO. Carlson, citing Edna Patterson, *Who named it? History of Elko County Place Names* (Elko: Warren L. and Mary J. Monroe, 1964), 63, relates that "Peko" was derived from the pokoe tea consumed by the Chinese.

Myrick's "Land Grants" paper is the source of information on the CP's land grant.

418. SCENE NEAR DEETH. Reports on land sales were included in the various *Annual Report[s] of the Commissioner of Railroads*, and the sales are summarized in Donaldson, 920. Adams, 17-18, 139-140, is the source on Nevada taxation and the CP.

420. SCENE AT MONUMENT POINT. Some travel by ox teams and wagons continued until the automobile age, though the volume certainly declined with the completion of the Pacific railroad. The *San Jose Mercury* of September 17, 1869 reported a large animal powered emigration that year, while emigrants in covered

wagons were noted in the *Reno Evening Gazette*, October 13, 1876. Likewise, steamship travel between the coasts via Panama also continued for many years after the completion of the Pacific railroad. When railroad builder Strobridge took his two daughters to visit the East in 1889, they travelled by way of Panama (*Alta*, February 25, 1889).

422. SALT LAKE FROM MONUMENT POINT. Butler Ives's activity was reported in the *Placer Herald*, April 21, 1866 and again in the *Virginia Trespass*, April 15, 1868. Huntington reported the adoption of the northern route in letters to E.B. Crocker on April 21, 1868 and to Hopkins on May 16. Huntington reported to E.B. Crocker that the UP was grading near Wells, Nevada in letters of September 22, and October 12, 1868. See also Spude, 5-7. The meeting that resolved the controversy between the CP and UP is described in Farnham.

Train travel over the CP was a leisurely affair. The *Annual Report of the Commissioner of Railroads* (1878-79, 37) said that express-passenger trains averaged 19 m.p.h., and were not permitted to exceed 36 m.p.h. Towne reported (*Railway Mail Transportation*, 63) that mail trains ran at 21 m.p.h. except in the Sierra where they were limited to from 14 to 18 m.p.h. In 1885, regular passenger trains ran from Oakland to Ogden in 41 hours while special tea trains

covered the distance in 38 hours (*Record-Union*, August 14, 1885). The Jarrett & Palmer run covered that distance in just over 24 hours (*Reno Evening Gazette*, June 5, 1876 and *Union*, April 9, 1883). Information on Harriman's May 1906 run comes from the *Reno Evening Gazette* of May 29, 1934.

424. RAILROAD CAMP NEAR VICTORY. The value "3,520 rails" is given by both Crofutt, 137, and Heath "A Railroad Record that Defies Defeat," 5. As it happens, 3,520 is exactly twice the product of 52,800 (10 miles in feet) divided by 30 (the presumed length of rails in feet). In fact, there were three minor "equations" (distance adjustments) within the "ten miles," which means the distance was not exactly 52,800 feet long. Furthermore, in that distance there were 18,365 feet of curves (ranging from 1° to 7°48'), and the actual length of the rail around the arc was greater than the length in 100-foot chords. While the minor net value of these effects can be calculated, there really is no point in doing so since there are also variables that we do not know. For instance, we do not know how foreman Coley's "10 miles and 56 feet" was determined. Nor do we know whether the 10 miles was between engineering stations 550 and 1078 or between 549 and 1077, which makes a difference as to how many feet were in which curve (of different degrees) at either end. Moreover, neither the precise rail length nor the gap left for expansion are known.

The identification of the iron crew comes from foreman Coley's paybook, reproduced in Heath's above cited article.

For a year, Huntington had chaffed at the constant delays in building track. His comment penned to E.B. Crocker on May 10, 1869, the day the gold spikes were driven, dripped with sarcasm: "I noticed by the papers that there were ten miles of track laid in one day on the CP, which was really a great feat, and more particularly so when we consider that it was done after the necessity for its being done had passed."

426. THE FIRST GREETING OF THE IRON HORSE.

Spude's "Promontory Summit" was the primary source for information about the events on May 10. He provided as well the story of the overland traveler, from a newspaper clipping in a scrapbook at Bancroft Library.

Digital searches of newspaper references disclose that for over 30 years after the event, the location where the CP and UP rails met was frequently called "Promontory Point." This presented some confusion after 1903, when a station of that name was established where the Lucin Cutoff touched the tip of the Promontory peninsula. Thereafter, "Promontory Summit" has grown in usage as the preferred term for the site of the meeting of the rails, and that is the term used in this work. While "Promontory Summit" was used in the press only a third as often as "Promontory Point" before 1903, there is contemporary justification for its use: While the document Huntington and Grenville Dodge negotiated in April 1869 specified a meeting of the rails at "the summit of Promontory Point," Congress recognized that as "Promontory Summit," and Huntington began using that term within days (Francaviglia, 98). The railroad station at that site initially was called "Terminus," but by 1874 was "Promontory," the name it bore until that railroad line was abandoned in 1942.

432. THE RIVAL MONARCHS.

The quote is from Capt. John C. Currier's version of events, published in *Golden Notes*.

434. MONARCHS FROM THE EAST AND THE WEST.

There are only few references to the colors of early rolling stock. However, as it happens, a reporter was so struck by the colors of *Jupiter* that he commented on it "gleaming in blue and crimson with gold" (*Bee*, March 20, 1869). Unfortunately, words do not disclose the exact shades and composition of the colors. However, in this case, Jim Wilke recognized that Scot-born Walter McQueen, the chief engineer of Schenectady Locomotive Works, was most likely decorating Schenectady locomotives in the crimson and Caledonian blue of the Caledonian Railway of Scotland.

436. THE LAST ACT.

The quote is from Currier's journal. The *Bee* of May 12, 1869 (taken from an *Alta* dispatch) reported that Strobridge entertained the press and officers of the 21st Regiment with his Chinese foreman at the head of the table.

438. RAILROAD AT OGDEN.

The date of sale and lease of the Promontory-Ogden line is from USPRC, 4748. Mary Ipsen's story is recorded in Mann, 124-134.

440 and 442. INTERNATIONAL.

The only railroad photographs Hart seems to have made after May 1869 were of the train of Pullman Palace Cars, which arrived in Sacramento in June, and that of the *Gov. Stanford* reproduced on page 26, probably made on the same occasion. The *Union* of June 21, 1869 mentions the photographing of *International*. This car was described in the *New York Times* of June 28, 1869.

444. SLEEPING CAR.

The story of the "Pioneer special" was told in the *Bee*, September 16, 1869. The *Union* of September 6 and the *Alta* of October 5, 1869 reported the activities of the Cincinnati Red Stockings. As late as 1881, emigrant cars were attached to freight trains and required nine to 11 days to travel from Omaha to San Francisco. The competition between the CP/SP and the Atchison, Topeka & Santa Fe, upon its completion into southern California, was credited with a marked improvement of emigrant service to the West Coast by the *Ashland Tidings*, November 25, 1887.

446. SILVER PALACE CAR.

The features which identify this as a Silver Palace are the vertical roof-support posts. For more on how the CP became an SP property, see Myrick's "Refinancing and Rebuilding the Central Pacific."

COMPANY NAME ABBREVIATIONS

CP = Central Pacific Railroad
PG&E = Pacific Gas & Electric Company
SP = Southern Pacific Railroad
SP&N = Sacramento, Placer & Nevada Railroad
SVRR = Sacramento Valley Rail Road
UP = Union Pacific Railroad

Canyon of the North Fork of the American River See p. 94.

467

Indian Viewing Railroad from Palisades. See p. 402."

BIBLIOGRAPHY

Adams, Romanzo. *Taxation in Nevada, A History*. Reno: Nevada Historical Society, 1918.

Bain, David Haward, *Empire Express, Building the First Transcontinental Railroad*. New York: Viking, 1999.

Basso, Dave. *Ghosts of Humboldt Region*. Sparks, Nev.: Western Printing, 1970.

Best, Gerald. *Snowplow: Clearing Mountain Rails*. Berkeley: Howell-North, 1966.

Bowie, Augustus J. Jr. *A Practical Treatise on Hydraulic Mining in California*. New York: Van Nostrand, 1905.

Buckley, Robert John. *Ireland as it is and as it would be under Home Rule*. Birmingham: Birmingham Daily Gazette, 1893.

Carlson, Helen S. *Nevada Places Names*. Reno: University of Nevada Press, 1974.

Choy, Philip P. *Canton Footprints: Sacramento's Chinese Legacy*. Sacramento: Chinese American Council of Sacramento, 2007.

Coleman, Charles M. *P. G. and E. of California; The Centennial Story of Pacific Gas and Electric Company 1852-1952*. New York: McGraw-Hill, 1952.

Conkling, Roscoe and William D. Shipmen. *The Central Pacific Railroad Company in Equitable Account with the United States*. New York: Henry Bessey, 1887.

Crofutt, George A. *Crofutt's New Overland Tourist and Pacific Coast Guide*. Omaha: Overland, 1884.

Curran, Harold. *Fearful Crossing: the Central Overland Trail through Nevada*. Las Vegas: Nevada Publications, 1982.

Currier, Capt. John C. [journal, published as] "First Train West," *Golden Notes* (April 1969).

Daggett, Stuart. *Chapters on the History of the Southern Pacific*. New York: Augustus M. Kelly, 1966.

Darby, William and Theodore Dwight Jr. "Baltimore and Ohio," *A New Gazetteer of the United States . . . .* Hartford: Edward Hopkins, 1833.

Davis, Sam P. *History of Nevada*. Reno: Elms Publishing, 1913.

Davis, Winfield J. *An Illustrated History of Sacramento County*. Chicago: Lewis Publishing, 1890.

Dodd, Charles H. "Over, around, and across; the Truckee Trail through Reno and Sparks, Nevada", *Overland Journal* (Spring 2004): 3-17.

Dodge, Grenville M. *How We Built the Union Pacific Railway and Other Railway Papers and Addresses*. [N.p., n.d.].

Donaldson, Thomas. *The Public Domain, its history, with statistics . . . .* Washington: Public Lands Commission, 1880.

Duncan, Jack E. *Donner Pass to the Pacific*. Newcastle, Calif.: 2001.

Durham, David L. *California's Geographic Names: a Gazetteer of Historic and Modern Names of the State*. Clovis: Quill Driver Books, 1998.

Farnham, Wallace D. "Shadows from the Gilded Age," *The Golden Spike*. Salt Lake City: Utah State Historical Society, University of Utah Press, 1973. 1-22.

Finlay, John. "The Awaking of the Comstock" *Overland Monthly* (November 1900): 445-65.

Flaherty, Darwin L. "The Naming of Reno, Nevada: A century-old mystery," *Nevada Historical Society Quarterly* (Fall 1984): 155-181

Francaviglia, Richard V. *Over the Range: A History of the Promontory Summit Route of the Pacific Railroad*. Logan, Utah: Utah State University Press, 2008.

Frederick, Charles. "Railroading Under Roof" *The Railway Conductor* (January 1922) 1-4. This article originally appeared in *Scientific American*.

Fulton, Robert Lardin. *The Epic of the Overland*, San Francisco: A.M. Robertson, 1925.

Gilliss, John R. "Tunnels of the Pacific Railroad" *Transactions of the American Society of Civil Engineers* I (1872): 153-69.

Gray, George E. *Central Pacific Railroad of California: Report*. Sacramento: H.S. Crocker, 1865.

Griswold, Wesley A. *A Work of Giants: Building the First Transcontinental Railroad*. New York: McGraw-Hill, 1962.

Gudde, Erwin G. *California Place Names: A Geographical Dictionary*, Berkeley: University of California, 1949.

Harris, Robert L. "The Pacific Railroad—Unopen" *Overland Monthly* 3 (1869): 244-252.

Haymond, Creed. *The Central Pacific Railroad Company: Its Relations to the Government*. San Francisco: H.S. Crocker, 1888.

[Heath, Erle] "From Trail to Rail: A History of the Southern Pacific Company" *Southern Pacific Bulletin*. (November 1926-March 1928) various pages.

_____. "A Railroad Record that Defies Defeat" *Southern Pacific Bulletin* (May 1928): 3-5.

_____. "Eye Witness Tells of 'Last Spike' Driving," *Southern Pacific Bulletin* (May 1926): 5-6.

_____. "First & Last: Pioneer SP Line and its only Surviving Builder Celebrate Birthdays," *Southern Pacific Bulletin* (May, 1937): 11.

Hersh, Lawrence K. *The Central Pacific Railroad across Nevada 1868 & 1997*. North Hollywood, 2000.

History of San Joaquin County, California. Los Angeles, 1923.

Huffman, Wendell W. "How the Comstock determined the course of the Central Pacific Railroad," *Nevada Historical Society Quarterly* (Spring 2007): 3-35.

_____. "Iron Horses along the Truckee; the Central Pacific Reaches Nevada" *Nevada State Historical Society Quarterly* (Spring 1995): 19-36.

_____. "Railroads Shipped by Sea," *Railroad History*, Bulletin 180, (Spring 1999): 7-30.

Hulse, James W. "The California-Nevada Boundary; The History of a Conflict," *Nevada Historical Society Quarterly* (1980): 87-109, 157-78.

Huntington, William S. and Charles Latimer. *Road-master's Assistant and Section-master's Guide.* New York: Railroad Gazette, 1872.

Jones, T.R. "Rough and Ready was the Early Day Motto," *Southern Pacific Bulletin* (August 1920): 23-24, and (part 2) "Days when hand brake setting was an art," *Southern Pacific Bulletin* (September 1920), 23.

Joslyn, David L. "How They Hauled a Hoisting Engine to the Summit of the Sierra Nevada Mountains in 1886 [sic]" *Bulletin of the Railway and Locomotive Historical Society* 32 (1933), 67-68.

Judah, Theodore D. *The Central Pacific Railroad of California.* San Francisco, Calif.: November 1, 1860.

_____. *Pacific Railroad: Report upon his Operation in the Atlantic States.* San Francisco, 1860.

Kibbey, Mead B. *The Railroad Photographs of Alfred A. Hart, Artist.* Sacramento: California State Library Foundation, 1996.

Knowles, Constance Darrow, "A History of Lumbering in the Truckee Basin from 1856 to 1936" (Forest Survey Division, California Forest and Range Experiment Station, October 26, 1942

Kraus, George. *High Road to Promontory: Building the Central Pacific across the High Sierra.* Palo Alto: American West, 1969.

Mann, David H. "The Undriving of the Golden Spike", *Utah Historical Quarterly.* 37, no. 1 (Winter 1969): 124-134.

Macaulay, Tom. "Ghosts of the Truckee River Canyon; Once Bustling Towns Gone but not Forgotten" *Sierra Sun* (September 15, 1997).

_____. "Were Bronco and Floriston the Same Place? *Nevada State Historical Society Quarterly* 39 (Summer 1996): 145-53.

McGlashan, H.D. "Water Resources of California" (Water Supply Paper 300, U.S. Geological Survey), 1913.

Menke, Arnold and Larry Mullaly's "The Great Transformation: Coal to Oil on the Southern Pacific" *SP Trainline* (Issue 85, Fall 2005): 15-38.

Myrick, David. *Railroads of Nevada.* Berkeley: Howell-North, 1962.

_____. "Refinancing and Rebuilding the Central Pacific: 1899-1910." *The Golden Spike.* Salt Lake City: Utah State Historical Society, University of Utah Press, 1973. 85-117.

Nevada Railroads Committee. *Evidence Concerning Projected Railways across the Sierra Nevada Mountains, from Pacific Tide Waters in California . . . .* Carson City: J. Church, 1865.

Nordhoff, Charles. *California: For Health, Pleasure, and Residence.* New York: Harper, 1873.

North, Edward P. "Blasting with Nitro-Glycerine" *Transactions of the American Society of Civil Engineers* I (January 1872): 15-22.

Phillips, D.L. *Letters from California: its mountains, valleys, plains, lakes, rivers, climate and productions. Also its railroads, cities, towns and people, as seen in 1876.* Springfield: Illinois State Journal, 1877.

"Pioneer days in Sparks and vicinity", *Nevada State Historical Society Papers* 5 (1926) 285-374.

Raymond, Anan S. and Richard E. Fike. *Rails East to Promontory: The Utah Stations.* Bureau of Land Management Utah; Livingston, Tex.: Pioneer Enterprises, 1997.

Richards, Gordon. "Boca Beer: the solution to a hot summer day" *Sierra Sun* (August 3, 2007).

Signor, John. *Donner Pass; Southern Pacific's Sierra Crossing* (San Marino: Golden West, 1985).

_____. *Southern Pacific Salt Lake Division* (Wilton and Berkeley: Signature Press, 2007).

Spier, Robert F.G. "Food Habits of Nineteenth-Century California Chinese," *California Historical Society Quarterly* (March 1958): 79-84.

Spude, Robert L. "Promontory Summit, May 10, 1869" (National Park Service, 2005).

Stevens, Thomas "Across America on a Bicycle" *Outing: An Illustrated Monthly Magazine of Recreation* 6 (April-September 1885). The portion relevant to the CP is on 41-52, 164-77.

Stewart, George R. *Donner Pass and Those Who Crossed It.* Menlo Park: Lane Books, 1964.

Stillman, Dr. J.D.B. "The Last Tie" *Overland Monthly*, 3 (1869): 77-83.

Strobridge, Idah Meacham. *Sagebrush Trilogy.* Reno: University of Nevada Press, 1990.

"Summit of the Sierras," *Friends' Intelligencer* 24 (February 1868): 797-98, 815-16, 831-37.

"Things as they are in America" *Chambers Journal of Popular Literature* (March 4, 1854): 131.

Thompson & West. *History of Sacramento County, California.* Oakland: 1880. Reprinted 1960.

_____. *History of the State of Nevada.* Oakland: 1881.

Townley, John M. *Tough Little Town on the Truckee: Reno 1868-1900.* Reno: Great Basin Studies Center, 1983.

Uzes, Francois D. *Chaining the Land.* Sacramento: Landmark Enterprises, 1977.

Vose, George L. *Manual for Railroad Engineers.* Boston: Lee and Shepard, 1881.

Wilder, Joel O. "The Way Pioneer Builders met Difficulties," *SP Bulletin* (November 1920): 23-5.

Wilson, Dick. *Sawdust Trails in the Truckee Basin; a History of Lumbering Operations.* Nevada City: Nevada County Historical Society, 1992.

Williams, Henry T. *The Pacific Tourist: Williams' Illustrated Guide to the Pacific R.R., California, and Pleasure Resorts across the Continent.* New York: 1876.

Willis, William Ladd. *History of Sacramento County.* 1913.

Winnemucca, Sarah. *Life Among the Piutes.* Boston: G.P. Putnam's Sons, 1883.

GOVERNMENT DOCUMENTS

An Act to aid in the construction of a railroad and telegraph line from the Missouri River to the Pacific Ocean, and to secure to the Government the use of the same for postal, military, and other purposes. Approved July 1, 1862.

An Act to amend an act entitled "An Act to aid in the construction of a railroad and telegraph line from the Missouri River to the Pacific Ocean, and to secure to the Government the use of the same for postal, military, and other purposes" approved July 1, 1862. Amendment of July 2, 1864.

An Act to amend an act entitled "An Act to aid in the construction of a railroad and telegraph line from the Missouri River to the Pacific Ocean, and to secure to the Government the use of the same for postal, military, and other purposes" approved July 1, 1862, and to amend and act amendatory thereof, approved July 2, 1864. Amendment of March 3, 1865.

An Act to amend an act entitled "An Act to amend an act entitled 'An Act aid in the construction of a railroad and telegraph line from the Missouri River to the Pacific Ocean, and to secure to the Government the use of the same for postal, military, and other purposes" approved July 1, 1862," approved July 2, 1864. Amendment of July 3, 1866.

Annual Report[s] of the Commissioner of Railroads. U.S. Department of Interior. 1881-1901.

[Crocker, Charles] testimony in *Report of the Joint Special Committee to Investigate Chinese Emigration,* U.S. Congress. Senate. 44th Cong., 2nd Sess. (1877), Sen. Rept. 689.

[Heuer, William H.] *Report on the survey of the Union and Central Pacific Railways,* February 2, 1877. U.S. Congress. House. 44th Cong., 2nd Sess. House Ex. Doc. no. 38.

_____. Field notebooks from the Corp of Engineers resurvey of the Pacific railroad, 1876. (Unpublished.)

Report[s] of the [California] State Board of Health. 1873 and 1882.

Report of Cases Determined in the Supreme Court of the State of California. 1906.

Testimony Taken by the United States Pacific Railway Commission. U.S. Congress. Senate. 50th Cong., 1st Sess., S. Ex. Doc. 51.

[Towne, Alban] testimony in *Railway Mail Transportation. Evidence.* U.S. Congress. Senate. 44th Cong., 2nd Sess., 1876. Mis. Doc. No. 20.

[Williamson, Robert S., et al.] *Report of the Special Commissioners* (January 25, 1869). U.S. Congress. Senate. 40th Cong. 3 Sess., Ex. Doc. 54.

_____. Report of the Commission to examine the Pacific Rail Road, May 14, 1869. (Unpublished.)

CENTRAL PACIFIC AND SOUTHERN PACIFIC DOCUMENTS

Annual Report[s] of the Board of Directors of the Central Pacific Railroad Company to the Stockholders for the years: 1872-87.

Annual Report[s] of the Central Pacific Railroad Company of California to the Secretary of State. 1862-68.

Annual Report[s] of the Southern Pacific Company. 1902-03.

The Central Pacific Railroad Company of California: Character of the Work, Its Progress, Resources, Earnings, and Future Prospects, With the Foundations and Advantages of Its First Mortgage Bonds. New York: Brown & Hewitt, February 1868.

List[s] of Agencies, Stations, etc. 1953-73.

List[s] of Officers, Agencies and Stations. 1888-1952.

Official List[s] of Officers, Stations, Agents. 1879-85.

Report[s] of the Chief Engineer. 1861-65, 1869.

Rules and Regulations for Employees [1868].

Station Numbers and Distances. 1882-83.

Bridge index [copy] MW 309. 1899.

Bridge Inspection Reports, 1961, 1986.

Profiles. [c1880-1900].

Track charts. 1967.

Right of Way and Track maps.

C.P. Huntington's invoice ledgers. [1863-69].

Montague, Samuel S. "Trestlings" September 1, 1869.

Montague, Samuel S. "Bridges" [1869].

"Buildings Humboldt Div. C.P.R.R." [1869].

"Buildings on the Salt Lake Division, C.P.R.R." [1869].

"List of Buildings on the Central Pacific Railroad from Sacramento to Winnemucca" [1869].

"List of Buildings on the Central Pacific Railroad from Truckee to Winnemucca" [1869].

"Shoshone Division List of Buildings" [1869].

Reports of the Commissioners appointed to examine the Central Pacific Railroad, 1864-69. These are the "commissioners reports" filed upon completion of individual sections of railroad.

MISCELLANEOUS UNPUBLISHED MATERIAL

Bowsher, Amos L. "Memorandum." CPRR Biographical Notes from the Lynn D. Farrar Collection, cprr.org.

Clement, Louis M. CPRR Biographical Notes from the Lynn D. Farrar Collection, cprr.org.

Graham, J.M. CPRR Biographical Notes from the Lynn D. Farrar Collection, cprr.org.

Gray, J.B. Notebook [n.d.].

Heath, Earl. "Interview with J.M. Graham." March 8, 1929. CPRR Biographical Notes from the Lynn D. Farrar Collection, cprr.org.

Huntington, Collis P. Papers, Syracuse University Library. Microfilm.

Jones, T.R. CPRR Biographical Notes from the Lynn D. Farrar Collection, cprr.org.

Judah Anna F. Reminiscences, Bancroft Library, University of California, Berkeley. Microfilm.

_____. Letter to Amos P. Catlin, December 1889.

Judah, Theodore D. Papers, Bancroft Library, University of California, Berkeley. Microfilm.

Montague, Samuel. CPRR Biographical Notes from the Lynn D. Farrar Collection, cprr.org.

Myrick, David. "Land Grants: Aids and Benefits to the Government and to the Railroads." 1969.

Partridge, A.P. "Reminiscences." CPRR Biographical Notes from the Lynn D. Farrar Collection, cprr.org.

Wilder, Joel O. CPRR Biographical Notes from the Lynn D. Farrar Collection, cprr.org.

Willumson, Glenn G. "Alfred A. Hart: Photographer of the Transcontinental Railroad" 1984, an unpublished MA thesis in art history, University of California, Davis.

PERIODICALS

Carson Daily Appeal.

Daily Nevada State Journal.

Dutch Flat Enquirer.

Elko Independent.

Engineers Monthly Journal (February 1900).

Folsom Telegraph.

Gold Hill Daily News.

Grass Valley National.

The Illustrated Photographer (May 29, 1868).

Mining & Scientific Press.

The Monthly Journal of the Brotherhood of Locomotive Engineers (March 1877).

Nevada City Gazette.

Nevada [City] Transcript.

Nevada State Journal.

New York Times.

Placer Herald.

Railway Age.

Reno Evening Gazette.

Reno Weekly Gazette Stockman.

Sacramento Bee.

Sacramento Record-Union.

Sacramento Reporter.

Sacramento Union.

San Francisco Call.

[San Francisco] Centennial Spirit of the Times (July 4 1876).

San Francisco Chronicle.

San Francisco Daily Alta California.

San Francisco Evening Bulletin.

San Jose Mercury.

Southern Pacific Bulletin.

Sunset (1898).

Truckee Tribune.

Virginia Daily Trespass.

[Virginia City] Territorial Enterprise.

Weekly Nevada State Journal.

Boca—Crossing of Little Truckee River'
See p. 288.

Bloomer Cut and Embankment.' See p. 66.

INDEX

Abboy, James N.: 286
Accidents/deaths: 24 64 110 184 186 204 212 214 230 262 270 272 298 380 382 392 406
Albee, George: 214
Alta: 118 120 122
American (station): 132
American River: 30 94 132 134 136
Angora, Angora Ranch: 314
Animals used in construction: 168 360 388
Antelope Creek: 40
Antelope Ridge: 48
Applegate: 76
Argenta: 318 374
Auburn: 68 70
Ayres, ___: 154

Baker, Jesse G.: 30
Ballast: 404
Balloon track: 166
Baltimore Ravine: 66
Banvard, Edgar M.: 120
Barth: 388
Basaltic Rocks: 332
Baseball: 16 444
Battle Mountain: 374
Bear River, Bear Valley: 108 178 180
Beckwith, Edward G.: 378
Beowawe: 378
Black Butte (Cisco Butte): 194
Black Point (Tunnel no. 8): 258
Blasting/drilling): 64 110 116 124 188 192 226 242 244 246 264 336 412
Bloomer Cut: 62 64 66 474
Blue, Jim: 76
Blue Canyon: 156 158 160 162
Boca: 288 298 473
Boca Mill & Ice Company, Boca Brewery: 288
Bowsher, Amos L.: 370 428
Bradley, Elisha: 112 146

Brakes/braking: 90 182
Birce & Smart: 182
Bridge (station): 366
Bridge, American River: 30 34
Bridge, Cape Horn: 96n
Bridge, Cascade (Upper and Lower): 228
Bridge, Gray Creek: 292 294
Bridge, Little Truckee: 288
Bridge, Long Ravine: 88 90
Bridge, Sacramento: 14 26
Bridge, 1st Humboldt: 364 366
Bridge, 2nd Humboldt: 384 386
Bridge, 1st Truckee River: 292 294
Bridge, 2nd Truckee: 302 304
Bridge, 3rd Truckee: 308 312
Bridge, 4th Truckee: 312 314
Bridge, 5th Truckee: 342
Bridges: 194 228 328 336 382 398
Bringham, Charles A.: 38
Brown, Arthur: 260
Brown, Joseph B. "Poker": 356
Brown's Hill: 356
Brown's Station: 354 356 358
Butte Canyon: 192 194 196

Cadwalader, Charles: 62 284
California & Oregon Railroad: 26 34
California Central Railroad: 14 34
California Pacific Railroad: 26
Camels: 52
Camp 20 (Cuba, Iceland): 292
Camp 24: 302 304
Camp 26: 308
Camp 37 (Vista): 324 326
Canyon Creek: 126 128
Cape Horn: 92 94 96 467
Cape Horn Mills, Caporn: 98
Capital (riverboat): 16 18
Carlin: 408 410
Carlin, William P.: 408
Carlin Canyon: 382
Carpenter Flat: 170

Carson & Colorado Railroad: 184 310
Casa Loma: 136
Cascade Lake: 228
Cascades bridges: 228
Casement, John S.: 276
Cement Ridge (Smart Ridge): 182
Cement Ridge (Tunnel no. 10): 272 274
Chalk Bluffs: 124
China Ranch: 144
Chinese: 58 78 144 150 188 224 242 356 378 380 392 428 436
Cincinnati Red Stockings Base Ball Club: 444
Circus train wreck: 262
Cisco: 200 202 204 206 210 212 216 218 234 276
Cisco, John J.: 200
Cisco Butte (Black Butte): 194
City of San Francisco (train): 186 382
Clark, James: 414n
Clark's Station: 330 414n
Clement, Flavius: 24
Clement, Lewis M.: 62 130
Clipper Gap: 74 76 78
Clipper Ravine: 78 80
Coal (see also locomotive fuel): 314
Coburn, Samuel S., Coburn's Station: 280
Coldstream: 126 276 278
Coley, George: 424
Colfax: 84 86 102
Comstock: 50 114 296 316 320
Conness, John: 28
Contractors: 48
Construction train: 350 370 378 380 388
Cottonwood Valley: 330
Coupling cars: 368
Crested Peak (Donner Peak): 254 266 274
Crocker, Benjamin R.: 54n 168

Crocker, Charles: 48 118
Crocker, Edwin B.: 28 46 48 118 386
Crocker's Spur (Tunnel no. 5): 226
Crossties: 60 66 122 136 288 354 358 362 372 396 428 430
Crystal Lake: 190 192
Crystal Peak: 310
Cuba (Iceland): 292
Culverts: 126 128 224 396
Currier, John C.: 436
Curve no. 235: 160
Curve no. 238: 160
Curve no. 385: 278
Curve no. 737: 398
Curves: 74n 130 158 160 278 334 382 394 398

Daley, Thomas: 424
Davidson, George: 300
Deep Gulch: 80
Deeth: 418
Depots, freight: 18 68 84 102 120 202 320
Depots, passenger: 14 40 44 120 202 212 216 318 358 414
Derby, Derby Dam: 340
Dickman, William: 12n
Dixie Cut: 110 448
Doan, Lattimer: 288
Donner Lake: 254 256
Donner Lumber & Boom Company: 306
Donner Party: 114 164 176 256
Donner Pass: 50 170 236 250 254
Donner Peak (Crested Peak): 254 266 274
Donner's Backbone (Schallenberger Ridge) 274
Drum, Frank G., Drum Forebay: 144
Dry Creek: 34
Duncan, Lucinda: 378n
Durant, Thomas: 430
Dust: 242 408 414

Dutch Flat, Dutch Flat Station 114
Dutch Flat Divide: 108 134 170
Dutch Flat & Donner Lake Wagon Road: 50 112 136 192 200 216 220 236 250 252 254 280
Dutch Ravine: 60

Eagle Gap: 306
Earthwork: 58 60 64 70 82 66 106 110 122 124 126 128 138 140 146 150 158 166
Echo Point: 188 190
Elevation: 14n 130 170
Elko: 412 414
Ellen, "Elle": 298
Elliott, George: 424
Emigrant Canyon: 382
Emigrant Gap: 166 170 172 174
Emigrant Gap Tunnel (Tunnel no. 2): 174 176 180
Engineering: 62 66 108 264
Essex: 310
Excursion trains: 36 96 270 286

Farad: 296
Finances: 54 56 68 168 322 416 418
Fires and fire protection: 190 268
Fleish: 306 308 310
Fleishhacker, Herbert and Mortimer: 296 306
Floods: 30 34
Floriston, Floriston Pulp & Paper Company: 296
Floriston Ice Company: 292
Forebay: 144
Fort Point: 146 148
Forty-Mile Desert: 350 352 354
Foulkes, John P. and George: 310
Frémont, John C.: 176 338
Frémont Canyon: 382
Friend, Joseph: 288
Fulda: 168 172
Furniss & Mahon's saloon: 68

Gardner, Melvin: 146
Gay, Elkanar: 146
George's Gap: 82
Giant Gap: 132
Giesendorfer, George: 82
Gilliss, James M.: 240n
Gilliss, John R.: 62 240
Glendale: 316
Gold Run: 112
Gorge: 132
Gradient: 40 72 130 138 148 158 164
Grading: 88 116 124 140 192 276 282 284 336 352 372 378 422
Graham, Joseph M.: 62 316 390
Granite Point: 360 362
Gravely Ford: 378n
Gray, Joseph, Gray's Station: 280 282 292
Gray Creek: 292, 294
Great Salt Lake: 420 422
Green Bluffs, Green Valley: 132
Gregory, James F.: 152
Griffith, Griffith: 46
Grizzly Hill (Tunnel no. 1): 150 152 154 162
Grubbing: 128
Guan Yu: 392
Guppy, Alonzo: 62 136n

Hafed: 330
Hamlin, Sylvester A.: 310
Harriman, Edward H.: 322 422
Hart, Alfred A., Hart's photography: 18 28 32 44 50 90 128 154 178 180 218 232 236 240 250 284 290 294 332 338 354 370 386 402 406 410 426 430 440
Haten, John: 294
Hayford Hill 100
Healey, M. J.: 312
Heaton, James, Heaton Station, Heatonville: 200
Henness Pass: 188
Herrick, ___: 154
Heuer, William H.: 152
Hewes, David: 432

Hog's Back (Moody Ridge): 130 132
Hollenbeck Orrin W.: 112
Hood, William: 62
Hopkins, Mark: 24 118 186 234
Hopkins Bluff: 186
Horse Ravine: 150
Hot Springs: 350 352
Houghton, Eliza: 256
Houghton, James F.: 300
Housewirth, Thomas: 206
Hubbard, Isaac M.: 30
Howden, James: 244
Humboldt Gate: 396
Humboldt Lake: 352 354 356
Humboldt River: 352 364 366 378 382 384 388 416
Humboldt River bridges: 364 366 384 386
Humbridge: 366
Huntington, Collis P.: 20 118 414
Hunter's Crossing: 314 316
Hussey, Ned: 154 396
Hydroelectric power: 144 296 306 308 314

Ice: 288 292 296 410
Iceland (Cuba): 292
Indians: 82, 358, 376 402
Inyo Marble Company: 310
Ipsen, Mary: 438
Iowa Hill: 100
Irishmen: 306 380 424
Ives, Butler: 62 300 422

Jarrett & Palmer Special: 422
Joyce, Patrick: 424
Judah, Edward Douglas: 62
Judah, Theodore D.: 12 62 102 108 114 130 170 176 378 430
Junction (Roseville): 14 34
Juniper Creek (Gray Creek): 292, 294

Kelleen, Edward: 424
Kennedy, Mike: 424
Kidder, John: 62 284 300
King, Warren: 314

Kirby, Paul: 284
Kodak: 366

Laborers: 58 78 88 188 218 224 230 242 272 360 362 364 366 378 380 386 388 392 400
Laborers, statistics: 58 88 242 300 386
Lake, Myron, Lake's Crossing: 316
Lake Ridge (Schallenberger Ridge): 274
Land: 416 418
Laws, Robert J.: 184
Little Blue Canyon: 136
Little Truckee River: 288
Lockwood: 330
Locomotive servicing facilities: 40 42 86 202 204 206 344 358 410
Locomotive fuel: 40 42 44 98 168 310 346 376 426
Locomotive water facilities: 26 40 342 352 354 358 364 388 398 404 416
Lone Tree Hill: 370
Long Ravine: 88 90
Loomis: 40 44
Loomis, James: 44
Lost Camp: 164
Lovell, Samuel W., Lovell's Ranch: 74
Lumbering: 16 82 98 102 122 162 182 228 280 282 288 306 310

Madden, ___: 154
Maggie's Bower: 404
Mail: 216 416
Manassas Gap: 308
Marmol: 310
Marriott, Frank: 432
McDowell, Irvin: 318
McNamara, Fred: 424
McWade, D.D.: 154
Meacham, George Washington and Idah: 362n
Meadow Lake: 200
Michigan City, Michigan Bluff: 100
Midas: 136

Mileage: 152
Miller, Edward H., Jr., Miller's Bluff: 186
Milligan, Samuel P.: 230n
Mills, Edgar: 428
Mines, mining: 108 112 314 374 388
Minkler, Henry: 276 414n 424
Mirage: 350
Mogul: 314
Monk, Hank: 302
Monument Point, Monument: 420 422
Moody Ridge (Hog's Back): 130
Montague, Samuel S.: 62
Morrison, J.J.: 44n
Mystic: 298

Nevada County Narrow Gauge Railroad: 90
New England Mills: 82
Newcastle: 50 54 56
Nixon, George S.: 358
Nixon, Robert: 310n
Norman, J.F.: 214
Norris & Rowe Circus: 262

Ogden: 438
Old Man Mountain: 182 186
Orel: 144
Owl Gap: 168

Pacific Gas & Electric Company: 144 182
Pacific Railroad Act: 20 22 32 68 112 130 158n 218 322 416
Paddleford, George F.: 412
Palisade: 402
Palisade Canyon: 378 380 382 384 386 388 396 400 402 404 406 468
Panama: 20 96 294 326 414
Panama Railroad: 20 294 440
Partridge, A.P.: 294 312
Peko: 416
Penryn: 46
Pine Creek (Trout Creek): 396 398
Pino: 44
Pioneer Stage Company: 216

Placerville & Sacramento Valley Railroad: 46 52 102
Pleasant Valley: 334
Powder Bluff: 382
Pratt, Robert H.: 220
Profile Rock: 290
Promontory Range: 420 438
Promontory Summit: 422 426 438
Prospect Hill: 136 138 140 142
Pullman, George M. and Pullman cars: 44 440 442
Pumpernickel Valley: 370

Quarries: 36 38 46 186 404

Rail: 20 46 136 222 326 334 362 368 372 394
Rail joints: 66 136 222 394 398
Rancho del Paso: 32 322
Rattlesnake Cliffs: 306
Rattlesnake Mountain (Red Mountain): 190 206
Rattlesnake Mountain (Reno): 322
Rebuilding railroad, second track: 74 90 96 104 132 150 152 160 174 182 186 246 324 332 336 340 350 358 382 384 398
Red Bluffs: 336 338
Red Mountain (Rattlesnake Mountain): 190 206
Red Spur (Tunnel no. 4): 226
Reed, Samuel: 430
Reese River, Reese River mining district, Reese River siding: 374
Reilly, G.: 286
Reno: 316 318 320
Reno, Jesse L.: 318
Rice's Ravine: 88 92 96
Riverboats: 12 14 16 18
Road Crossings: 70
Roads (other than DF&DL) and highways: 52 74 76 90 104 114 124 172 216 248 250 252 254 292 302 328 330 336 360 408 420
Robbers Ravine: 92
Rock Ravine: 72
Rocklin: 36 38 40 42

Rolling stock: 36 86 344 358 442
Rolling stock—decoration of: 156 434
Rolling stock—dump cars: 142
Rolling stock—freight cars: 156 116
Rolling stock—naming of locomotive: 28
Rolling stock—locomotive components: 92 210
Rolling stock—locomotives CP no. 1 *Gov. Stanford*: 24 26 36
Rolling stock—locomotives CP no. 3 *C.P. Huntington*: 30 94 100
Rolling stock—locomotives CP no. 4 *T.D. Judah*: 100
Rolling stock—locomotives CP no. 5 *Atlantic*: 34 36 52
Rolling stock—locomotives CP no. 6 *Conness*: 28 30 46 56
Rolling stock—locomotives CP no. 7 *A.A. Sargent*: 22
Rolling stock—locomotives CP no. 8 *Nevada*: 86
Rolling stock—locomotives CP no. 9 *Utah*: 86
Rolling stock—locomotives CP no. 11 *Arctic*: 406
Rolling stock—locomotives CP no. 14 *Oneonta*: 222
Rolling stock—locomotives CP no. 22 *Auburn*: 134
Rolling stock—locomotives CP no. 25 *Yuba*: 214 216
Rolling stock—locomotives CP no. 26 *Sampson*: 348
Rolling stock—locomotives CP no. 27 *Goliah*: 348
Rolling stock—locomotives CP no. 32 *Ajax*: 16
Rolling stock—locomotives CP no. 33 *Achilles*: 16
Rolling stock—locomotives CP no. 45 *Majestic*: 42
Rolling stock—locomotives CP no. 46 *Unicorn*: 16n
Rolling stock locomotives CP no. 47 *Griffin*: 16n

Rolling stock—locomotives CP no. 50 *Champion*: 376
Rolling stock—locomotives CP no. 60 *Jupiter*: 422 426 434
Rolling stock—locomotives CP no. 62 *Whirlwind*: 426
Rolling stock—locomotives CP no. 63 *Leviathan*: 418
Rolling stock—locomotives CP no. 108 *Stager*: 374 414
Rolling stock—locomotives CP no. 93 *Oakland*: 100
Rolling stock—locomotives SVRR *Sacramento*: 238
Rolling stock—locomotives UP no. 60 or 66: 426
Rolling stock—locomotives UP no. 119: 434
Rolling stock—locomotives WP letter E *San Mateo*: 282 286 368
Rolling stock—locomotives, use of: 376
Rolling stock—passenger cars: 156 178 440
Rolling stock—passenger cars— Dining cars: 44 440 442
Rolling stock—passenger cars— Silver Palace cars: 446
Rolling stock—passenger cars— Sleeping cars: 444 446
Rolling stock—snowplows: 172 202 208 212
Rolling stock—track-laying cars: 362 372
Roseville (Junction): 14 34 40
Route of railroad: 102 130 134 170 274 278
Russell, Donald J.: 64

Sacramento: 12 14 16 18 20 22 26 38
Sacramento River bridge: 14 26
Sacramento, Placer & Nevada Railroad: 32 46
Sacramento Valley Railroad: 12 22 50 54 84 102 216
Sacramento wharf: 14 16 18 20 440

Safford, Anson P. K.: 432
Sailor Ravine: 166
Salvia: 340
Sargent, Aaron A.: 22
Savage, Abraham O.: 328
Sawtooth Ridge: 134 136
Schaffer, George: 282
Schallenberger, Moses: 274
Schallenberger Ridge: 274 278 284
Secret Ravine: 40 100 102 104
Secret Town: 102 104
Sentinel Rock: 388
Seymour, Silas: 430
Shady Run: 136
Shaw, Mike: 424
Shed 10: 196
Sheep Ranch: 330
Shipping: 16 20 24 294 320 326 414 440
Signal Peak (Red Mountain): 190
Smallpox: 298 380 392 412
Smart, Smart Ridge (Cement Ridge): 178 182
Snow: 176 196 204 206 208 210 212 224 228 230 258 270 276 384 386
Snowsheds, snow galleries: 162 176 184 190 196 198 212 230 232 234 250 260 262 264 266 268 479
Soldiers: 432 434
Southern Pacific Railroad: 274 324 332 446
Sparks, John; Sparks: 322
Spikes: 430 432
Stanford, Leland: 24 100 118 420 428 430 446
Stanford, Phillip: 278
Stanford, Stanford Curve: 278
Starbuck, John: 82
State boundary: 300
Stevens Party: 338
Stone walls: 150 270 272
Strobridge, James H.: 64 118 242 270 362 370 380 390 412 420n 424 430 436
Strobridge, Samuel: 362n 430
Strong, Daniel: 108 114 170

Strong's Canyon: 276
Sullivan, David J.: 276 428
Sullivan, Mike: 424
Summit Tunnel (Tunnel no. 6): 236 238 240 244 246
Summit: 234
Sunday trains: 50
Switches: 122 346

Tangents: 32 44 158
Taxation: 418
Telegraph: 188 300 358 370 428
Terry, Wallace: 288
Thanksgiving Day: 390
Todd, John: 428
Towle Brothers: 122 164
Toy, W. J. Toy: 358
Track laying: 66 136 154 226 276 282 302 326 334 340 352 356 362 372 388 394 400 424
Trackwalkers: 262
Train speed: 80 208 414 422
Trap Spur (tunnel no. 3): 224 226
Travel: 420 426 436 444
Trestle, Auburn: 74
Trestle, Butte Canyon: 74 194 196
Trestle, Clipper Gap: 78
Trestle, Clipper Ravine: 78 80
Trestle, Deep Gulch: 80
Trestle, Long Ravine: 74 88
Trestle, Newcastle: 54 56 58 74
Trestle, Secret Town: 74 102 104
Trestles: 28 30 54 56 72 74 78 80 88 102 104
Trestles, Lovell's ranch: 74
Trestles, Sacramento: 28 30
Tritle, Frederick A.: 432
Trout Creek (Pine Creek): 396 398
Truckee: 280 282
Truckee Meadows: 316 322
Truckee (Paiute): 338
Truckee River: 218 284 286 292 294 296 302 304 306 308 310 312 314 328 330 334 336 338 340 342 344
Truckee River bridges: 292 294 302 304 308 312 314 342
Truckee River General Electric

Company: 296 306
Tunnel Hill: 106
Tunnel no. 0: 80
Tunnel no. 1 (Grizzly Hill): 150 152 154 162
Tunnel no. 2 (Emigrant Gap): 174 176 180
Tunnel no. 3 (Trap Spur): 224 226
Tunnel no. 4 (Red Spur): 226
Tunnel no. 5 (Crocker's Spur): 226
Tunnel no. 6 (Summit Tunnel): 236 238 240 244 246
Tunnel no. 7: 248 256
Tunnel no. 8 (Black Point): 258
Tunnel no. 9: 270
Tunnel no. 10 (Cement Ridge): 272 274
Tunnel no. 11: 274
Tunnel no. 12 (Tunnel Spur): 276
Tunnel no. 13: 278
Tunnel no. 14: 284n
Tunnel no. 15: 298 300
Tunnel no. 35 (Hopkins's Bluff) 186
Tunnel no. 36 (Miller's Bluff): 186
Tunnel no. 37 (Echo Point): 190
Tunnel no. 41 (Summit Tunnel): 246
Tunnel Spur (Tunnel no. 12): 276
Tunnels: 80 96 106 186 190 240 248

Union Pacific Railroad: 78 218 224 226 332 402 420 426 428 438

Verdi: 310
Victory: 424
Virginia & Truckee Railroad: 310 320
Vista: 326
Von Schmidt, Allexey: 300

Wadsworth: 216 318 322 342 344 346 348
Wadsworth, James S.: 318
Wagons and stagecoaches: 52 112 120 202 216 218 220 246 250 252 254 302 420

Water ditches: 108 112 124 126 138 142 148
Watkins, Carlton E.: 24
Weather: 112 176 194 196 204 206 208 210 212 224 228 230 258 270 276 364 412
Weimar: 82
Wells Fargo & Company: 216 416
Western Pacific Railroad (19th century): 286 320 388 438
Western Pacific (20th century): 320n 332
White Plains, White Plains Hill: 350
White Pine mining district: 374
Whitmarsh, Samuel Hooker: 362n
Willment, George: 68
Wilson, Andrew B.: 170
Wilson Creek, Wilson Ravine, Wilson Valley: 168 170
Winnemucca: 368
Women: 68 118 380 390
Woodruff, Thomas T.: 446
Woodshed (station): 168

Yerba Buena Island: 318
Yuba Pass: 184
Yuba River: 180 087

*Snow Gallery around Crested Peak.'
See p. 262.*

COLOPHON

Book design, typesetting, and final map art by Nancy Peppin,
Nancy Peppin Graphic Arts, Reno, Nevada

Fonts used: Adobe Caslon Pro, a variation of Caslon, created in 1722
by William Caslon (1692–1766), and Postoffice, a contemporary font
by an unknown creator, based on several 19th-century wood typefaces

Pages: printed on 140gsm Chinese matte
Printed and bound by Asia Pacific Offset, Hong Kong, China

The cover venticular image was printed by VueThru, Las Vegas,
Nevada, from a photographic file created by Howard Goldbaum.

Published by Nevada State Railroad Museum
2180 S. Carson Street
Carson City, Nevada 89701

The Waiting for the Cars website, waitingforthecars.com, features
stereo cards and anaglyphs not included in this book, as well as other
interactive features. There are links to order additional paper 3D
glasses, or professional models.